vol. One

P U R G A T O R Y   K A B U K I

Written and Illustrated by

Yasushi Suzuki

Translators: *Daniel Sullivan &*
Asako Otomo

Senior Translator: *Toshikazu Hosaka*

English Adaptation: *Ailen Lujo*

Editor: *Sue Yang*

Production: *Bryce Gunkel*

V.P of Operations: *Yuki Chung*

President: *Jennifer Chen*

DrMaster Publications Inc.
4044 Clipper Ct.
Fremont, CA 94538
www.DrMasterbooks.com

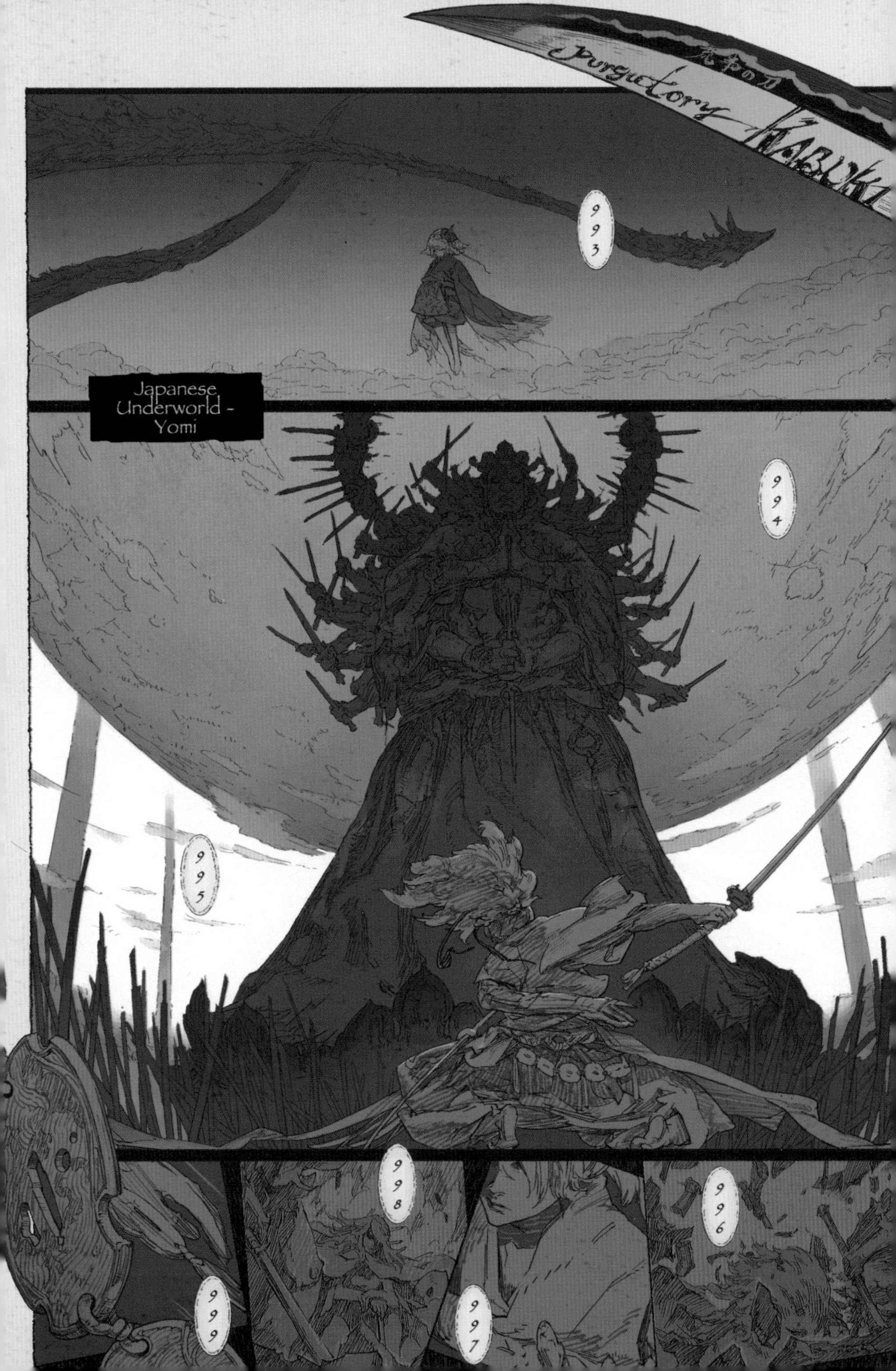
Purgatory KABUKI
993
Japanese Underworld - Yomi
994
995
996
997
998
999

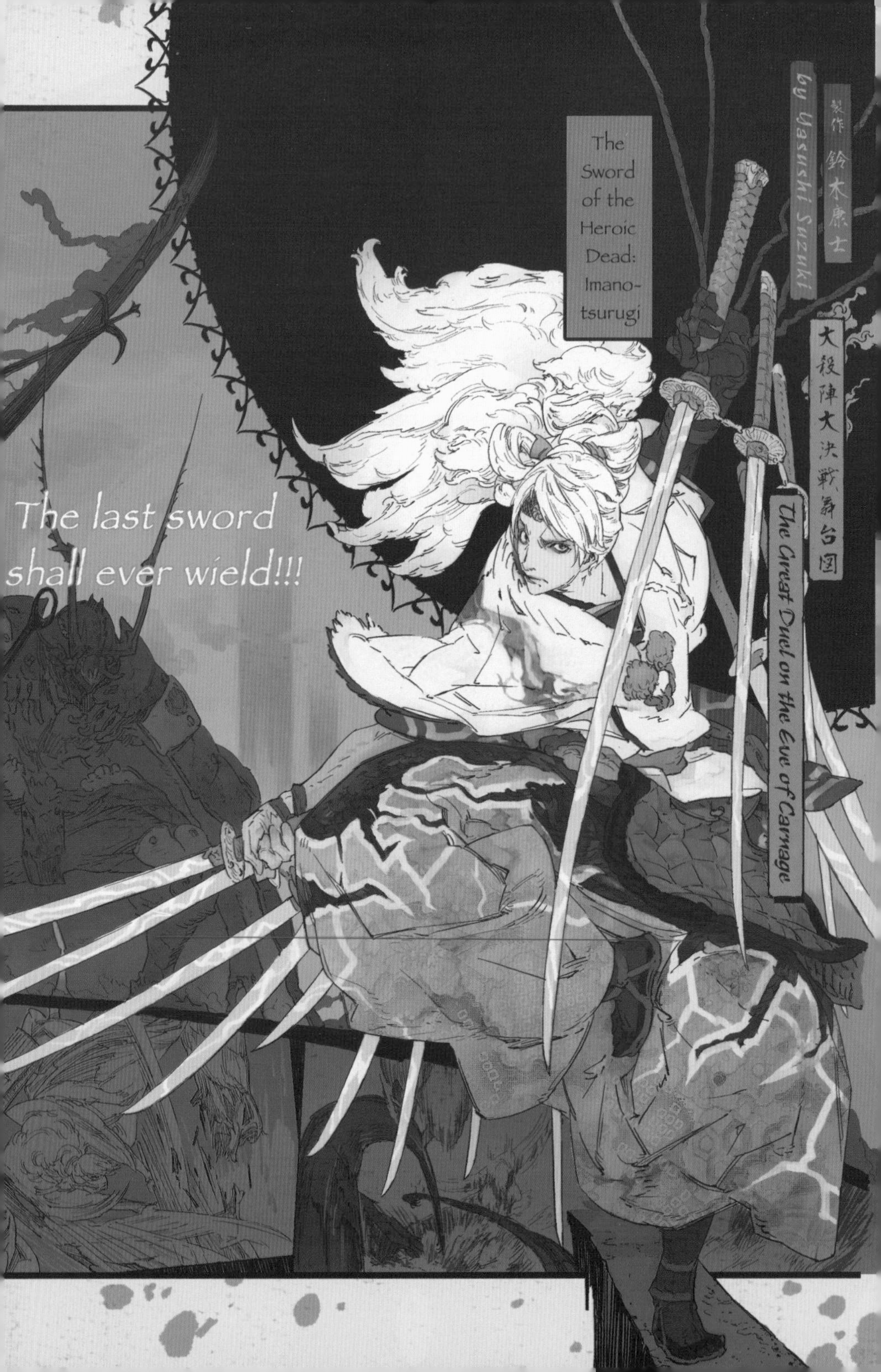
The Sword of the Heroic Dead: Imano-tsurugi
製作 鈴木康士
by Yasushi Suzuki
大殺陣大決戦舞台図
The Great Duel on the Eve of Carnage
The last sword shall ever wield!!!

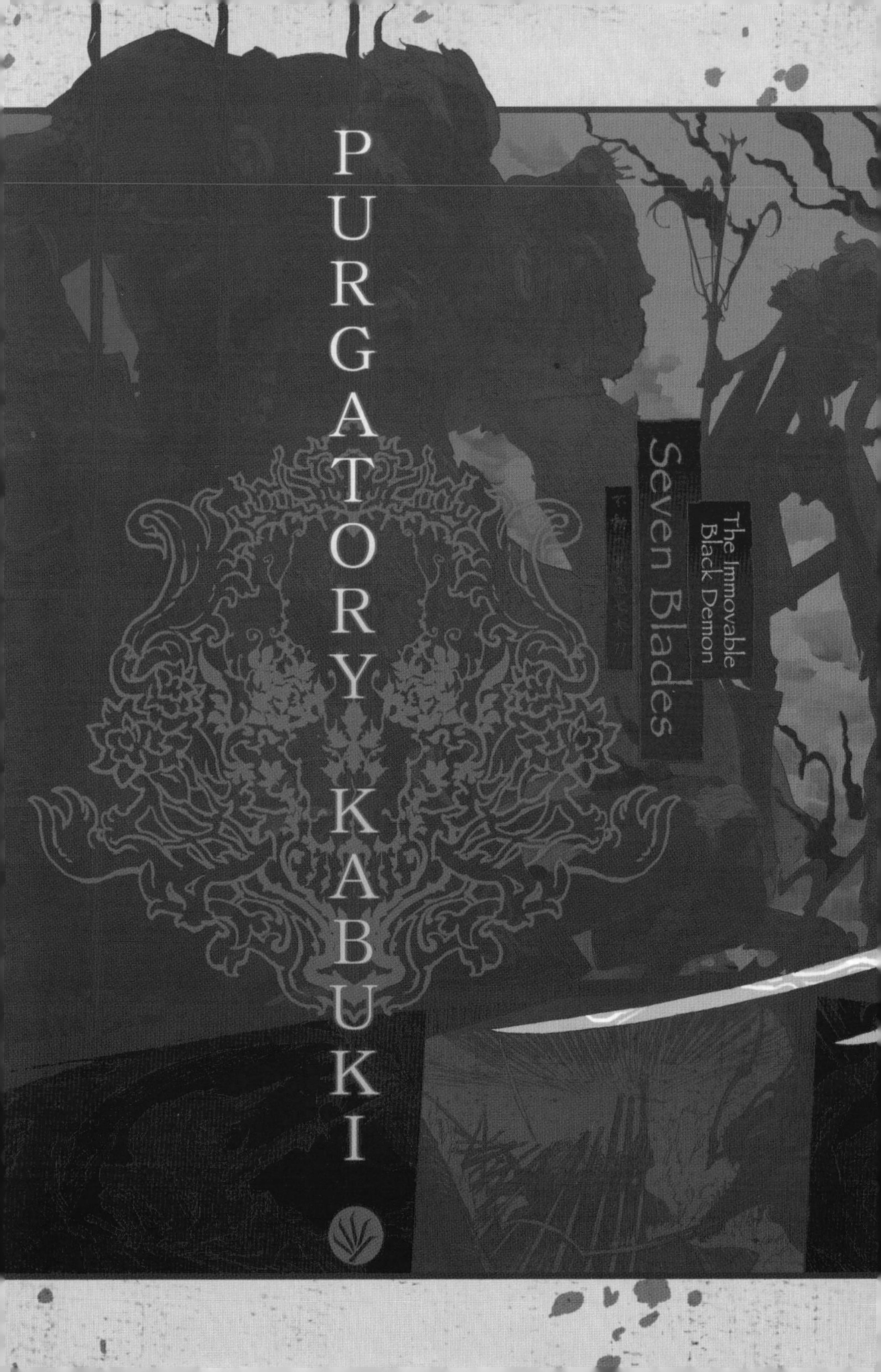
PURGATORY KABUKI
Seven Blades
The Immovable Black Demon

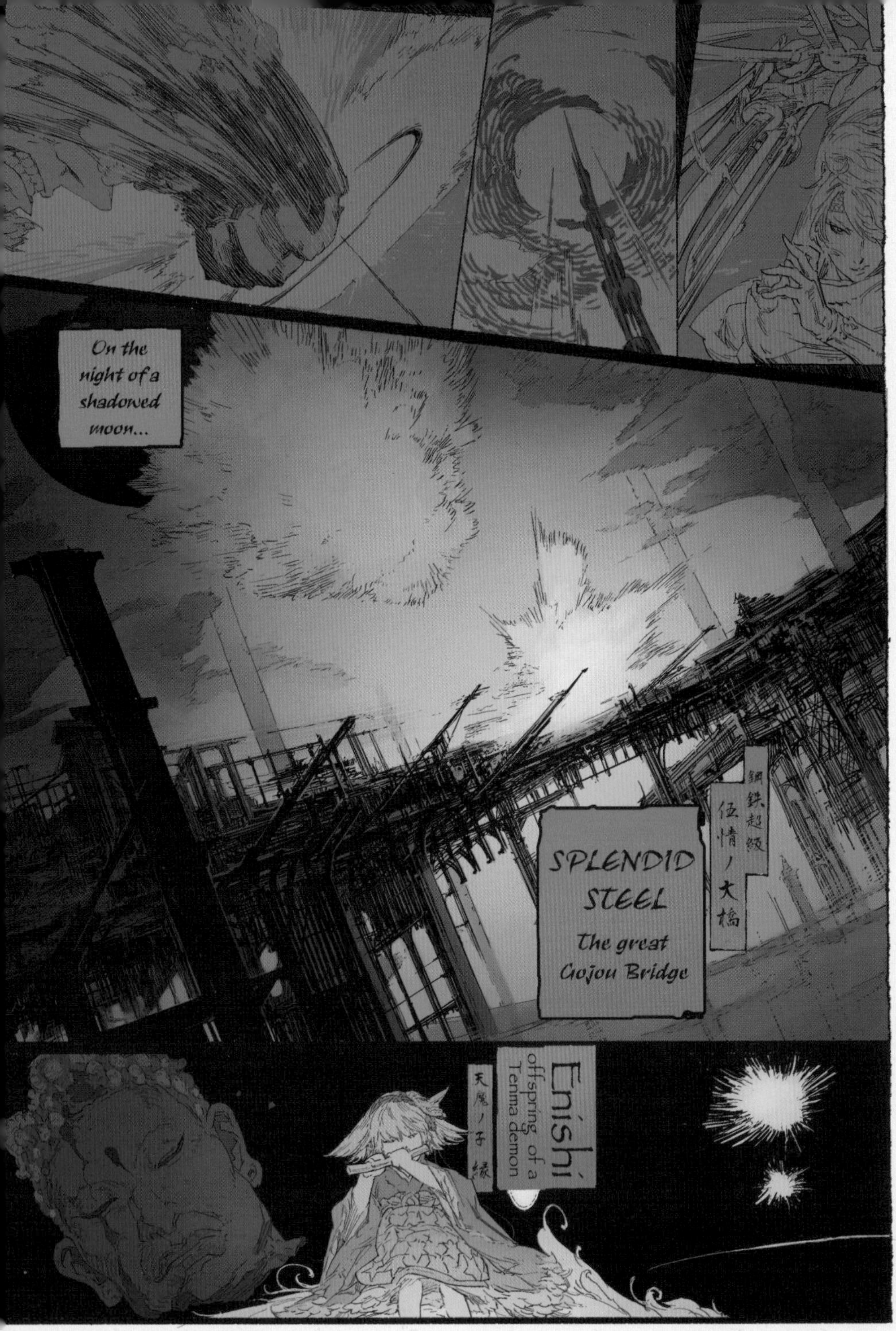
On the night of a shadowed moon...
鋼鉄超級
伍情ノ大橋
SPLENDID STEEL
The great Gojou Bridge
天魔ノ子 縁
Enishi
offspring of a Tenma demon

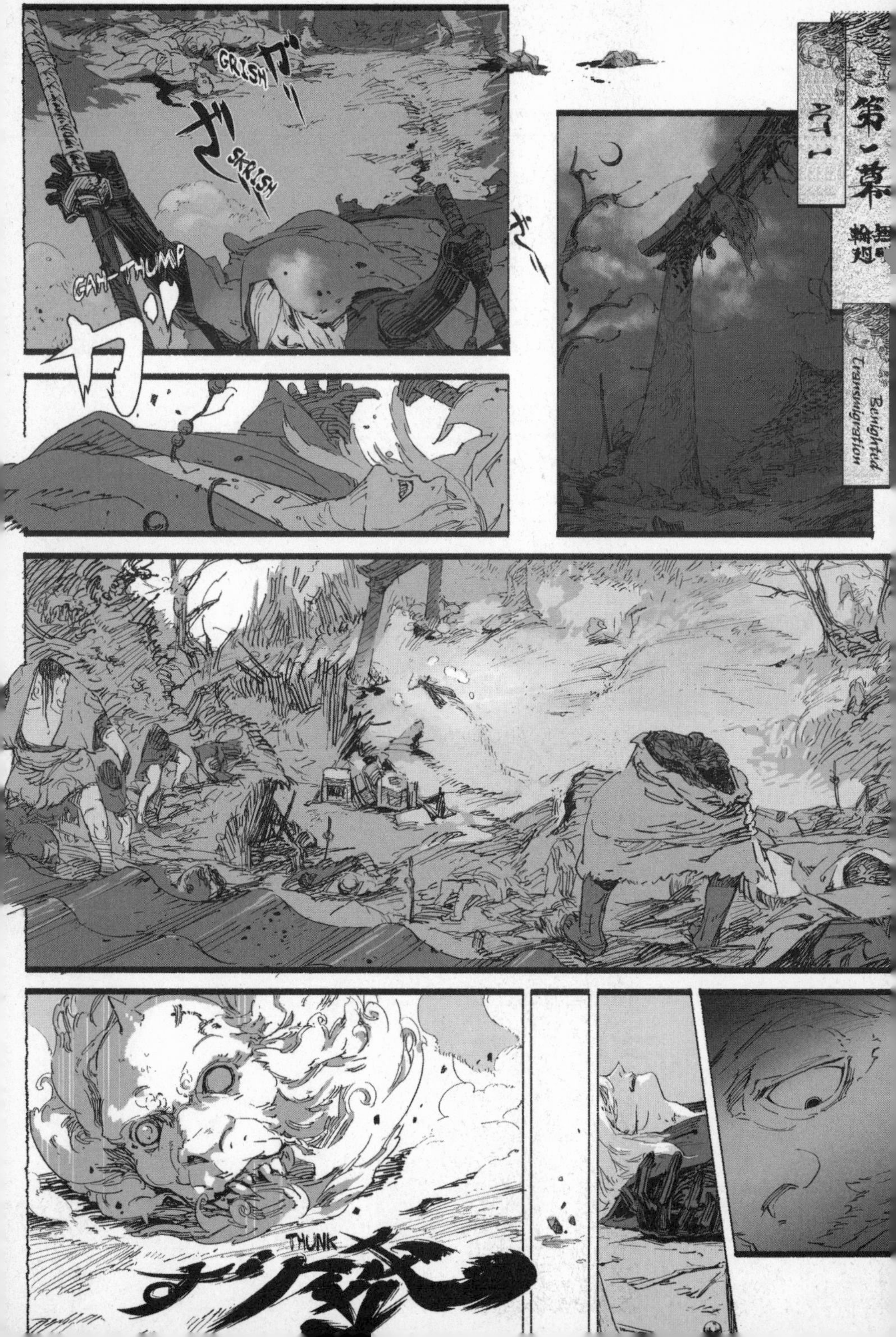
第一幕
ACT I
無明輪廻
Benighted Transmigration
GRISH
SKRISH
GAH-THUMP
THUNK

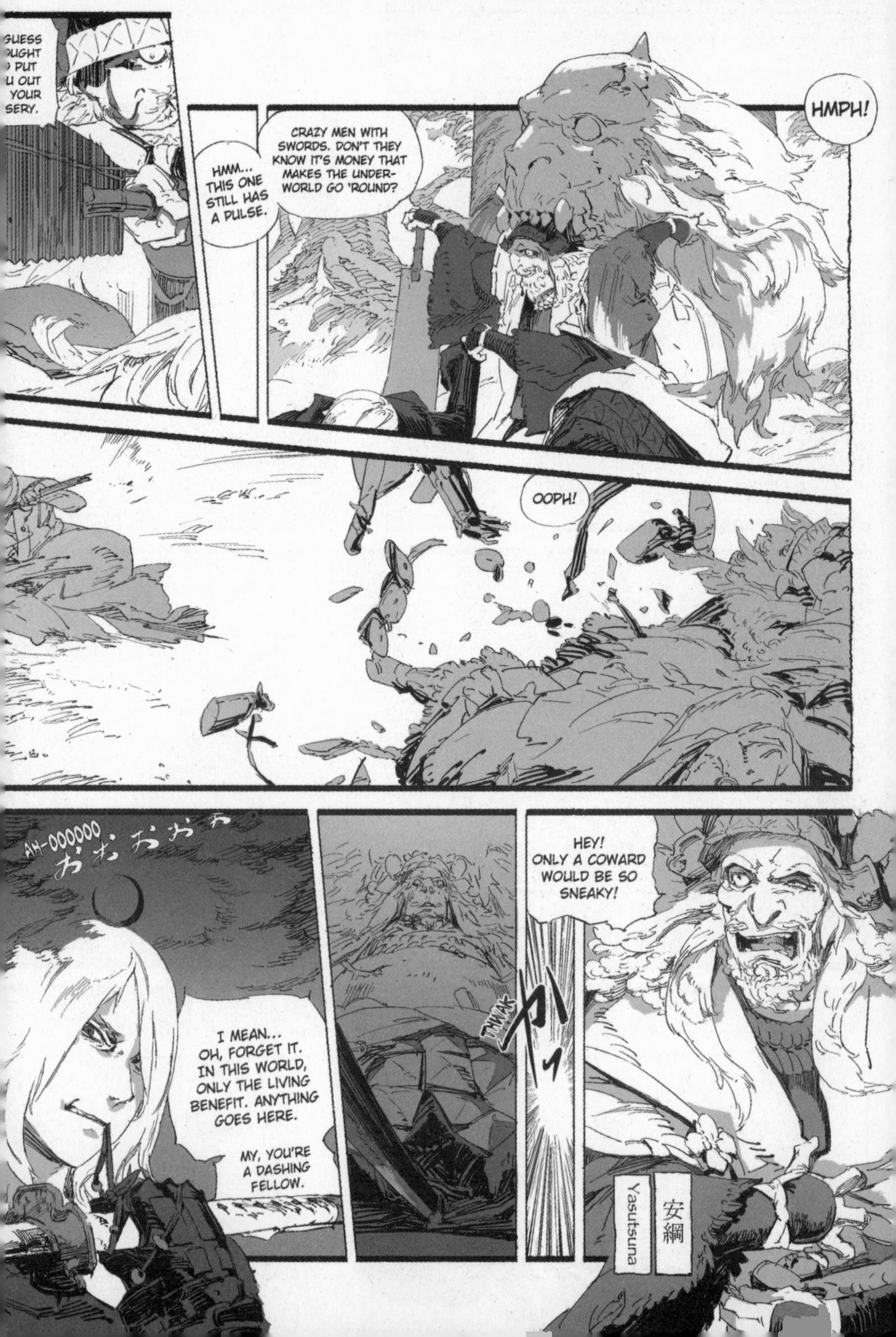

GUESS
OUGHT
PUT
U OUT
YOUR
SERY.
HMM... THIS ONE STILL HAS A PULSE.
CRAZY MEN WITH SWORDS. DON'T THEY KNOW IT'S MONEY THAT MAKES THE UNDER-WORLD GO 'ROUND?
HMPH!
OOPH!
AH-OOOOOO
おおおおお
I MEAN... OH, FORGET IT. IN THIS WORLD, ONLY THE LIVING BENEFIT. ANYTHING GOES HERE.
MY, YOU'RE A DASHING FELLOW.
THWAK
HEY! ONLY A COWARD WOULD BE SO SNEAKY!
安綱
Yasutsuna

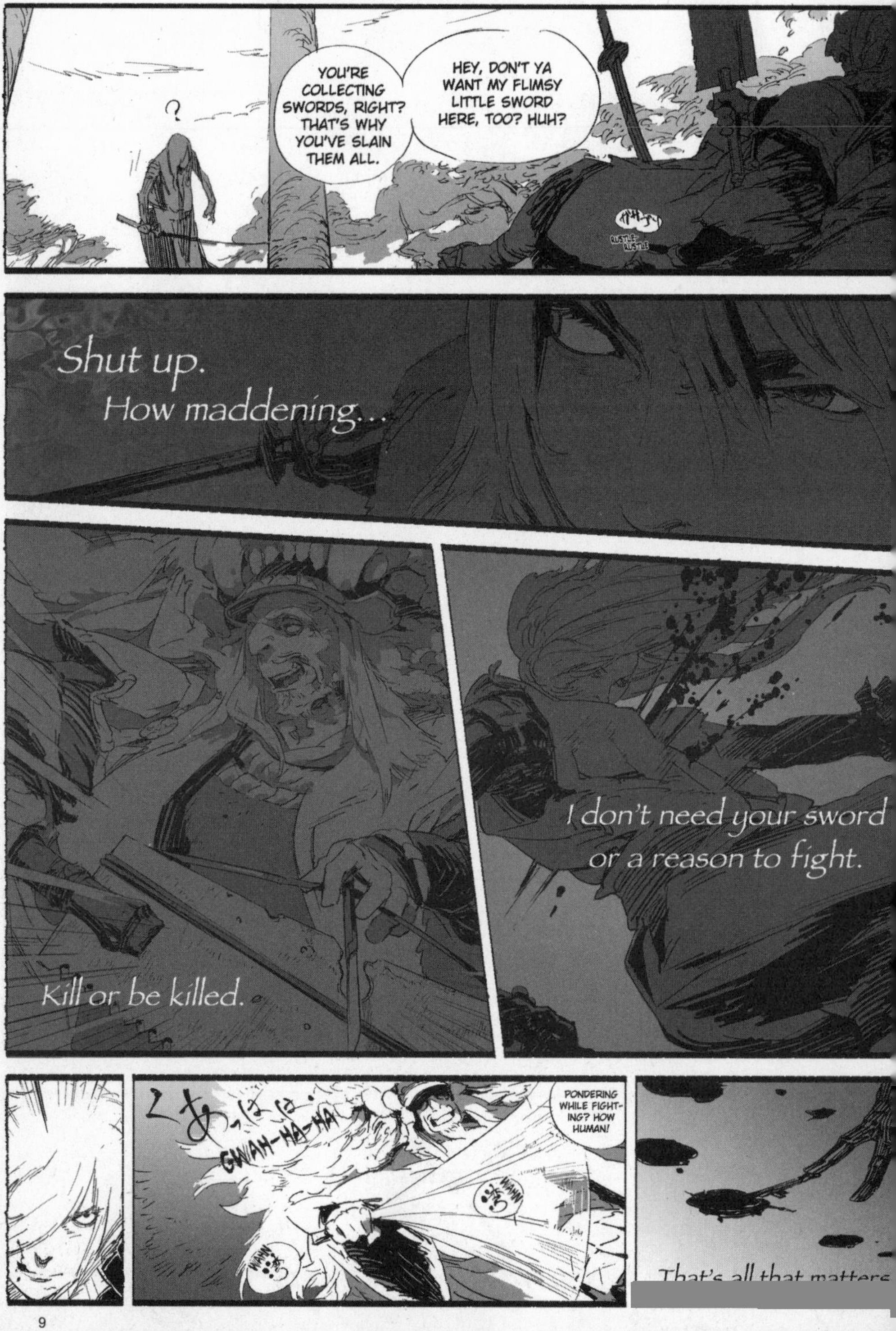

?
YOU'RE COLLECTING SWORDS, RIGHT? THAT'S WHY YOU'VE SLAIN THEM ALL.
HEY, DON'T YA WANT MY FLIMSY LITTLE SWORD HERE, TOO? HUH?
RUSTLE RUSTLE
Shut up.
How maddening...
Kill or be killed.
I don't need your sword
or a reason to fight.
GWAH-HA-HA
PONDERING WHILE FIGHT-ING? HOW HUMAN!
WAHN
WAHN
That's all that matters

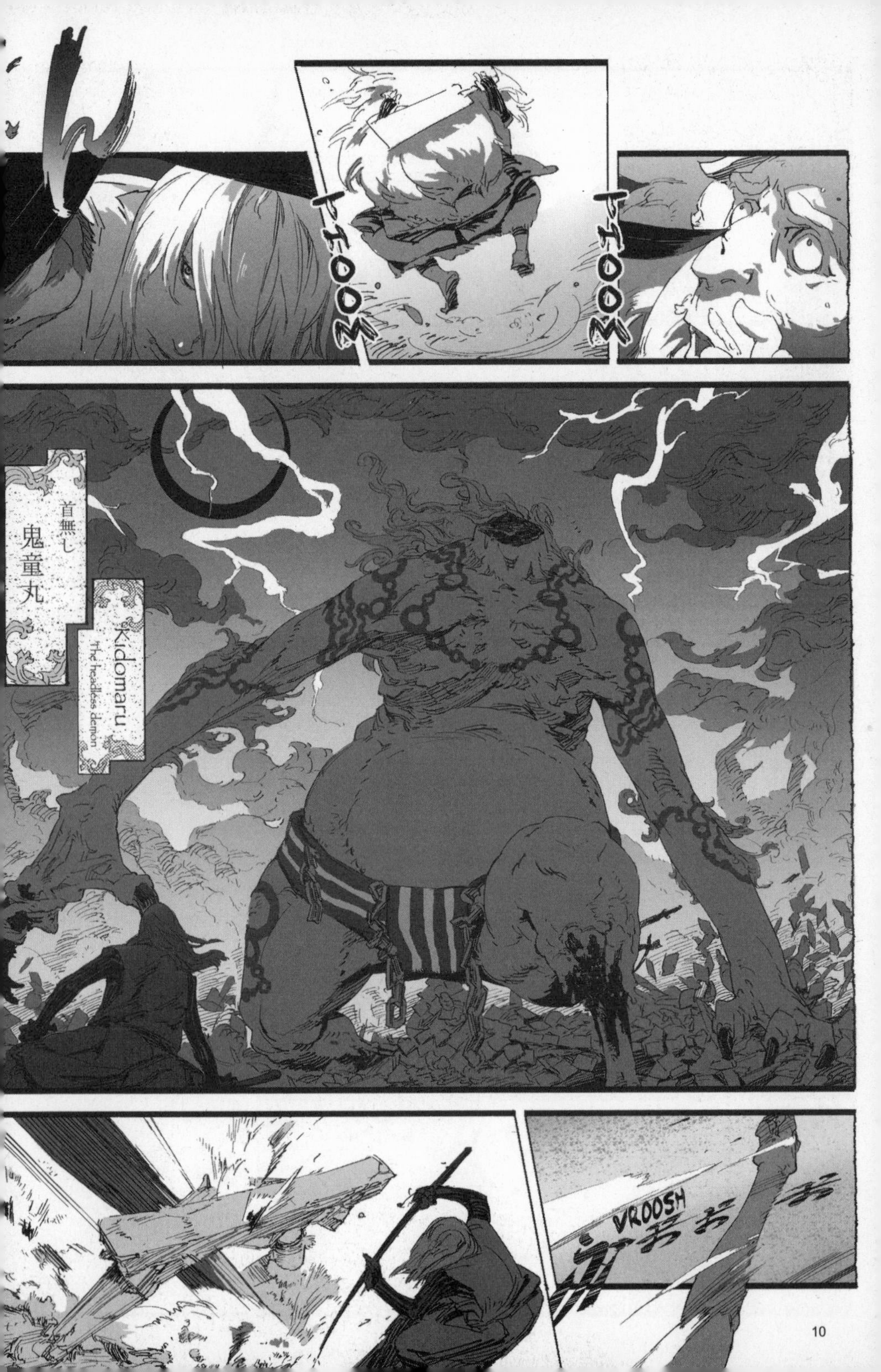

FWOOM
FWOOM
首無し
鬼童丸
Kidomaru
The headless demon
VROOSH

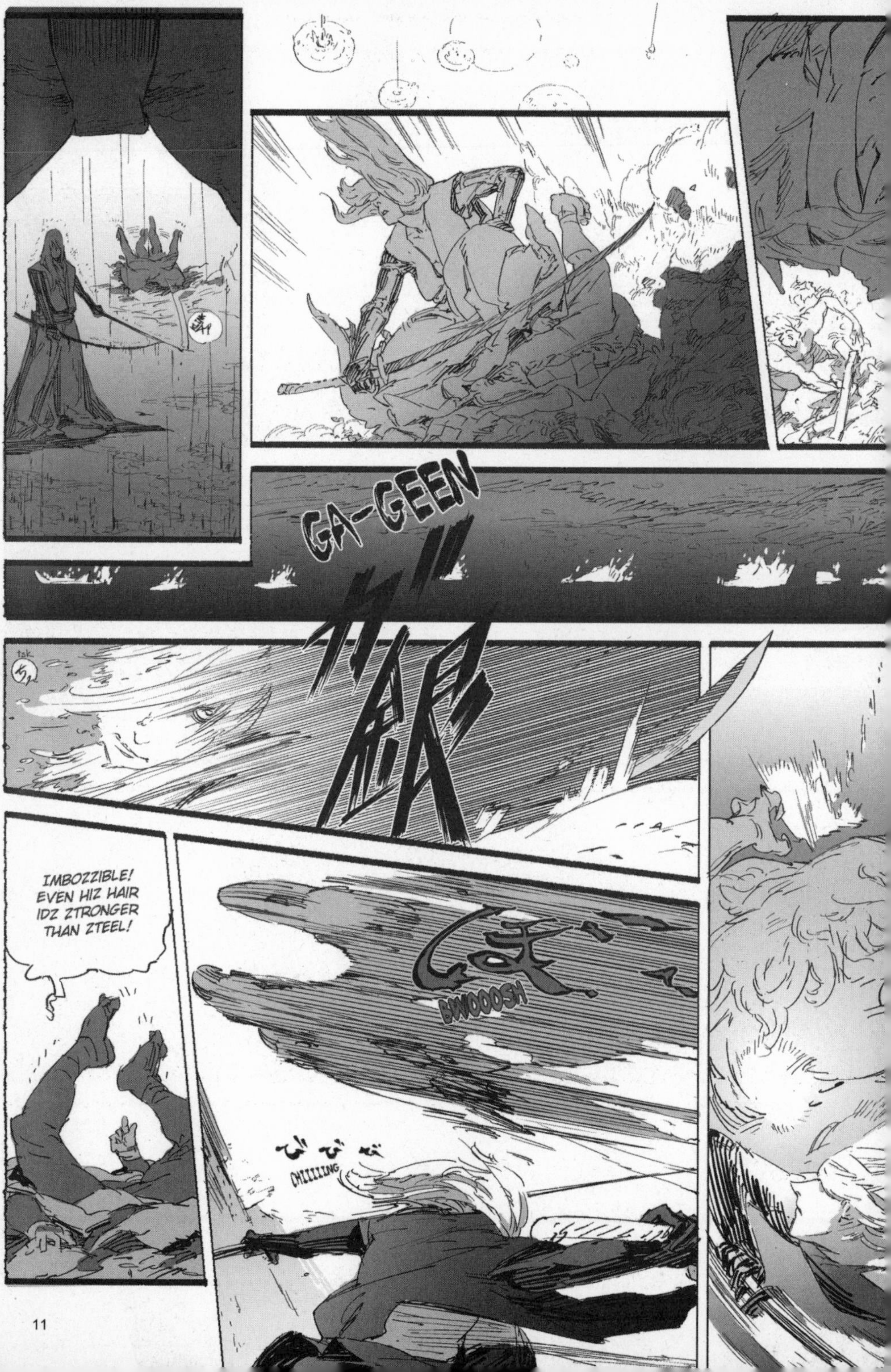

tsk
GA-GEEN
IMBOZZIBLE! EVEN HIZ HAIR IDZ ZTRONGER THAN ZTEEL!
BWOOOSH
CHIIIIING

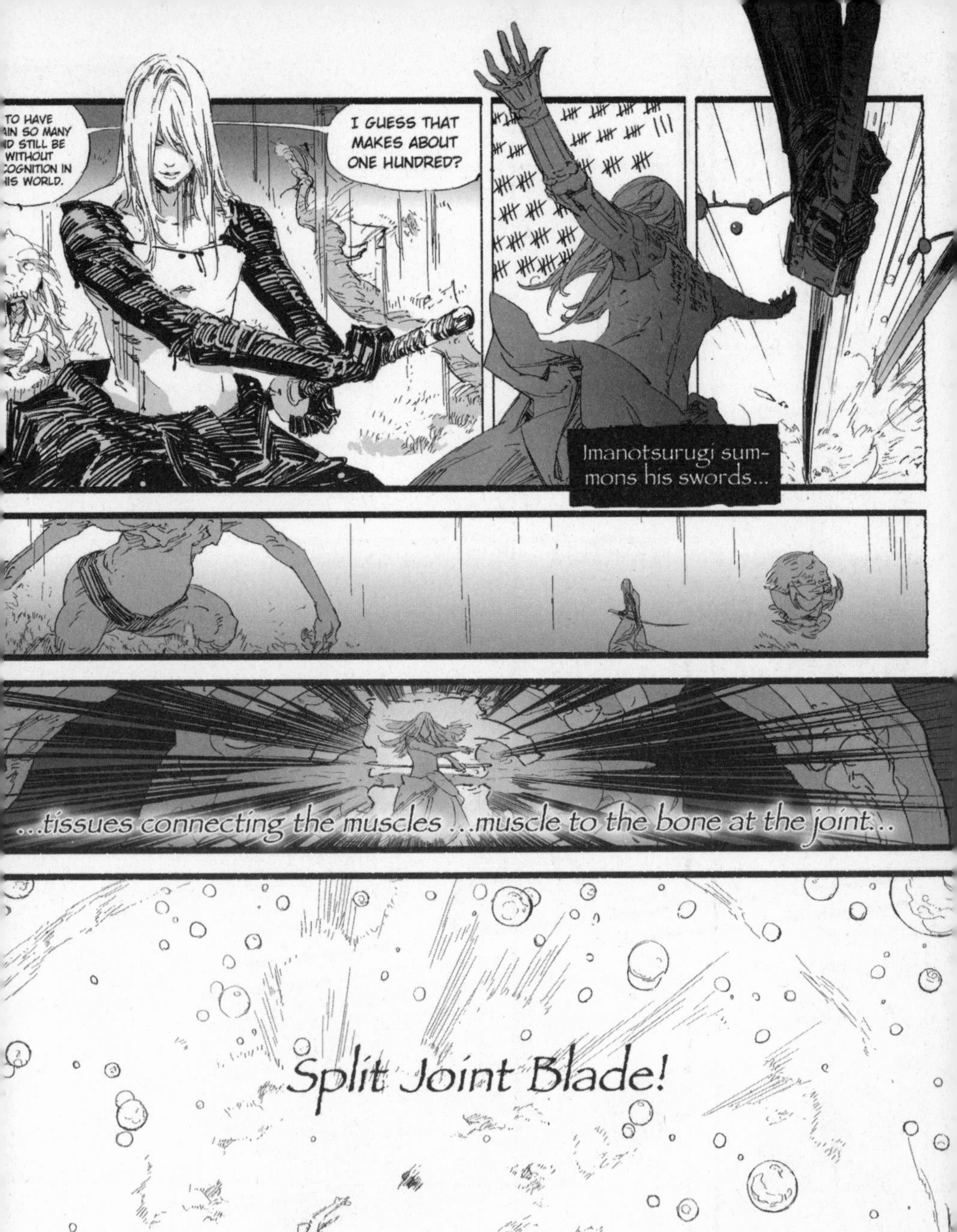

TO HAVE AIN SO MANY ID STILL BE WITHOUT COGNITION IN HIS WORLD.
I GUESS THAT MAKES ABOUT ONE HUNDRED?
Imanotsurugi summons his swords...
...tissues connecting the muscles ...muscle to the bone at the joint...
Split Joint Blade!

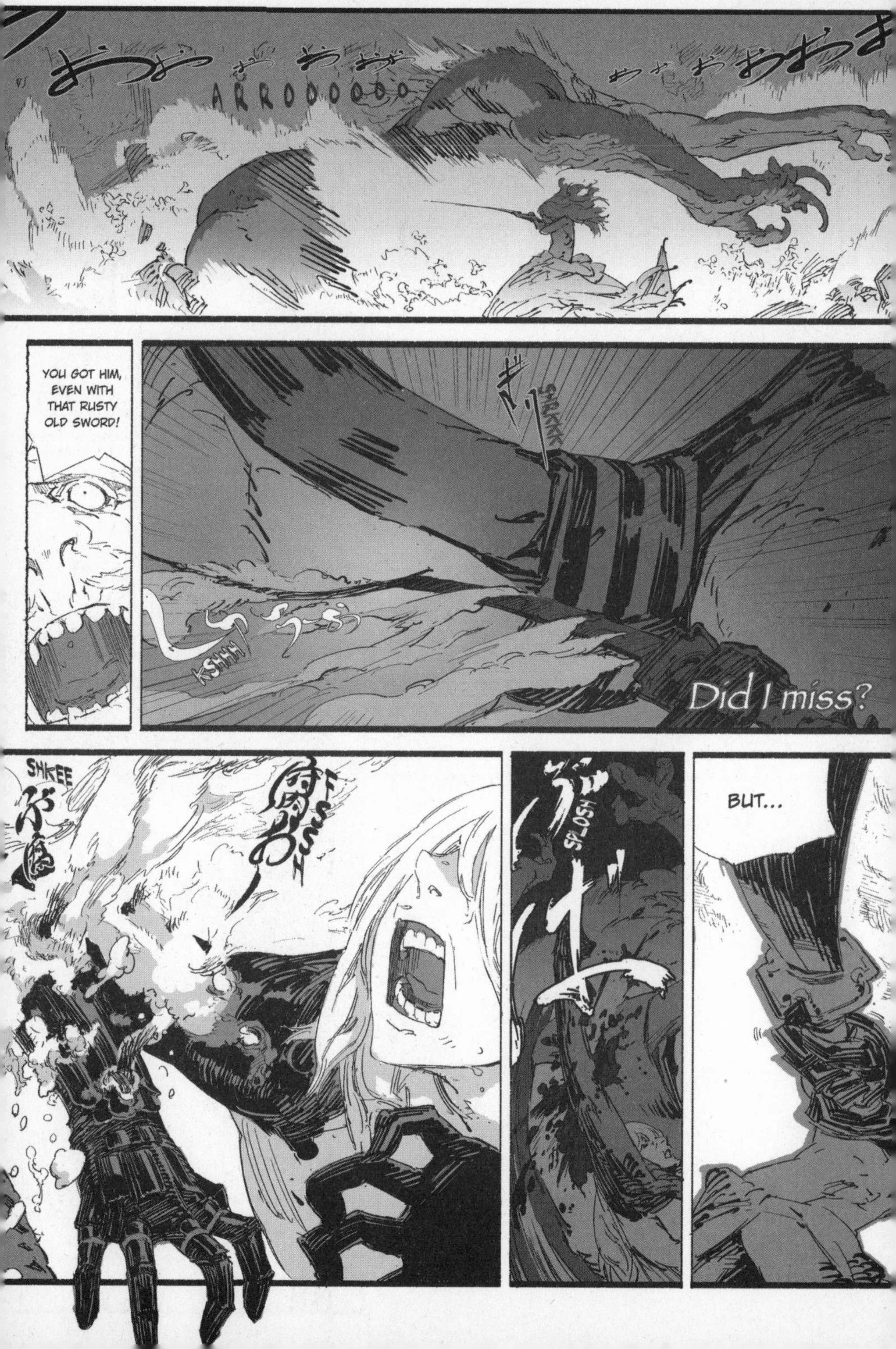
ARROOOOOO
YOU GOT HIM, EVEN WITH THAT RUSTY OLD SWORD!
SHRKKK
KSHHH
Did I miss?
SHREE
FSSSH
SPLOSH
BUT...

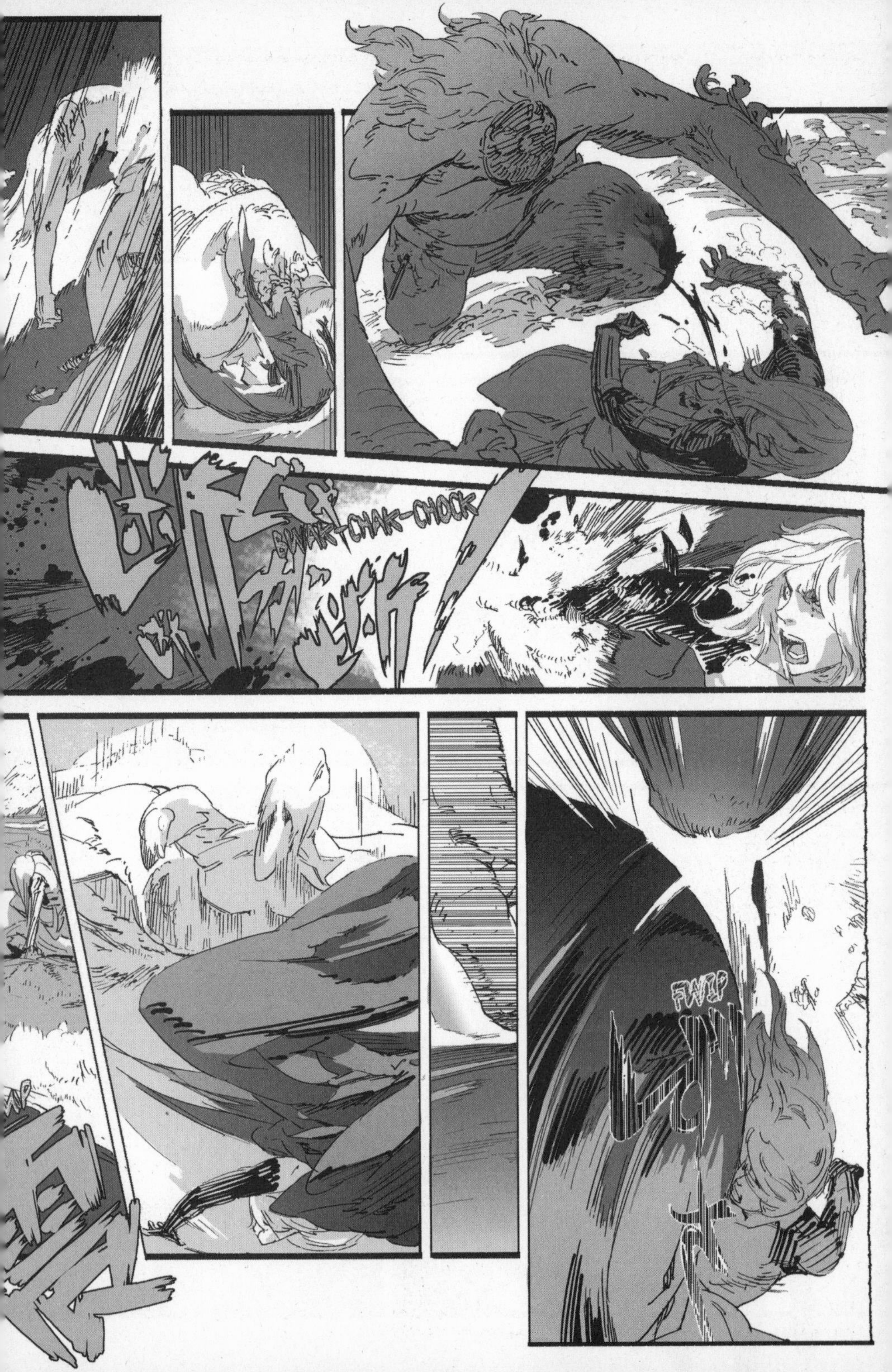
BWAR-CHAK-CHOCK
FWIP

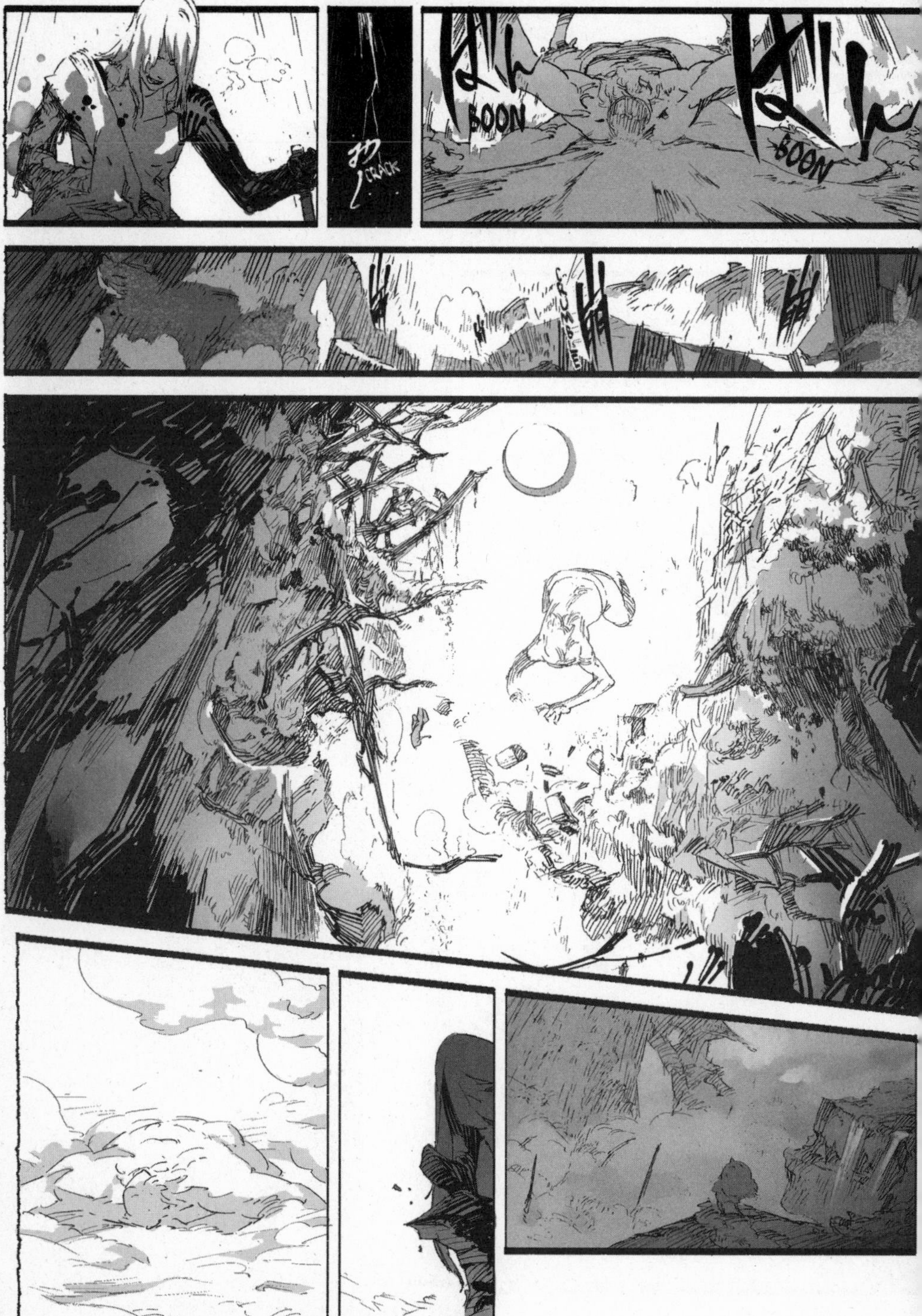
CRACK
BOON
BOON

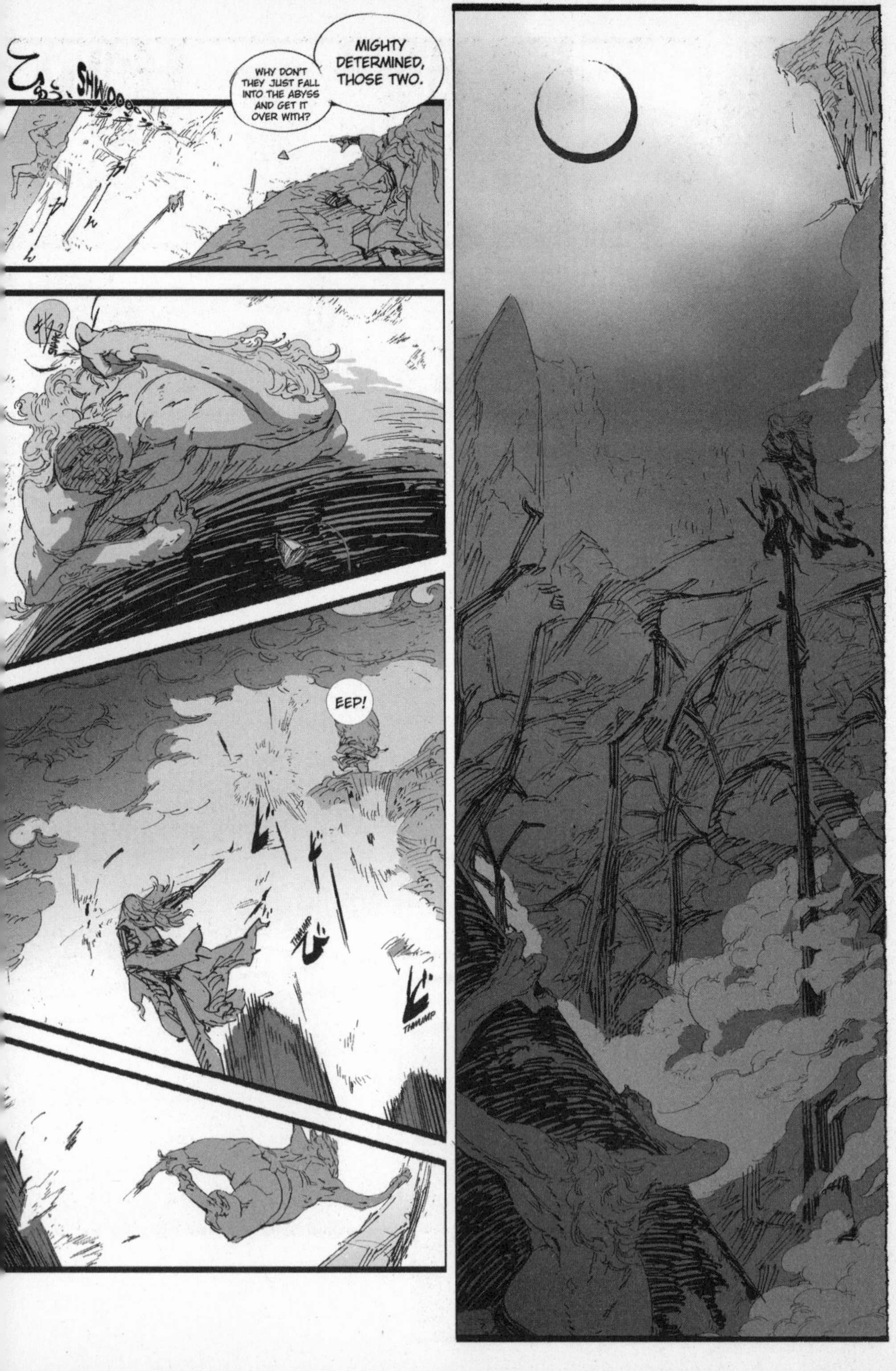

SHWOOO
MIGHTY DETERMINED, THOSE TWO.
WHY DON'T THEY JUST FALL INTO THE ABYSS AND GET IT OVER WITH?
EEP!
THMMP
THMMP

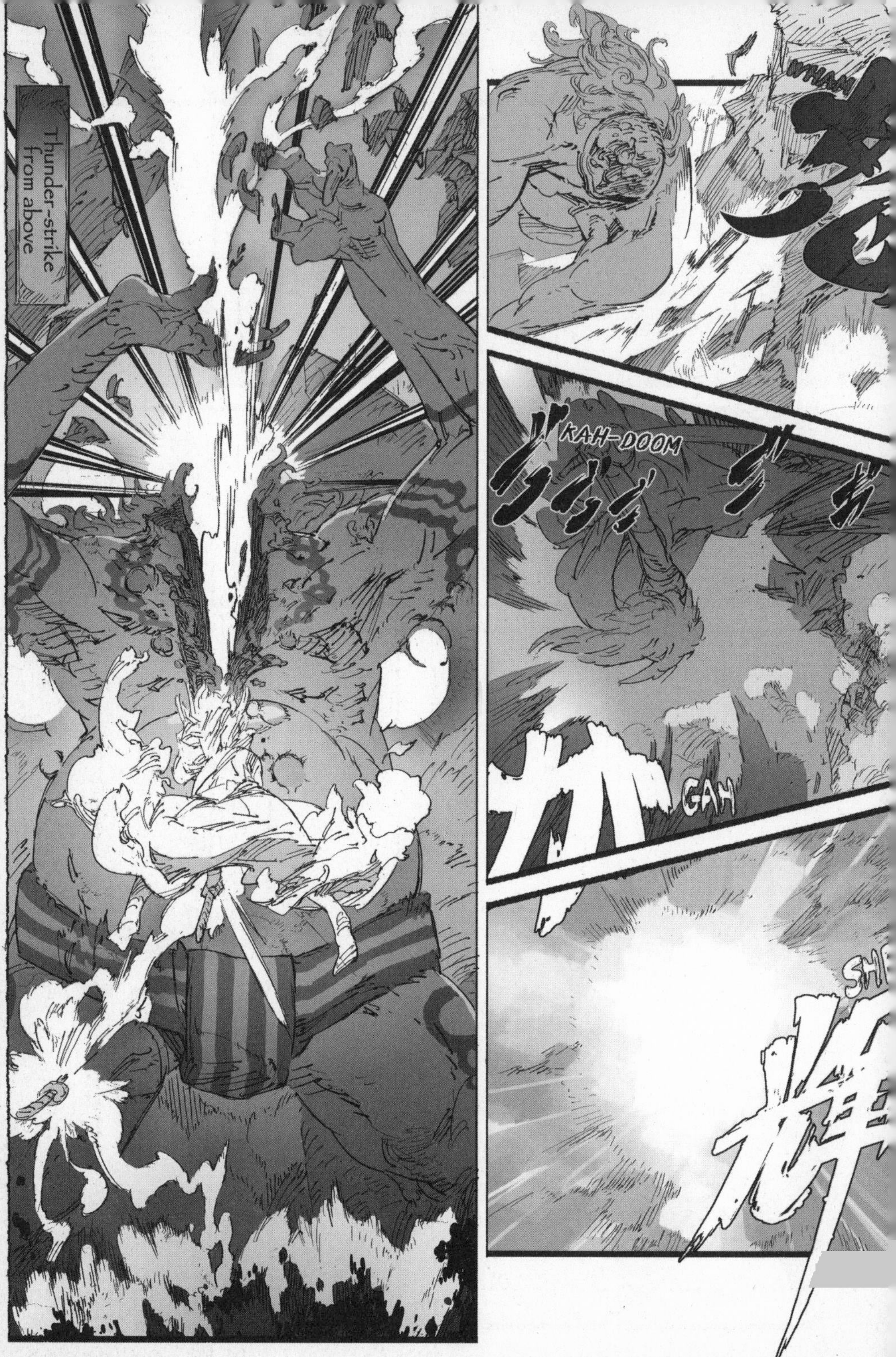
Thunder-strike from above
WHAM
KAH-DOOM
GAH

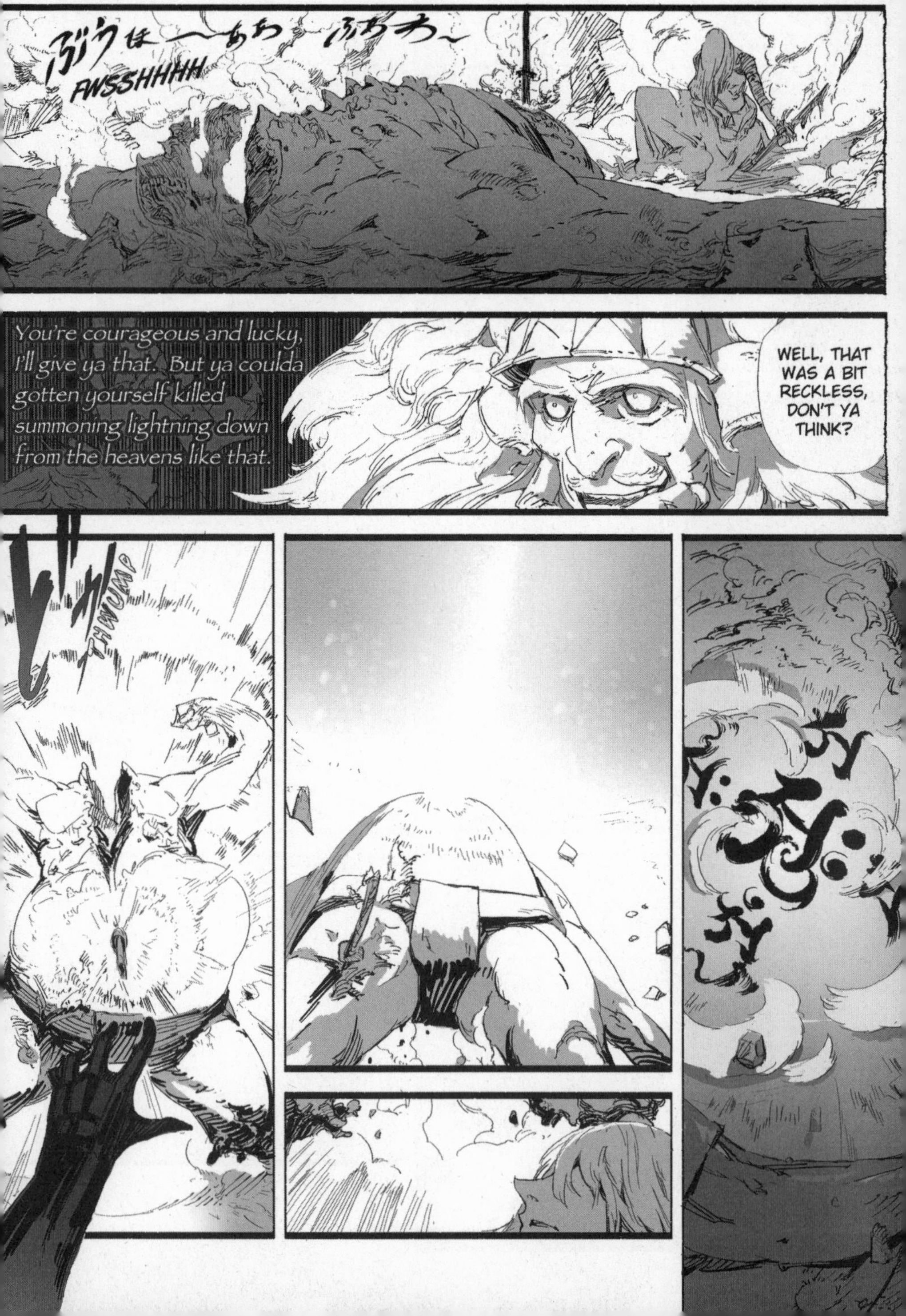
ぶしゅ～ ぶわ～
FWSSHHHH
WELL, THAT WAS A BIT RECKLESS, DON'T YA THINK?
You're courageous and lucky, I'll give ya that. But ya coulda gotten yourself killed summoning lightning down from the heavens like that.
THWUMP

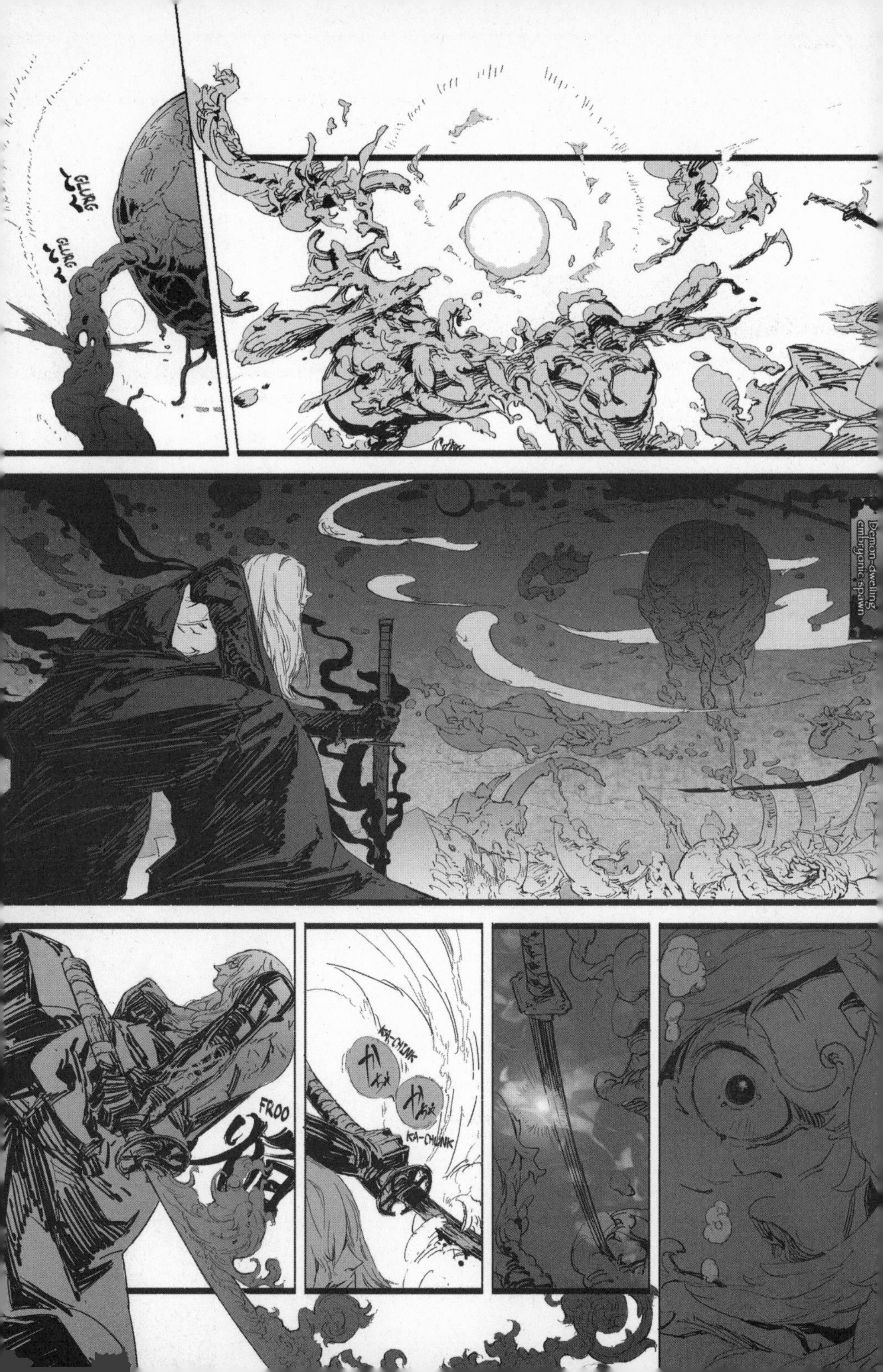
GLURG
GLURG
Demon-dwelling embryonic spawn
FROO
KA-CHUNK
KA-CHUNK

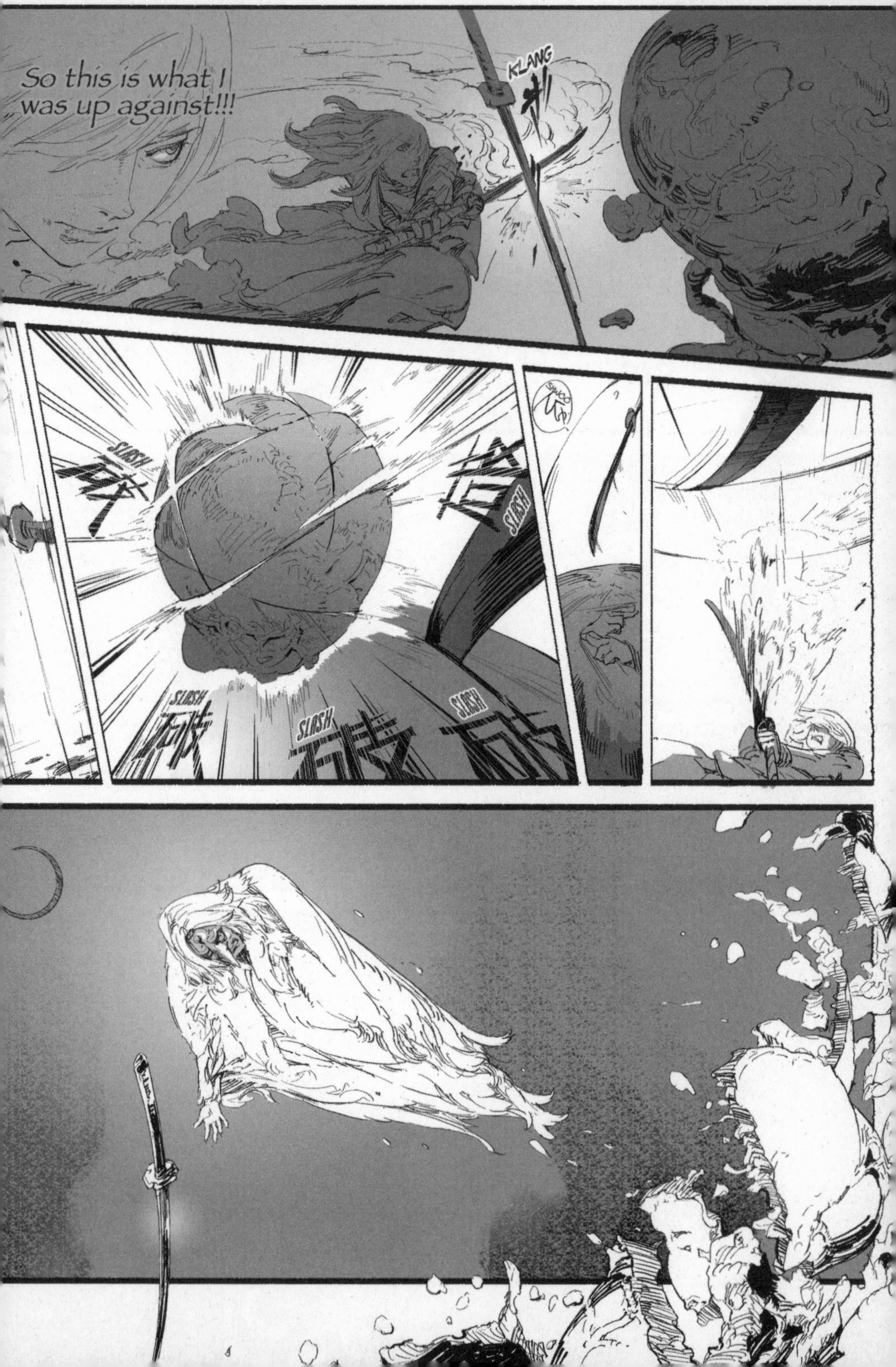

So this is what I was up against!!!
KLANG
SHWOO
SLASH
SLASH
SLASH
SLASH
SLASH

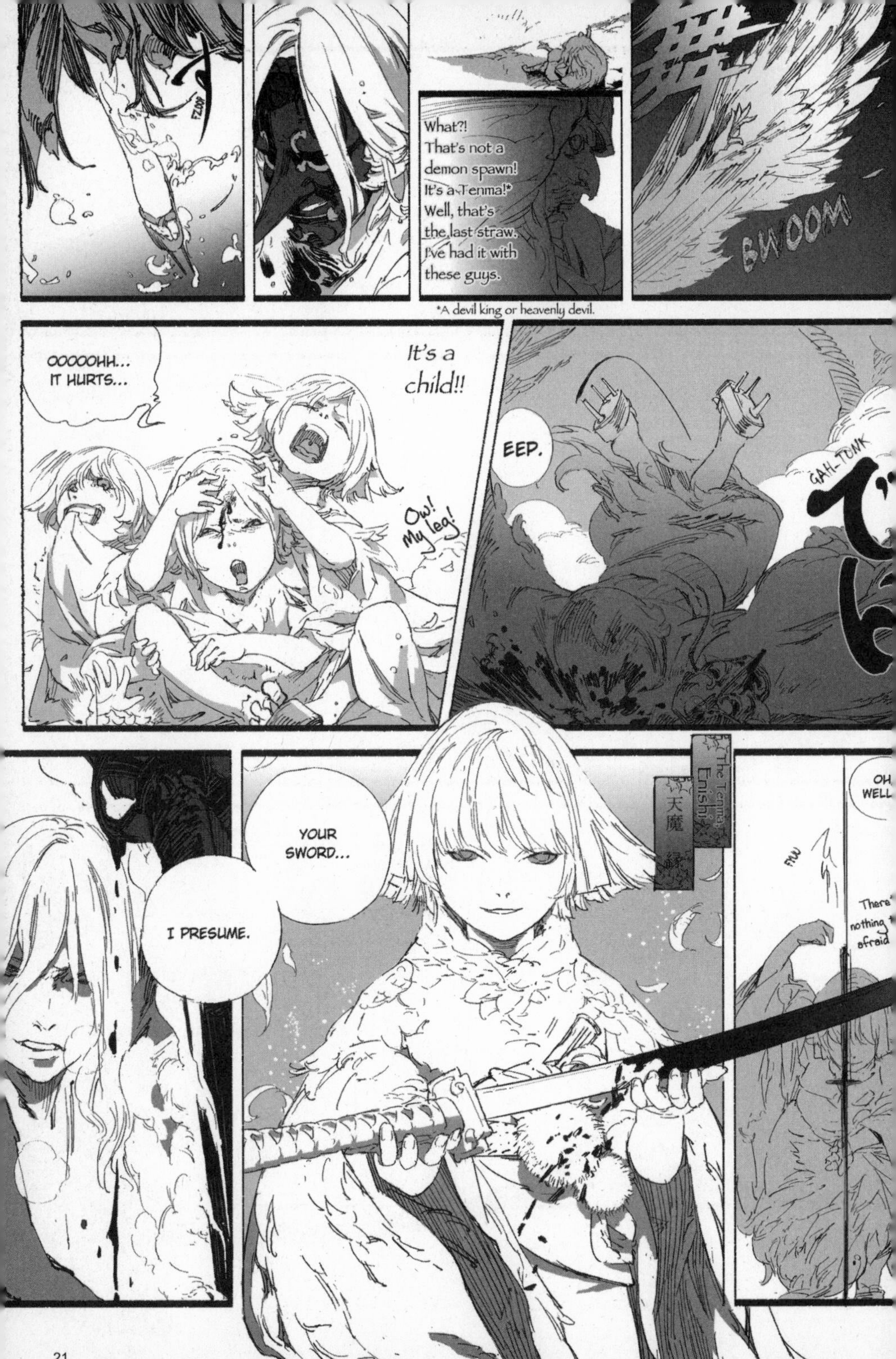

FZOOP
What?! That's not a demon spawn! It's a Tenma!* Well, that's the last straw. I've had it with these guys.
BWOOM
*A devil king or heavenly devil.
OOOOOHH... IT HURTS...
It's a child!!
Ow! My leg!
EEP.
GAH-TUNK
YOUR SWORD...
I PRESUME.
The Tenma Enishi
天魔 縁
FWU
OH, WELL
There's nothing to be afraid

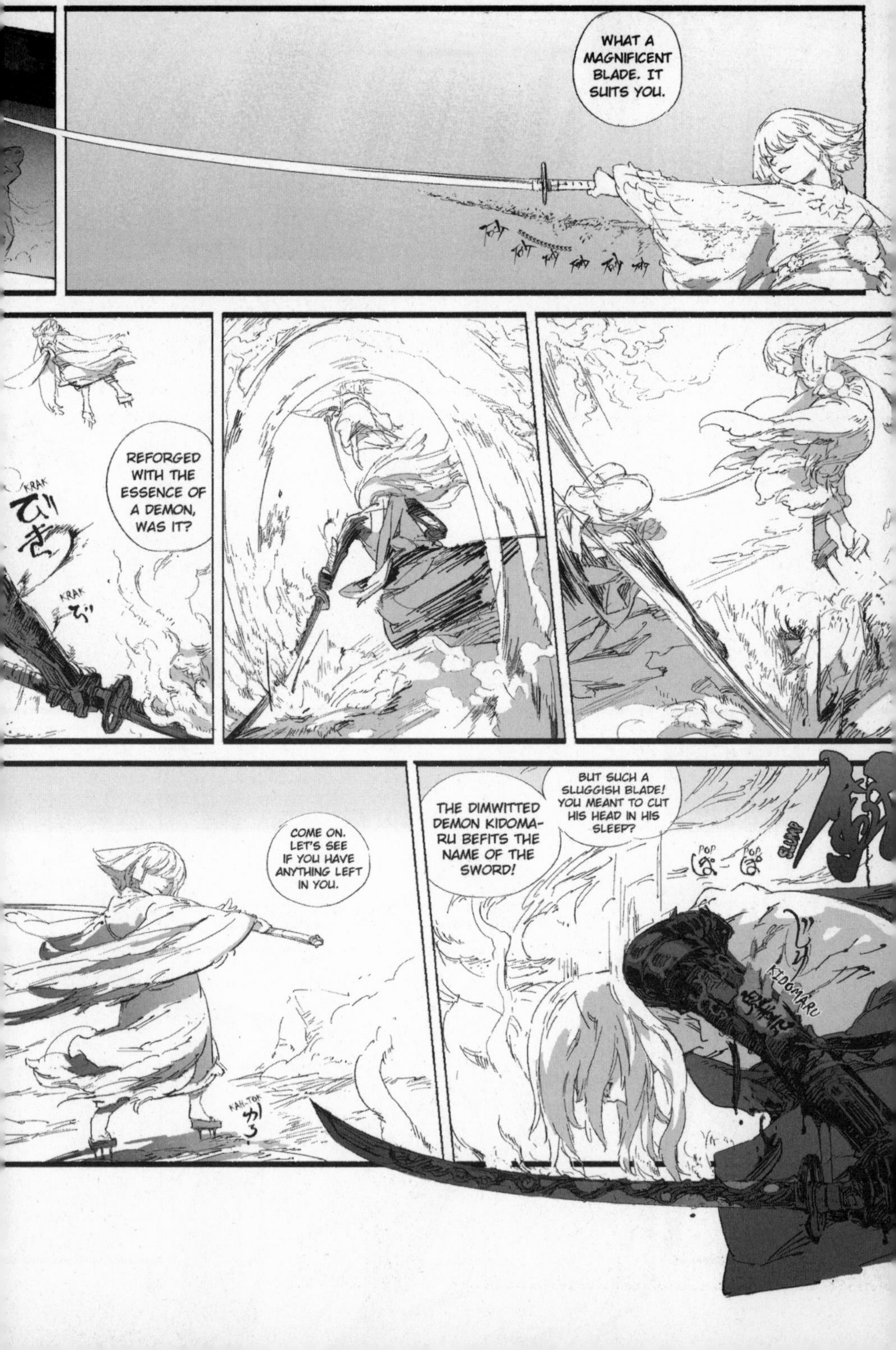

WHAT A MAGNIFICENT BLADE. IT SUITS YOU.
REFORGED WITH THE ESSENCE OF A DEMON, WAS IT?
KRAK
KRAK
COME ON. LET'S SEE IF YOU HAVE ANYTHING LEFT IN YOU.
KAH-TON
BUT SUCH A SLUGGISH BLADE! YOU MEANT TO CUT HIS HEAD IN HIS SLEEP?
THE DIMWITTED DEMON KIDOMA-RU BEFITS THE NAME OF THE SWORD!
POP
POP
SLUMP
KIDOMARU

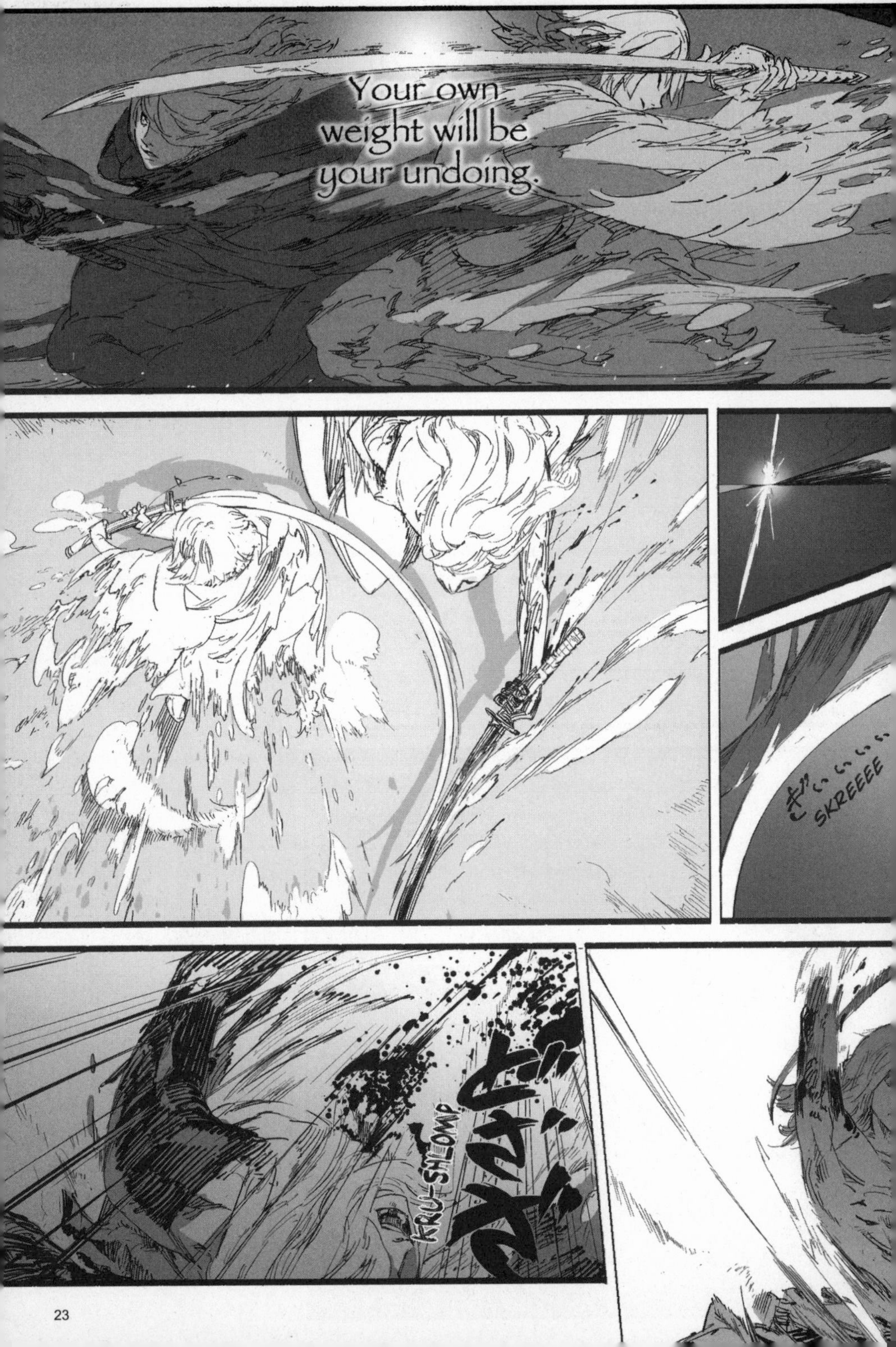
Your own weight will be your undoing.
SKREEEE
KRU-SHLOMP

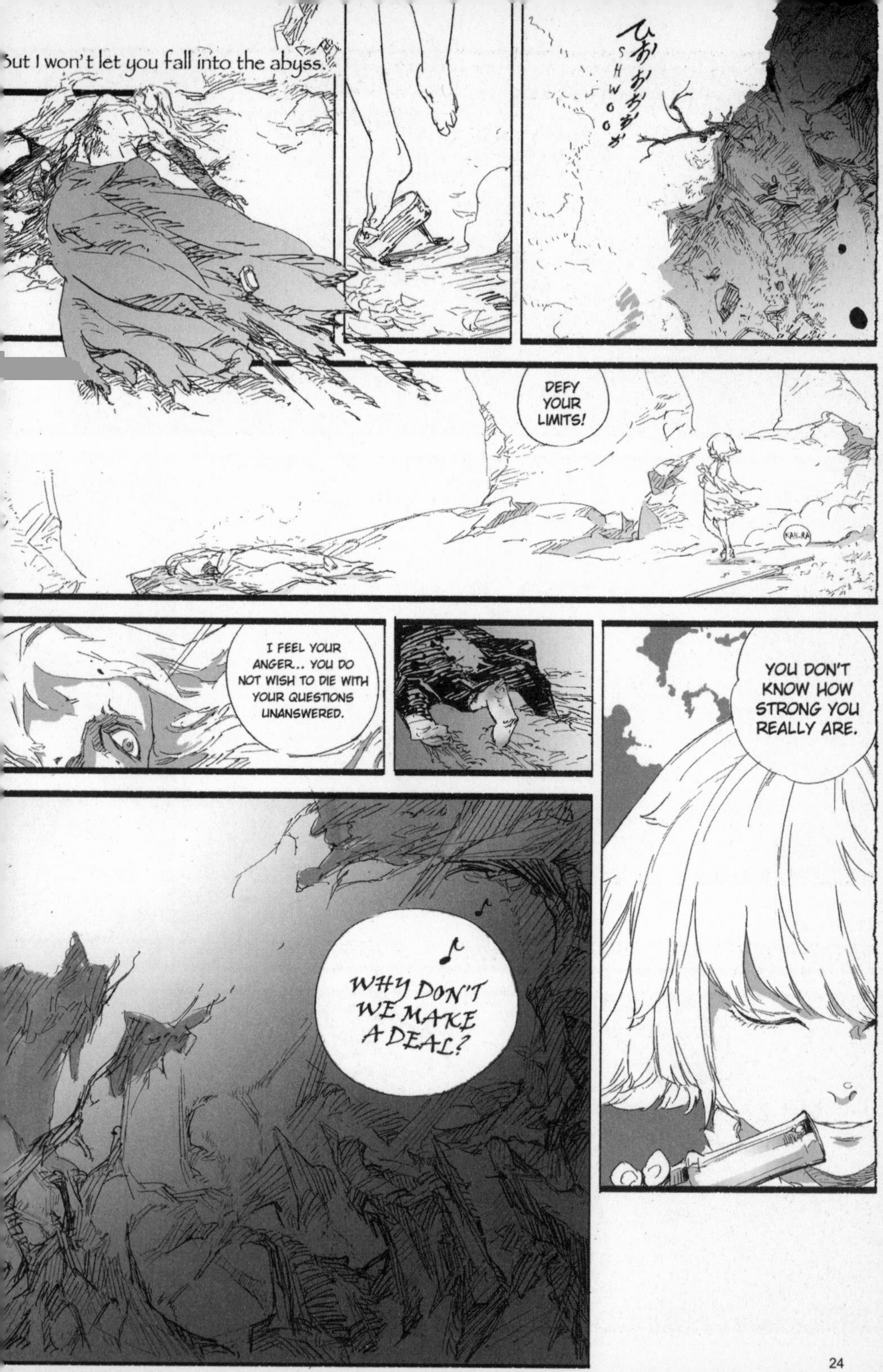
But I won't let you fall into the abyss.
SHWOOO
DEFY YOUR LIMITS!
KAH-RA
I FEEL YOUR ANGER.. YOU DO NOT WISH TO DIE WITH YOUR QUESTIONS UNANSWERED.
YOU DON'T KNOW HOW STRONG YOU REALLY ARE.
WHY DON'T WE MAKE A DEAL?

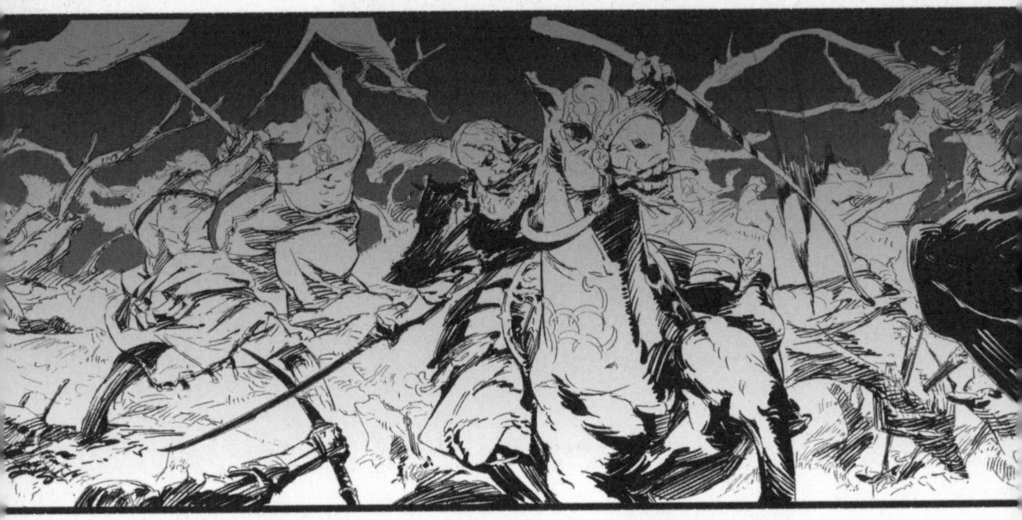

Behold, the great Gojou Bridge, the bridge of the dead.

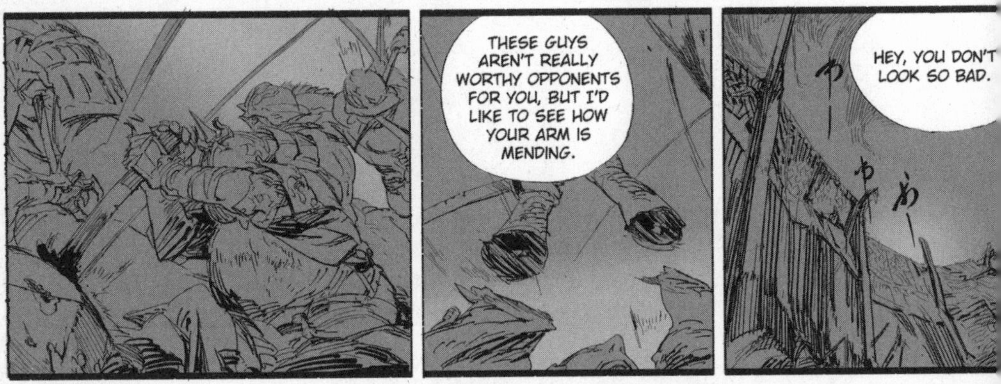
THESE GUYS AREN'T REALLY WORTHY OPPONENTS FOR YOU, BUT I'D LIKE TO SEE HOW YOUR ARM IS MENDING.
HEY, YOU DON'T LOOK SO BAD.

A hell of unlimited bloodletting. A world without hope for salvation.

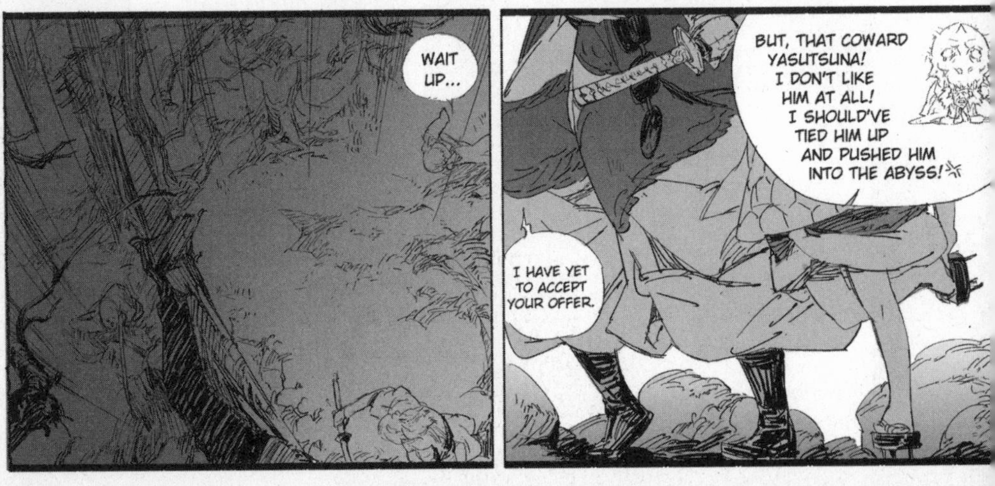
WAIT UP...
BUT, THAT COWARD YASUTSUNA! I DON'T LIKE HIM AT ALL! I SHOULD'VE TIED HIM UP AND PUSHED HIM INTO THE ABYSS!
I HAVE YET TO ACCEPT YOUR OFFER.

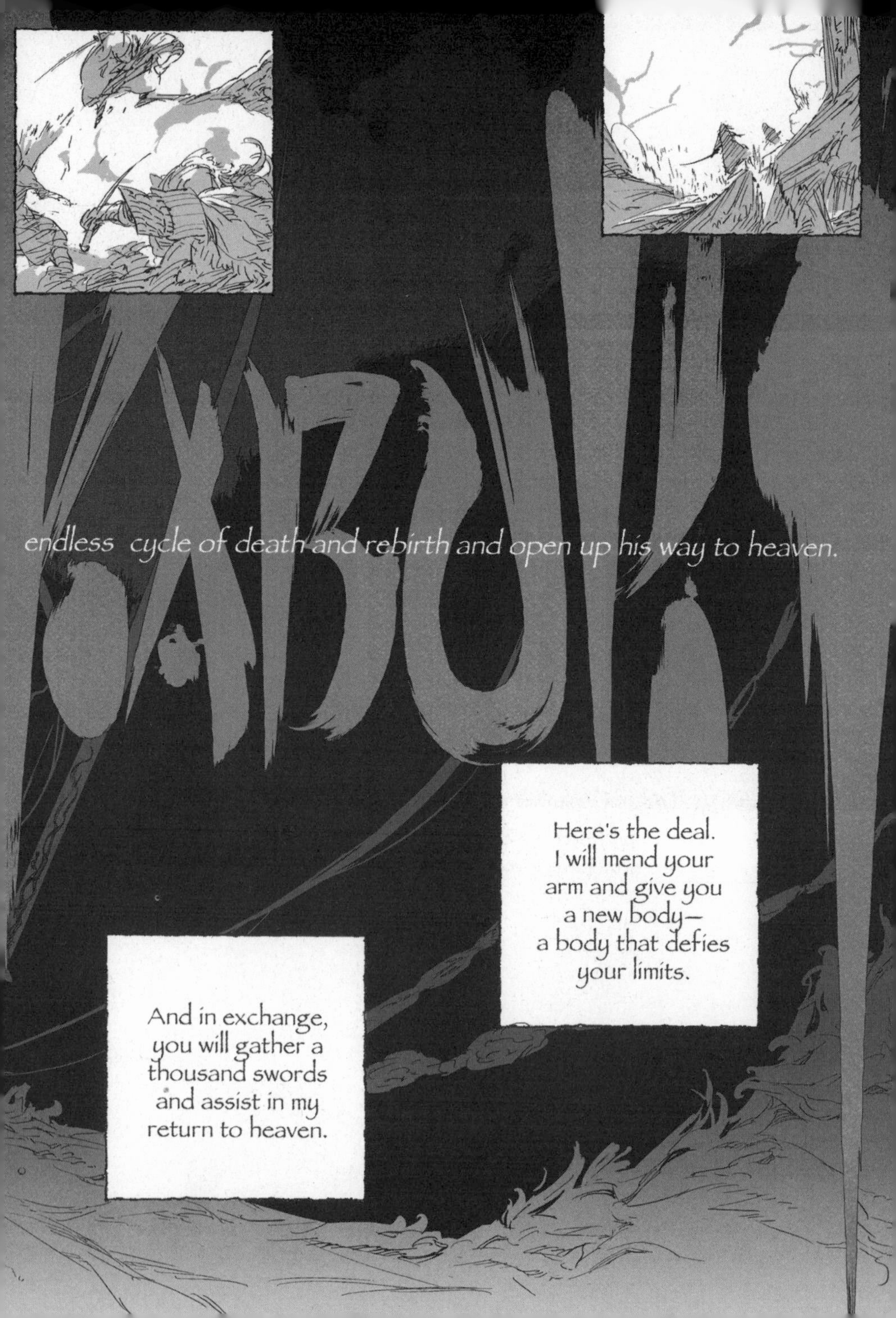
endless cycle of death and rebirth and open up his way to heaven.
Here's the deal. I will mend your arm and give you a new body— a body that defies your limits.
And in exchange, you will gather a thousand swords and assist in my return to heaven.

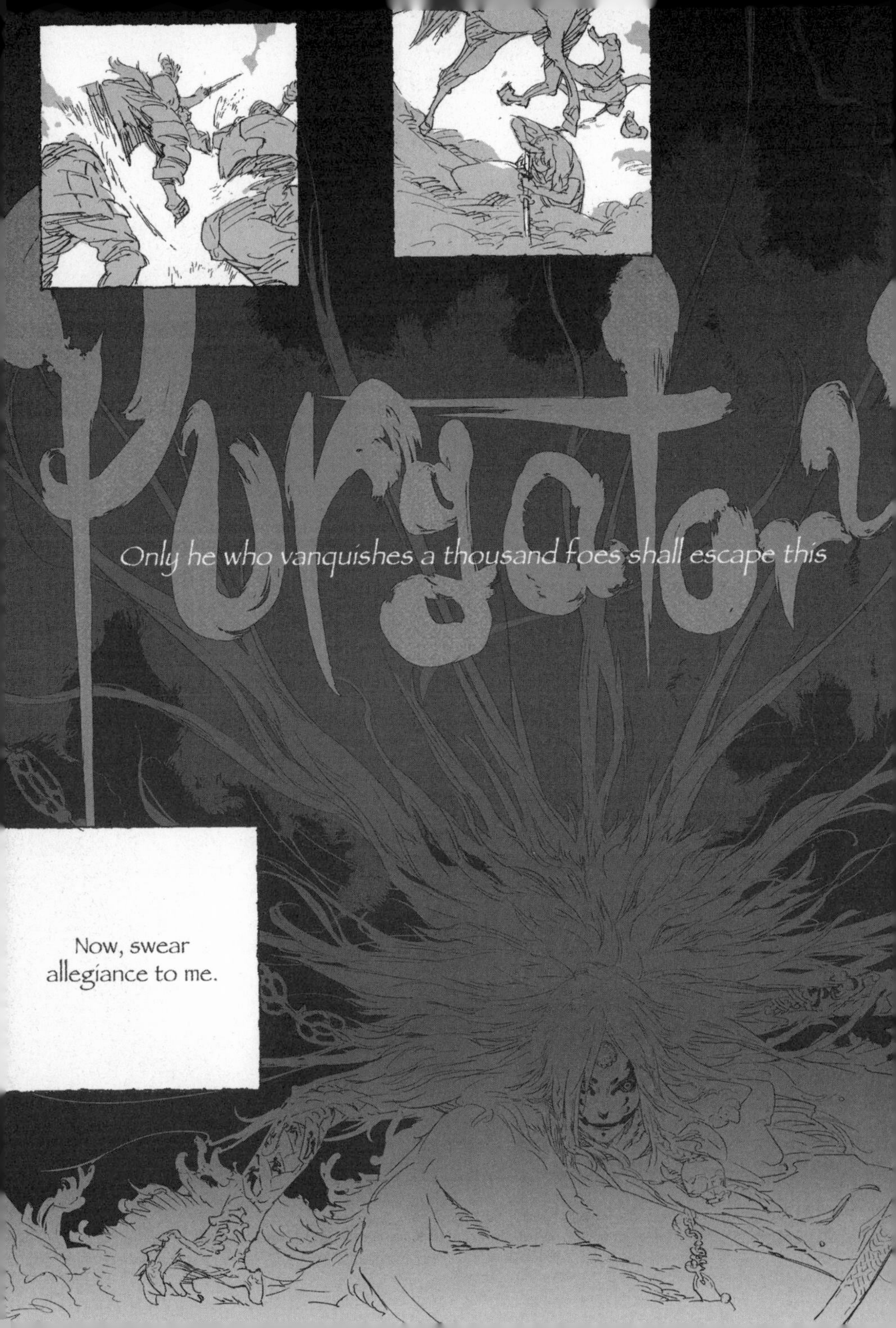
Purgatory
Only he who vanquishes a thousand foes shall escape this
Now, swear allegiance to me.

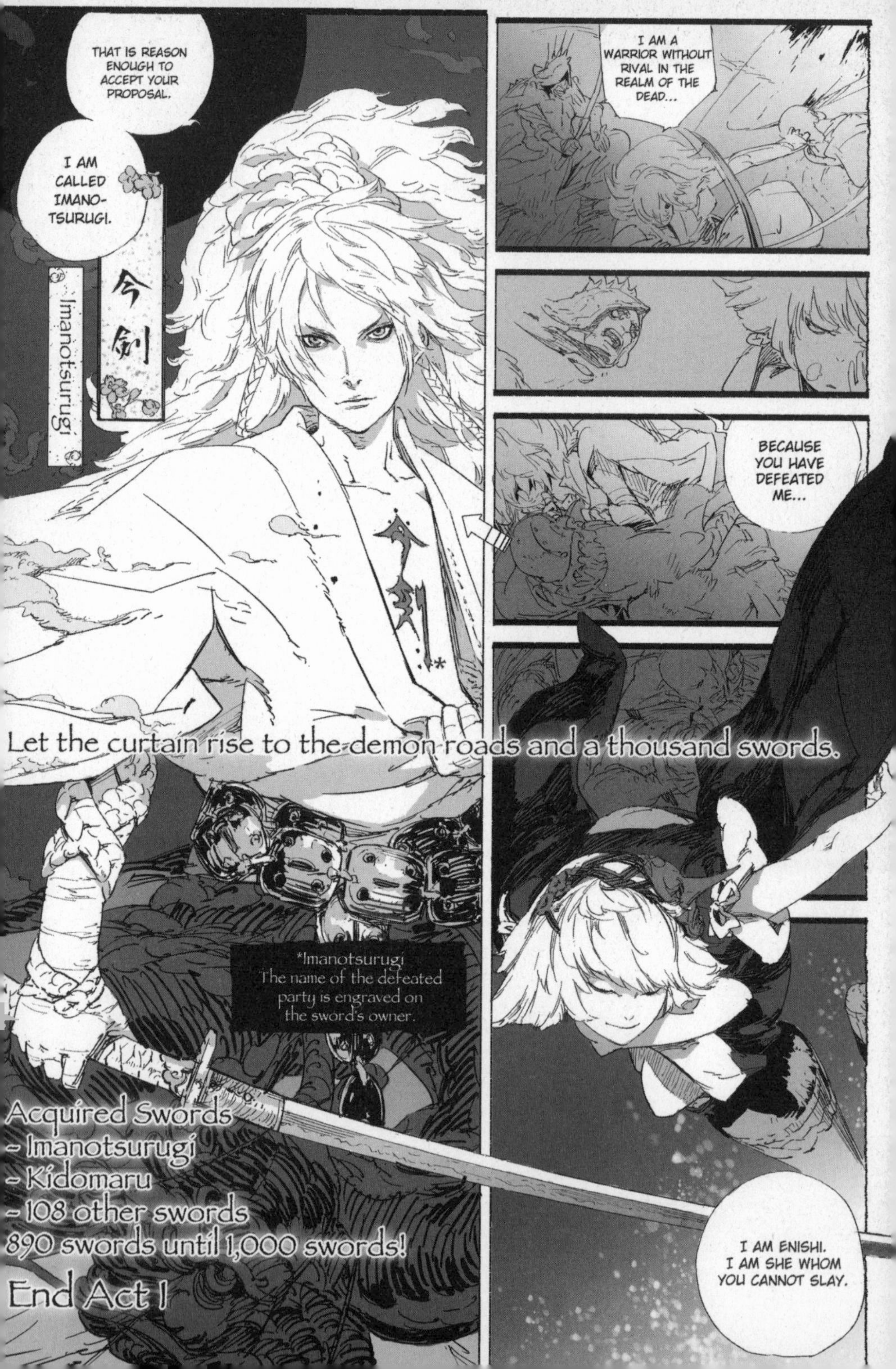
THAT IS REASON ENOUGH TO ACCEPT YOUR PROPOSAL.
I AM CALLED IMANO-TSURUGI.
今剣
Imanotsurugi
I AM A WARRIOR WITHOUT RIVAL IN THE REALM OF THE DEAD...
BECAUSE YOU HAVE DEFEATED ME...
Let the curtain rise to the demon roads and a thousand swords.
*Imanotsurugi
The name of the defeated party is engraved on the sword's owner.
I AM ENISHI. I AM SHE WHOM YOU CANNOT SLAY.
Acquired Swords
- Imanotsurugi
- Kidomaru
- 108 other swords
890 swords until 1,000 swords!
End Act I

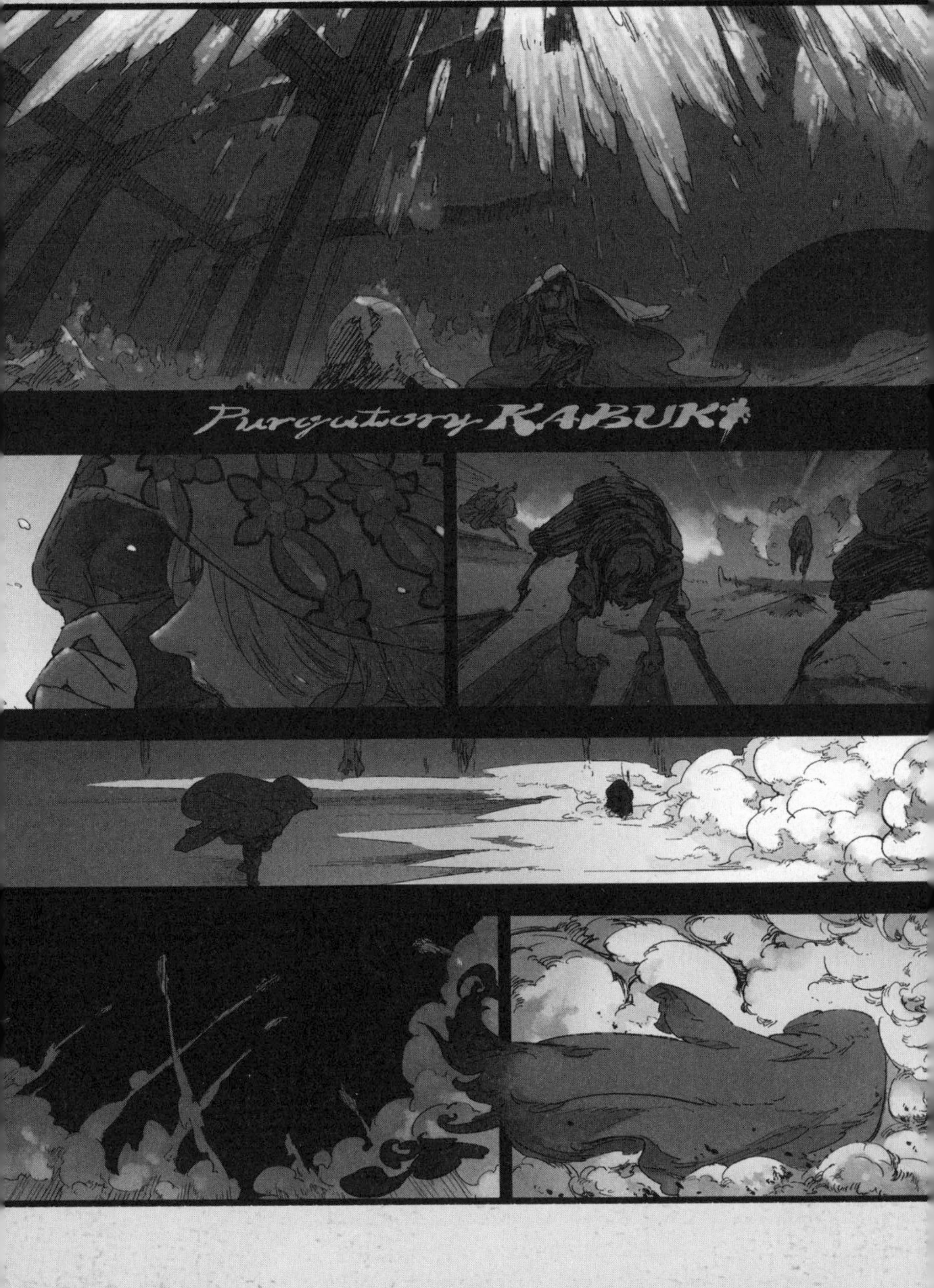
Purgatory KABUKI

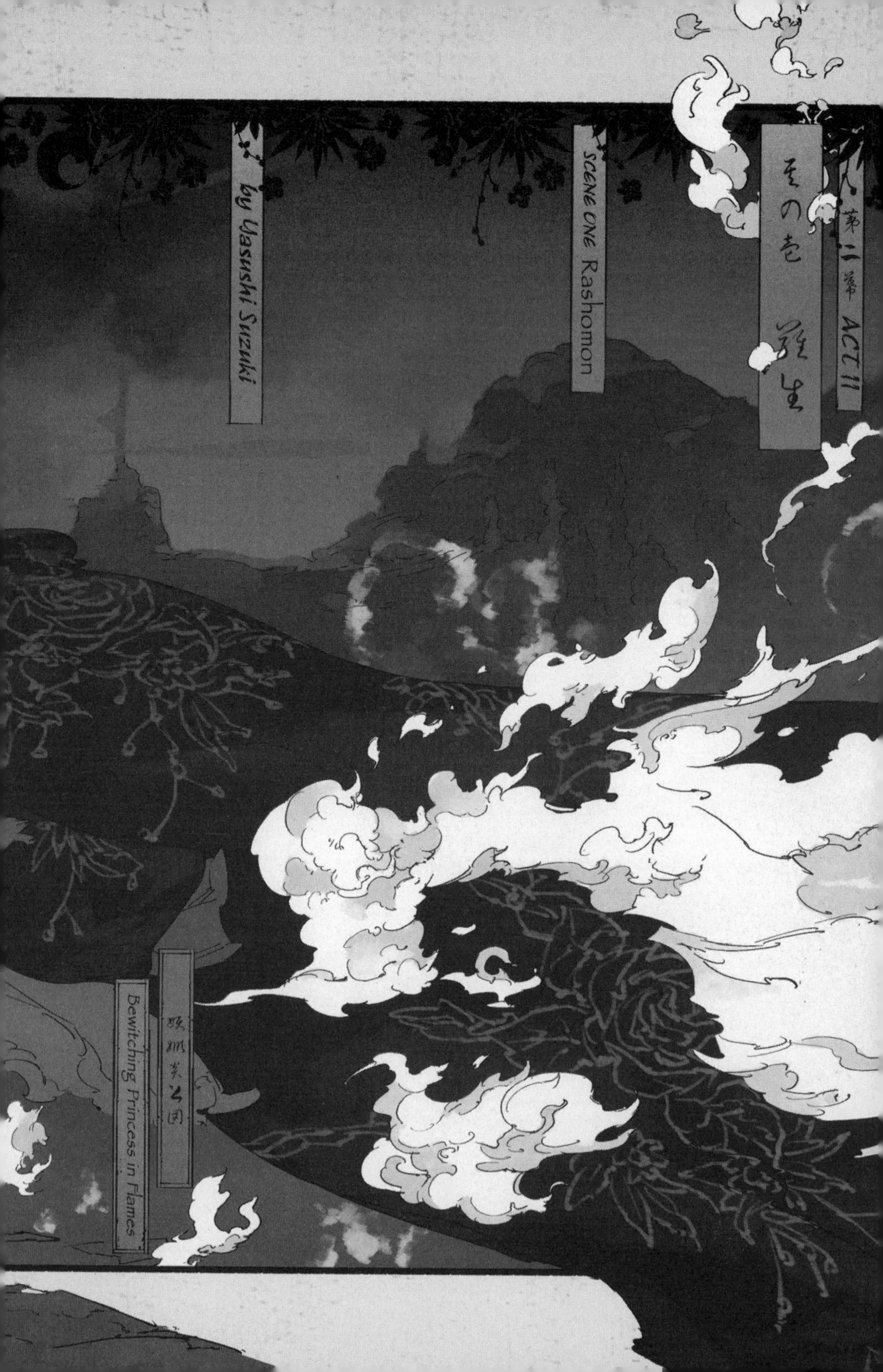
第二幕 ACT II
其の壱 羅生
SCENE ONE Rashomon
by Yasushi Suzuki
Bewitching Princess in Flames

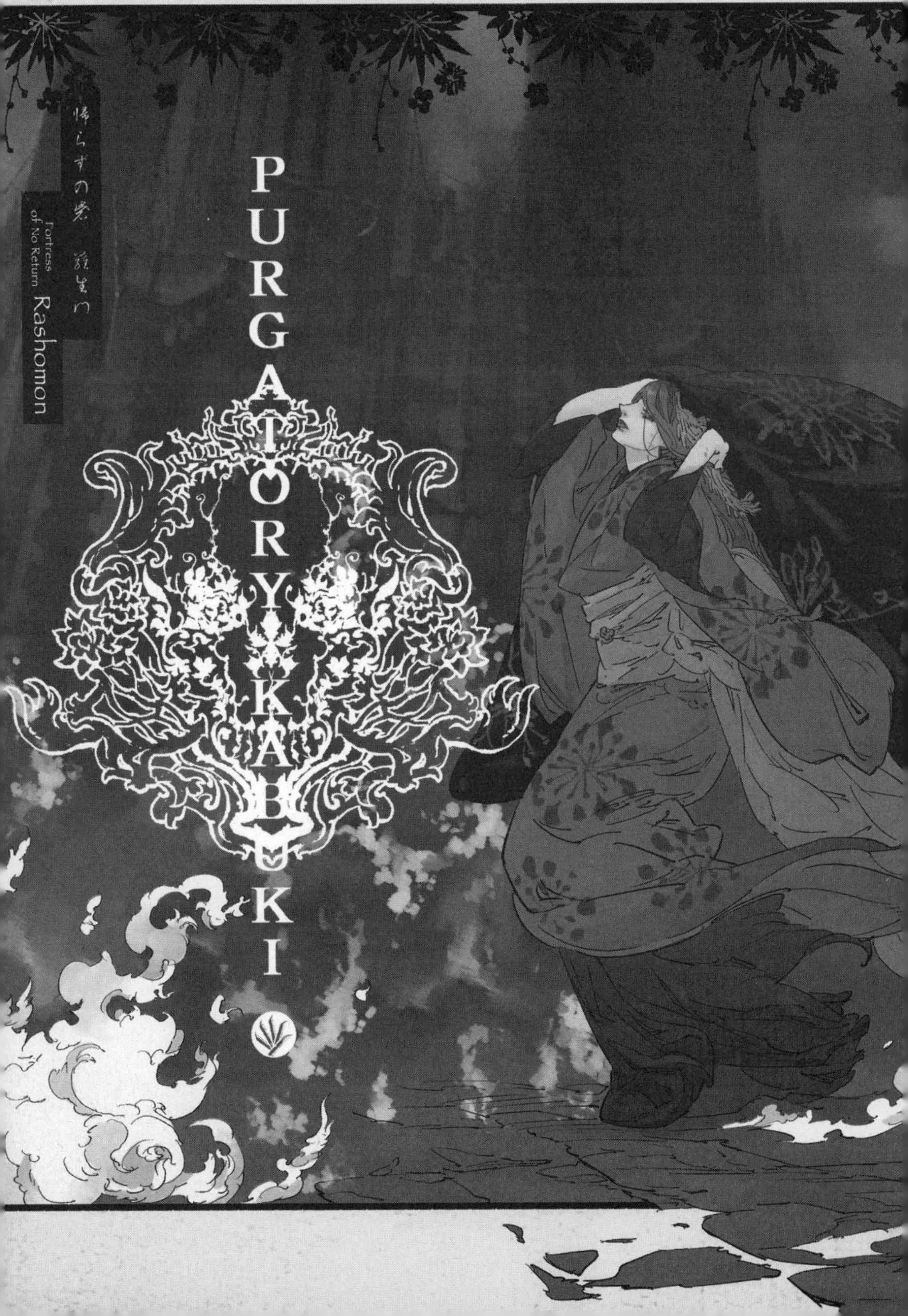
帰らずの砦 羅生門
Fortress of No Return
Rashomon
PURGATORY
KABUKI

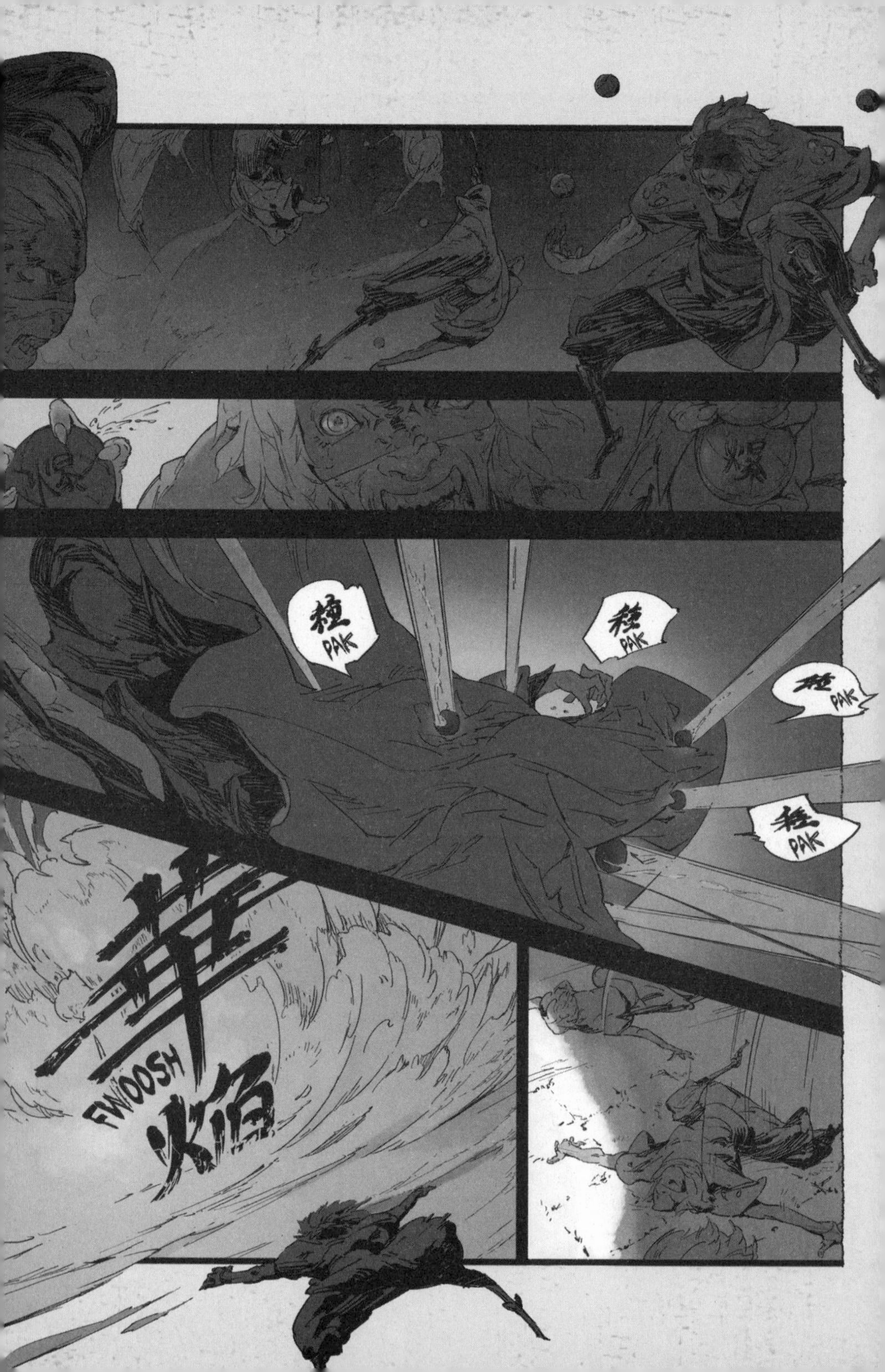
種 PAK
PAK
PAK
PAK
FWOOSH

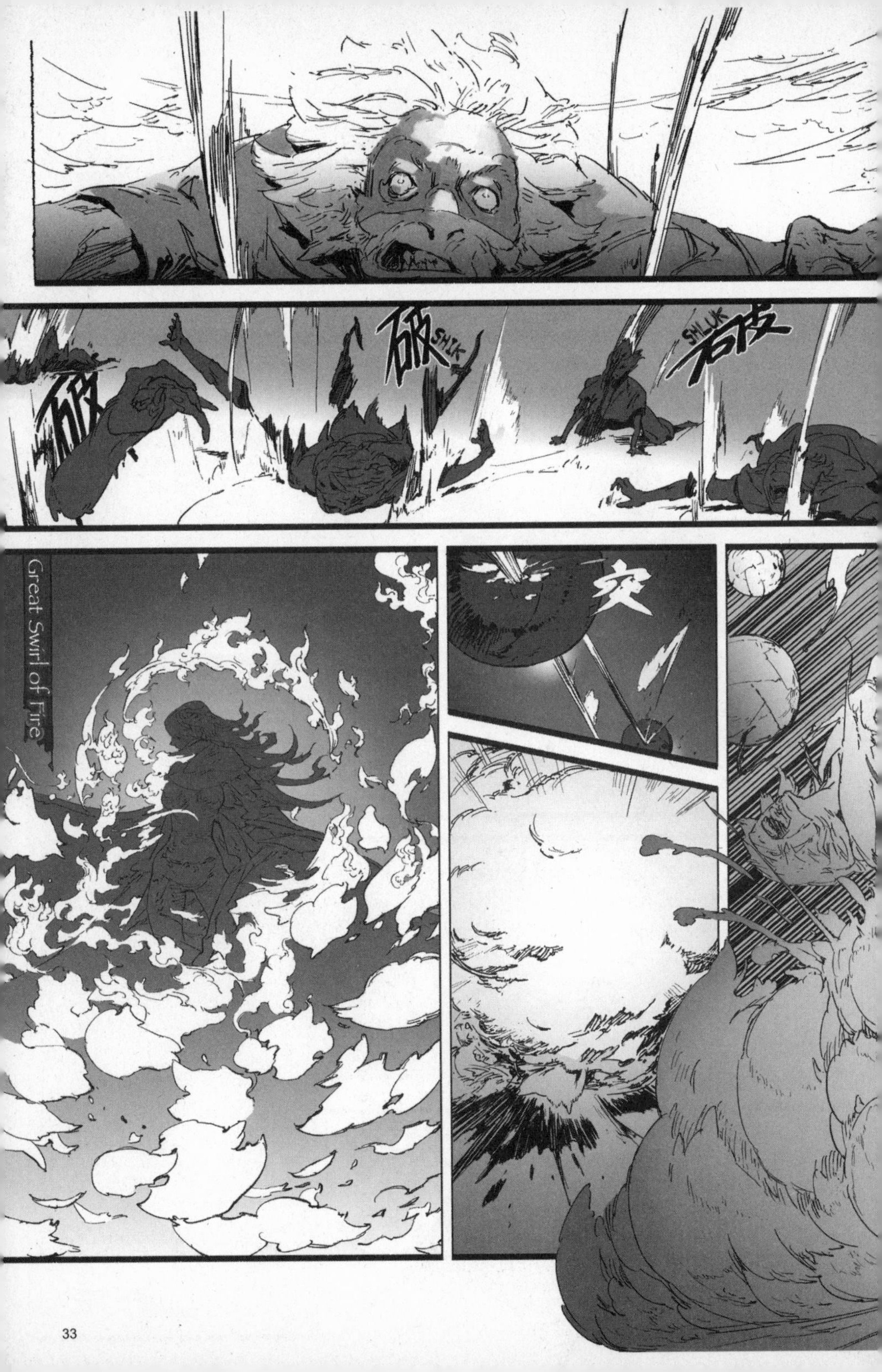
破
SHLUK
破
SHIK
破
Great Swirl of Fire

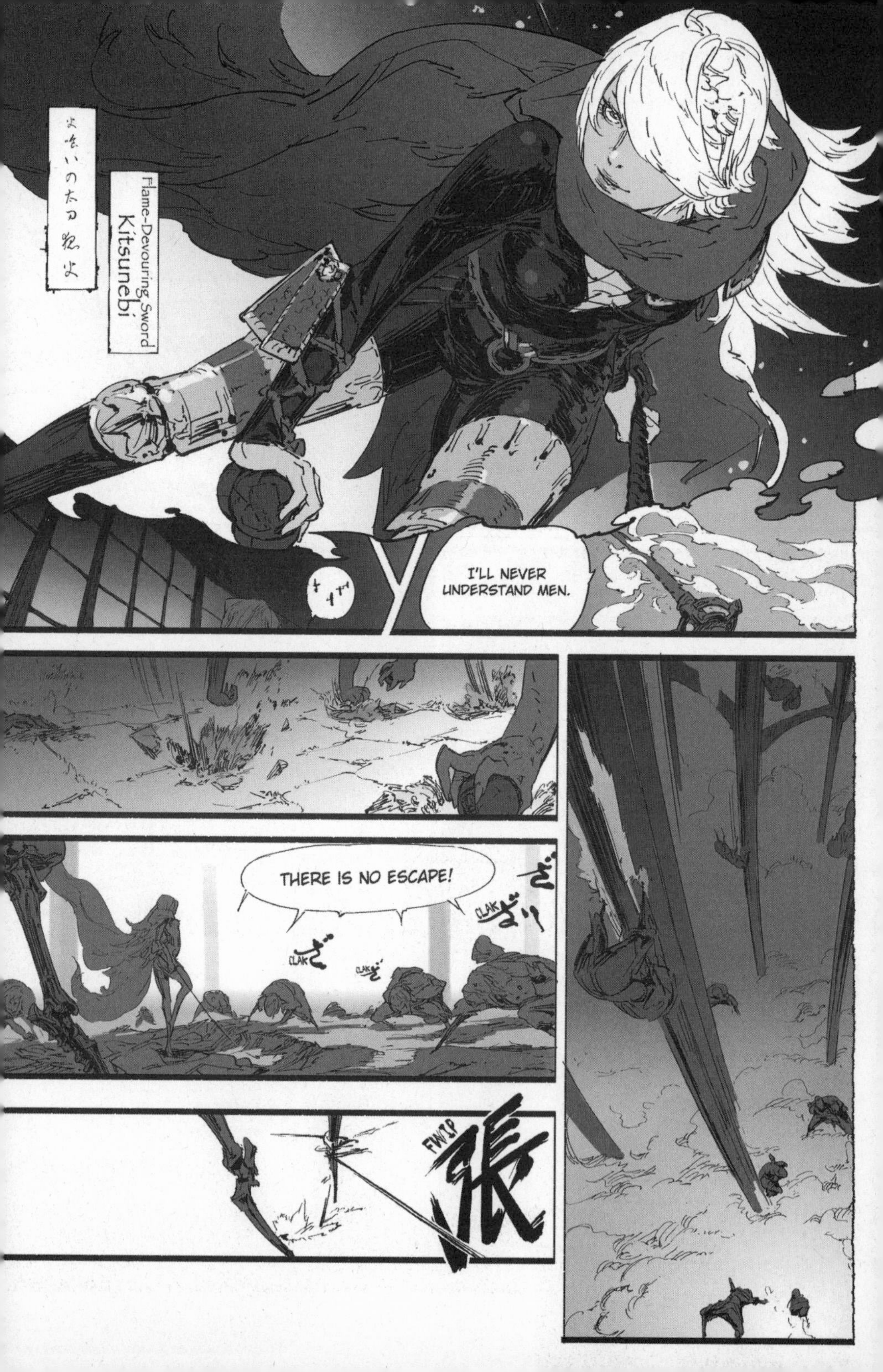
Flame-Devouring Sword Kitsunebi
I'LL NEVER UNDERSTAND MEN.
THERE IS NO ESCAPE!
CLAK
CLAK
CLAK
FWIP

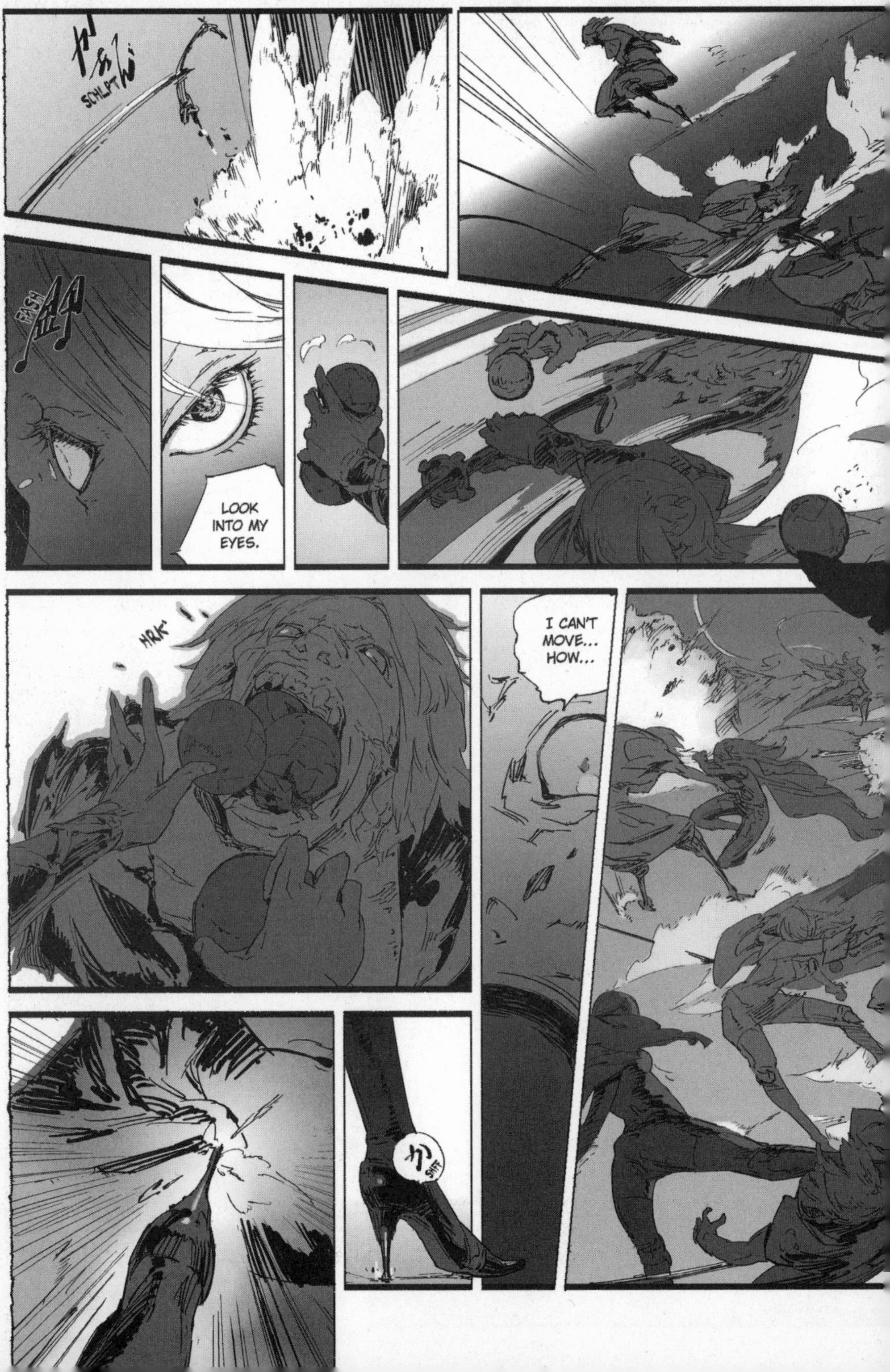
SCHLPT
FASH
LOOK INTO MY EYES.
HRK
I CAN'T MOVE... HOW...
SHFF

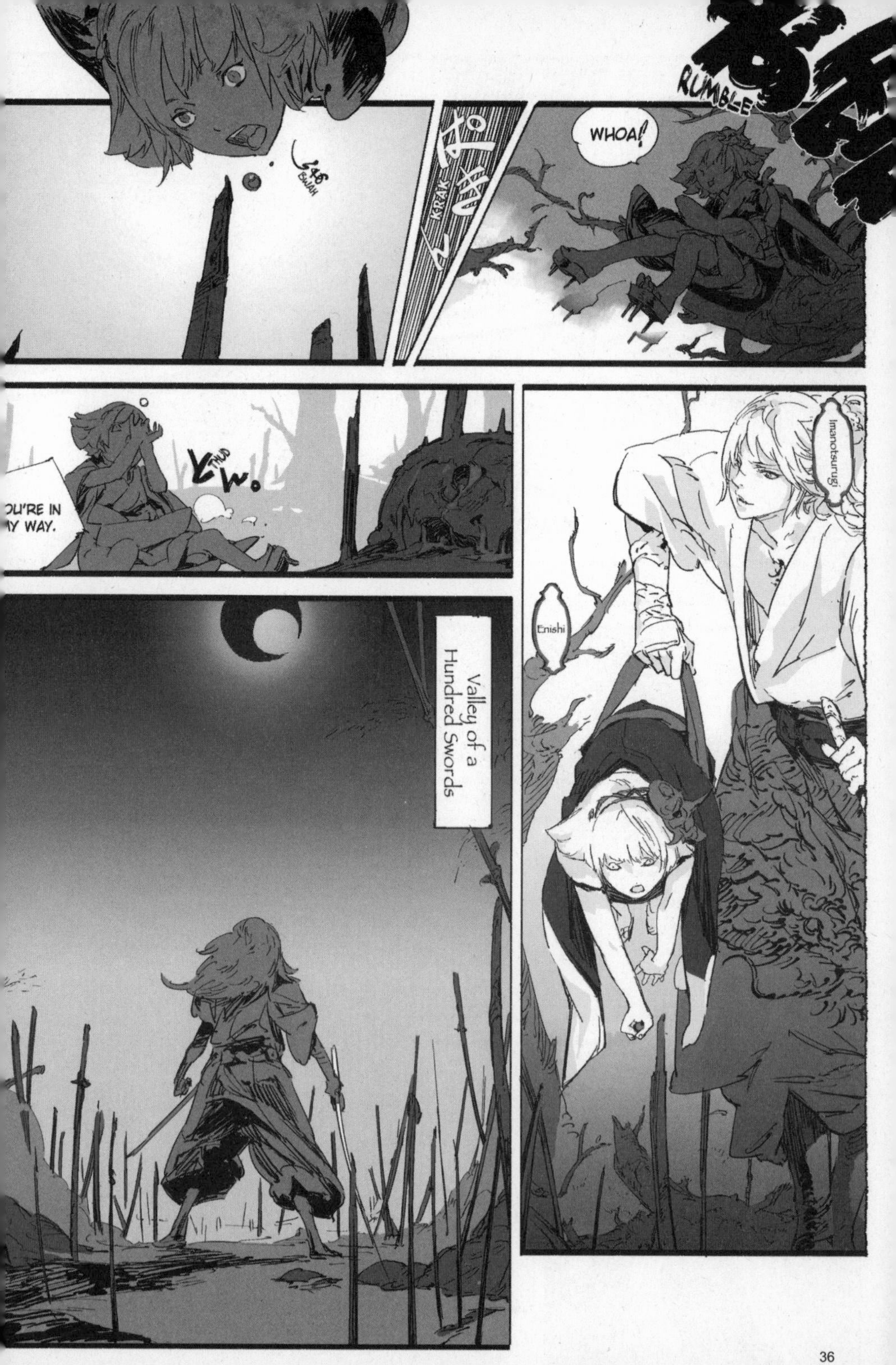
RUMBLE
WHOA!
KRAK
BWAH
Imanotsurugi
Enishi
THUD
OU'RE IN
Y WAY.
Valley of a Hundred Swords

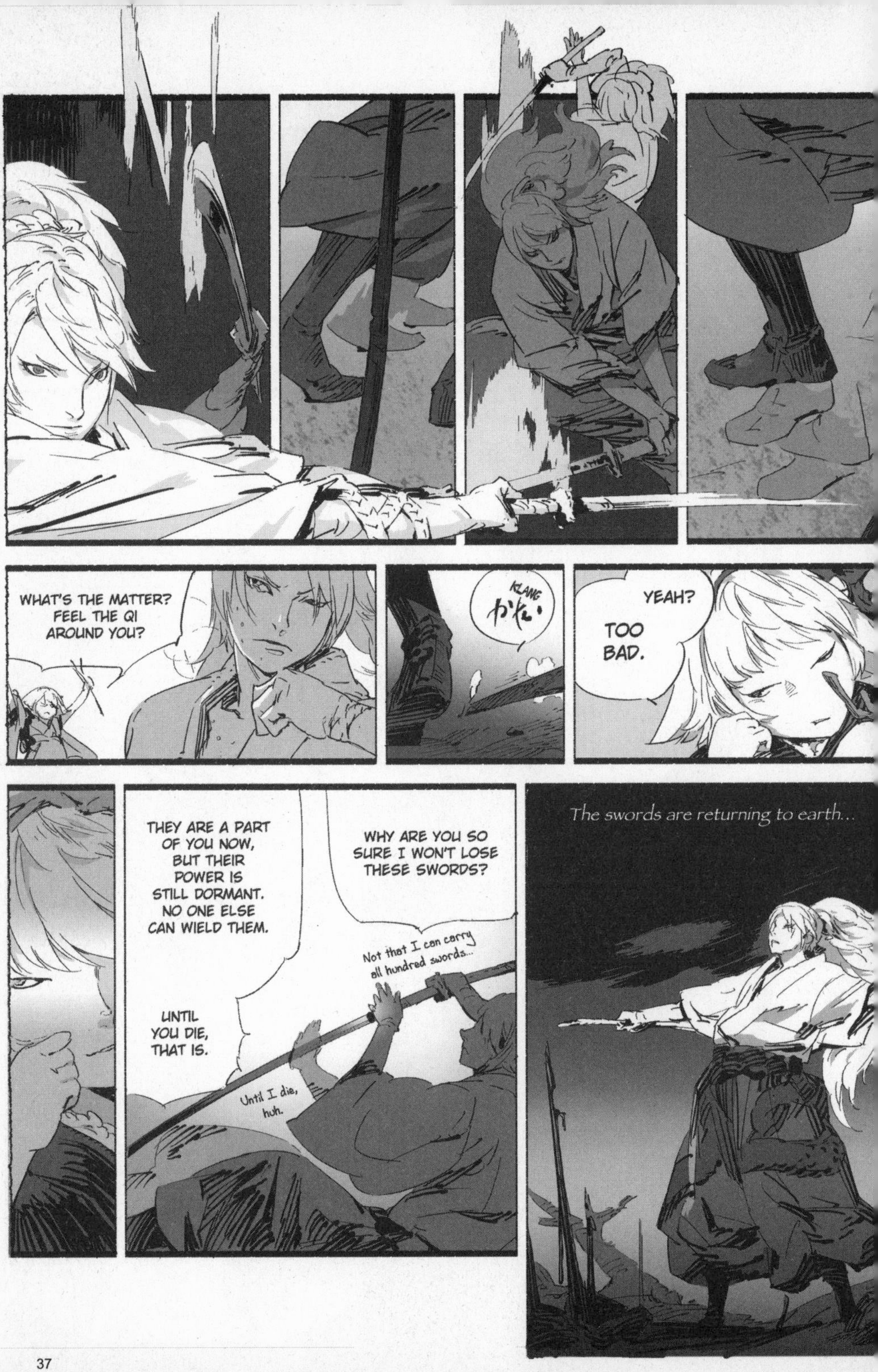
WHAT'S THE MATTER? FEEL THE QI AROUND YOU?
KLANG
YEAH?
TOO BAD.
THEY ARE A PART OF YOU NOW, BUT THEIR POWER IS STILL DORMANT. NO ONE ELSE CAN WIELD THEM.
UNTIL YOU DIE, THAT IS.
WHY ARE YOU SO SURE I WON'T LOSE THESE SWORDS?
Not that I can carry all hundred swords...
Until I die, huh.
The swords are returning to earth...

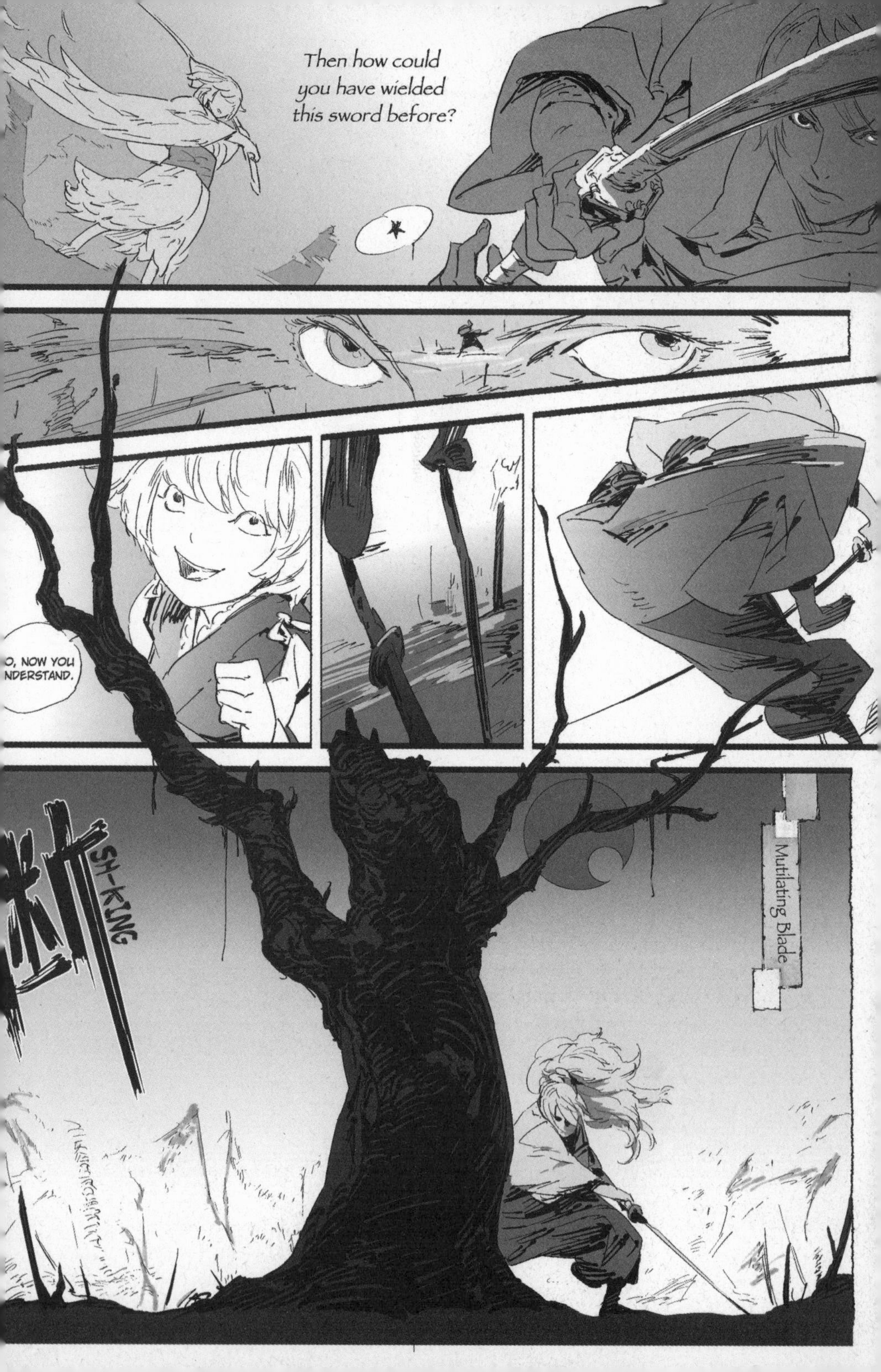
Then how could you have wielded this sword before?
O, NOW YOU
NDERSTAND.
SH-KING
Mutilating Blade

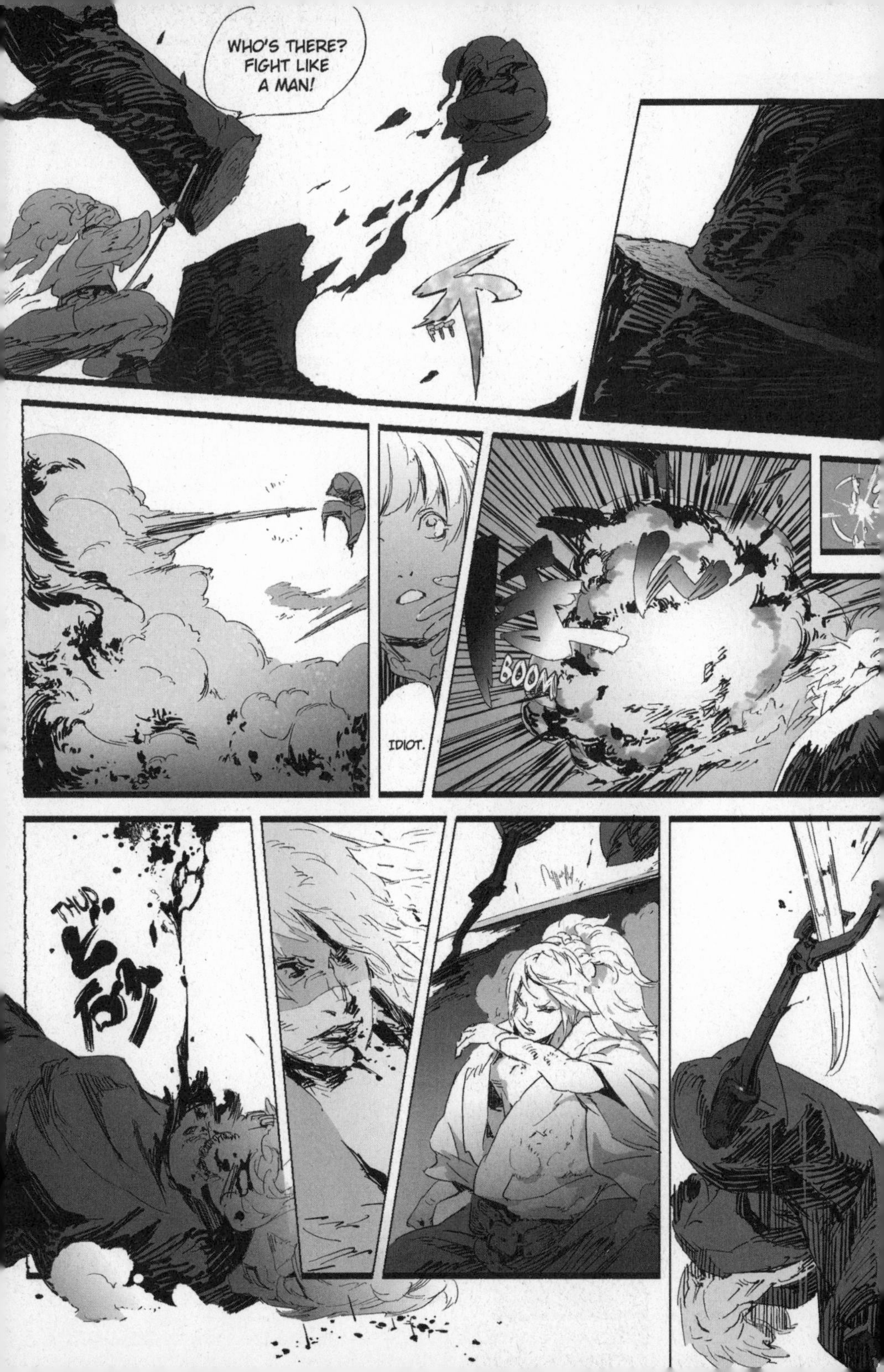
WHO'S THERE? FIGHT LIKE A MAN!
BOOM
IDIOT.
THUD

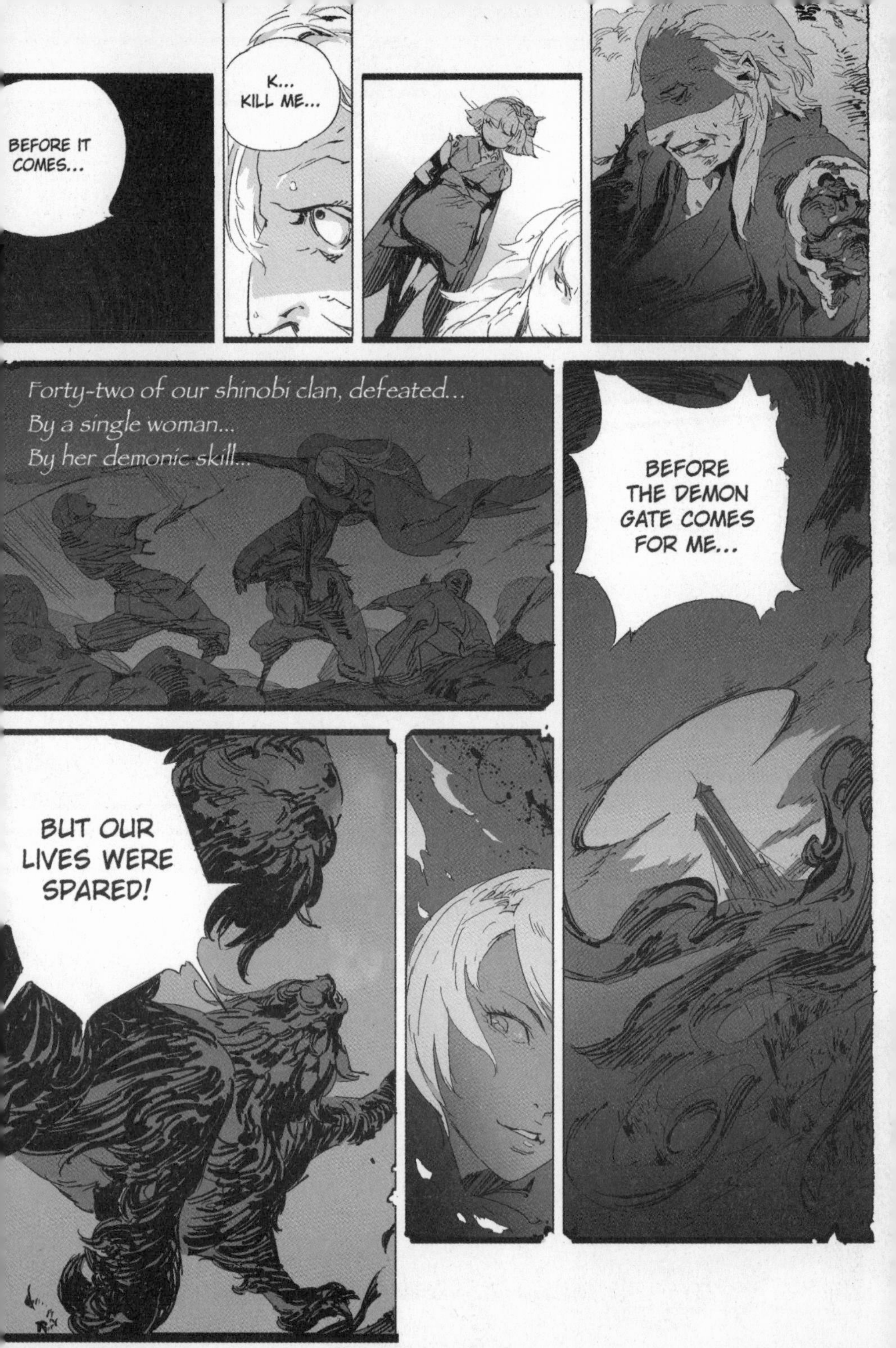
BEFORE IT COMES...
K... KILL ME...
Forty-two of our shinobi clan, defeated...
By a single woman...
By her demonic skill...
BEFORE THE DEMON GATE COMES FOR ME...
BUT OUR LIVES WERE SPARED!

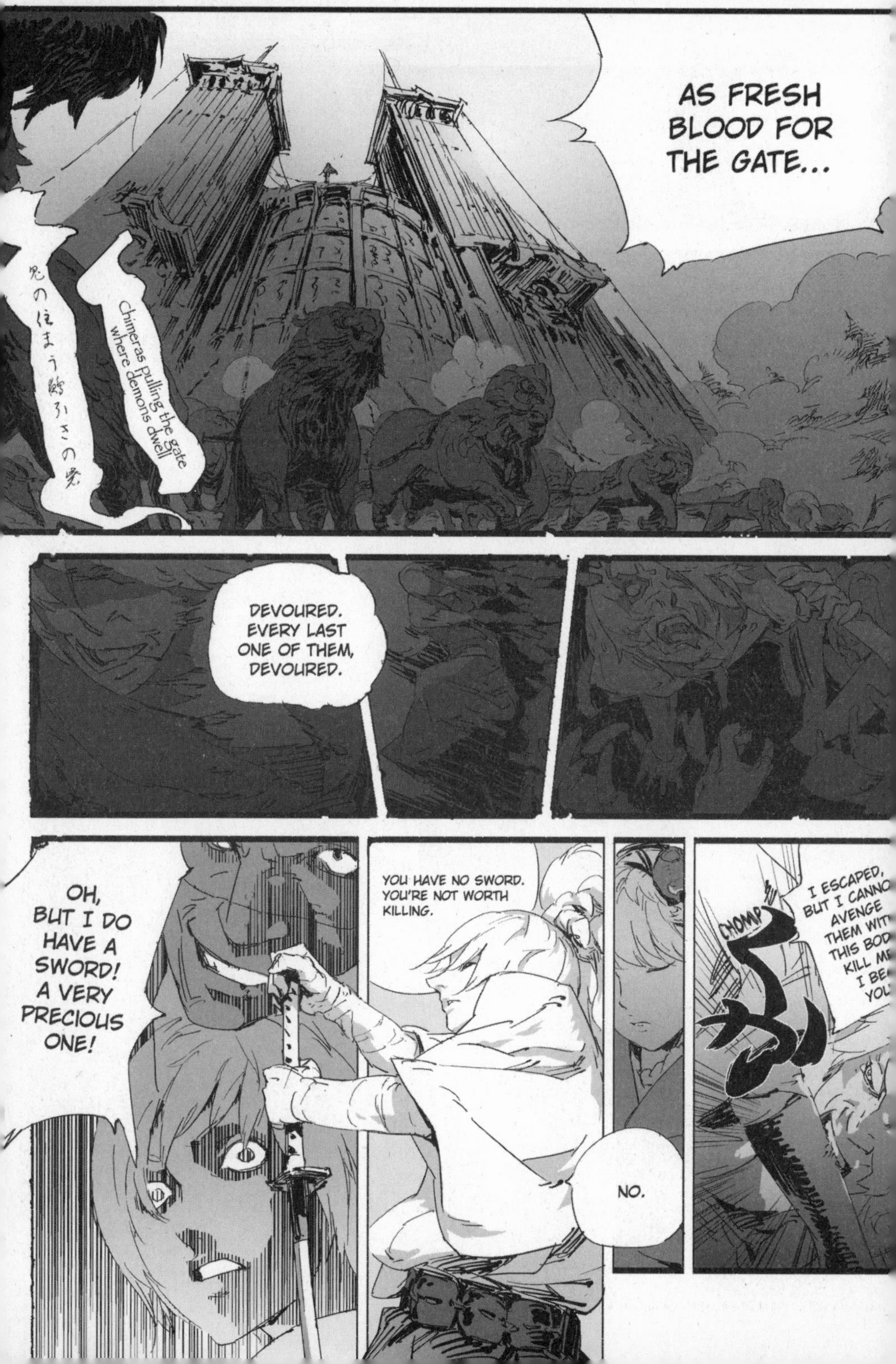
AS FRESH BLOOD FOR THE GATE...
Chimeras pulling the gate where demons dwell
DEVOURED. EVERY LAST ONE OF THEM, DEVOURED.
OH, BUT I DO HAVE A SWORD! A VERY PRECIOUS ONE!
YOU HAVE NO SWORD. YOU'RE NOT WORTH KILLING.
NO.
CHOMP
I ESCAPED, BUT I CANNO AVENGE THEM WIT THIS BOD KILL M I BE YOU

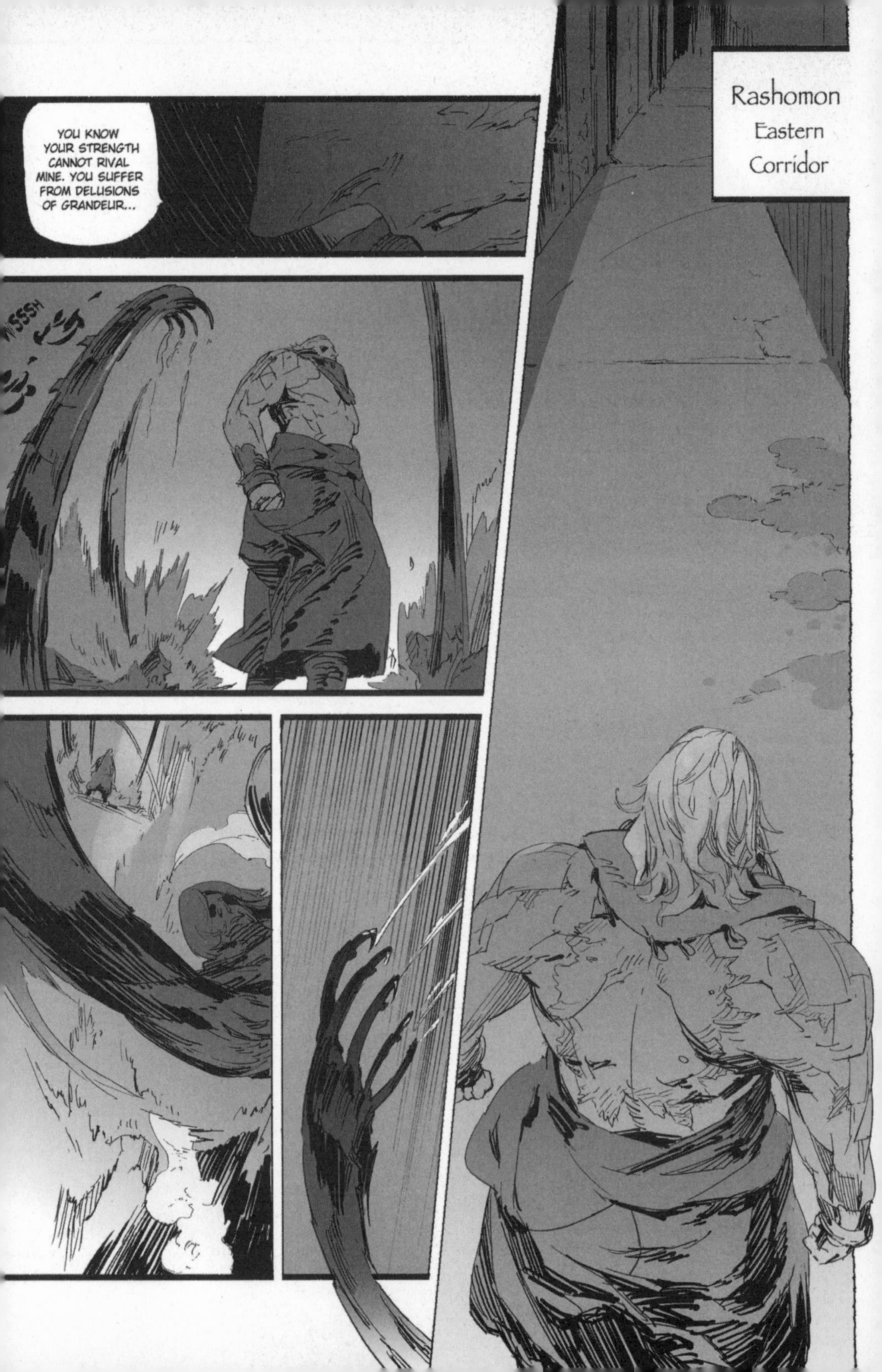
Rashomon
Eastern
Corridor
YOU KNOW YOUR STRENGTH CANNOT RIVAL MINE. YOU SUFFER FROM DELUSIONS OF GRANDEUR...
WSSSH

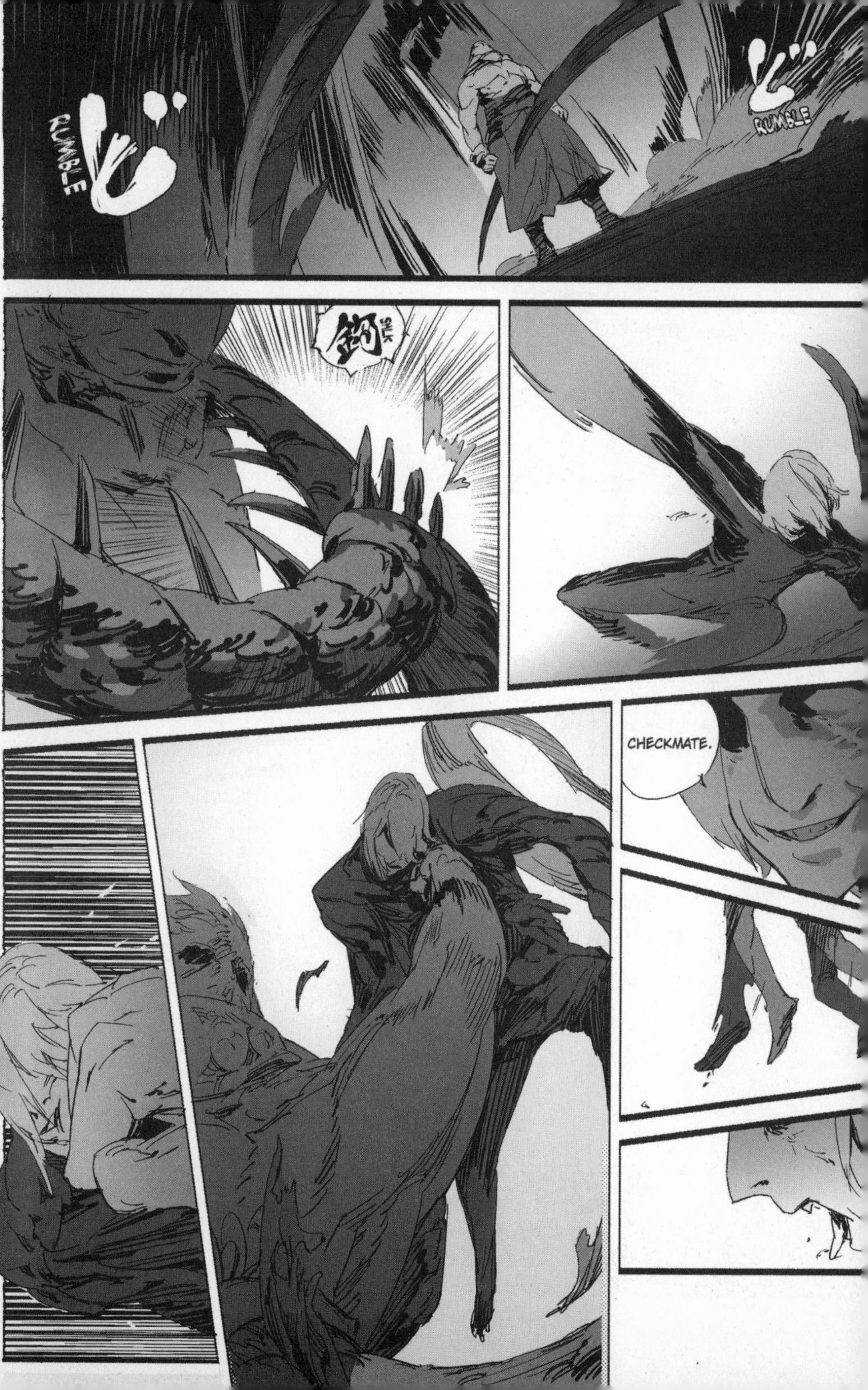
RUMBLE
RUMBLE
SHLK
CHECKMATE.

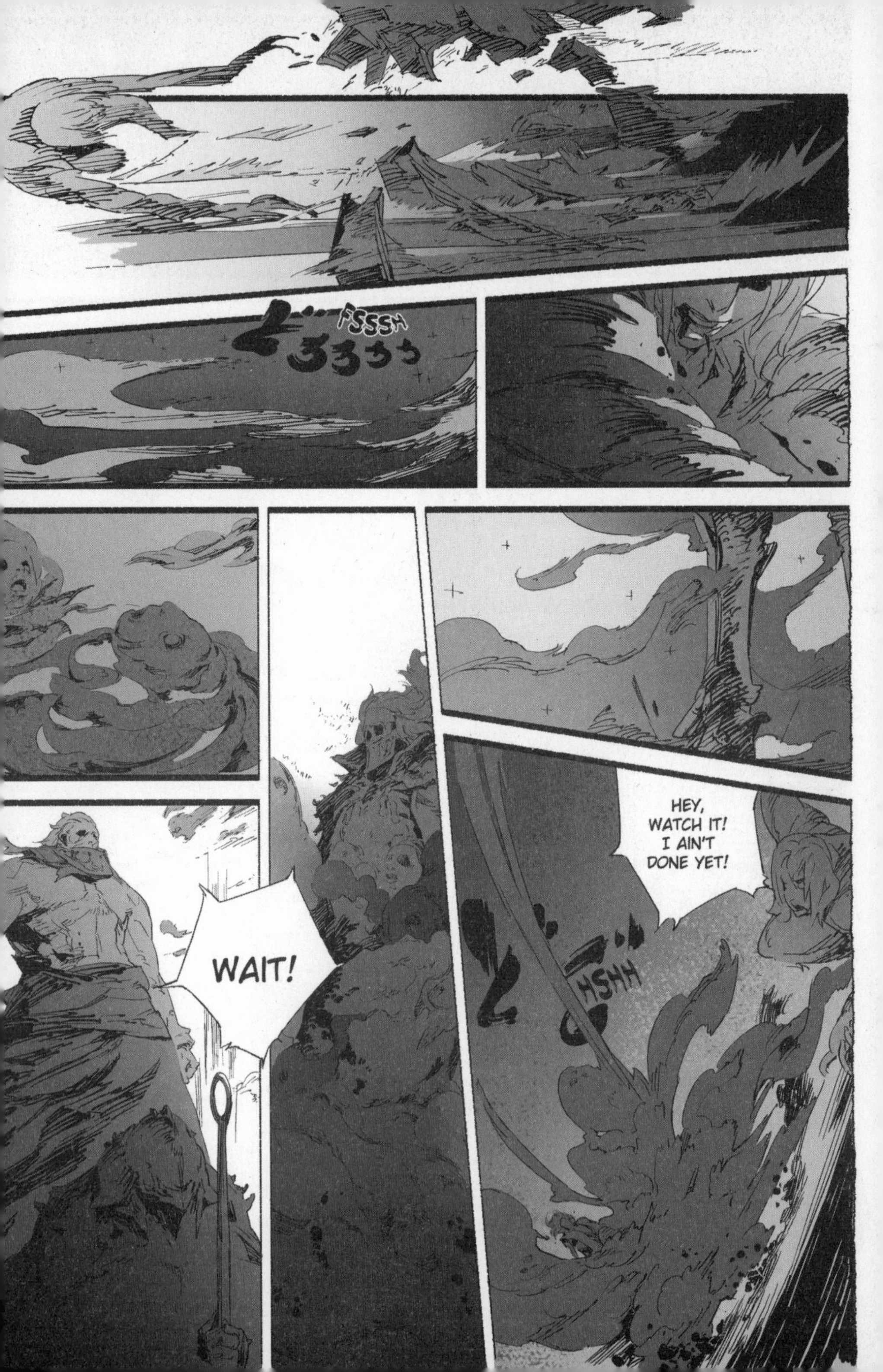
FSSSH
WAIT!
HEY, WATCH IT! I AIN'T DONE YET!
HSHH

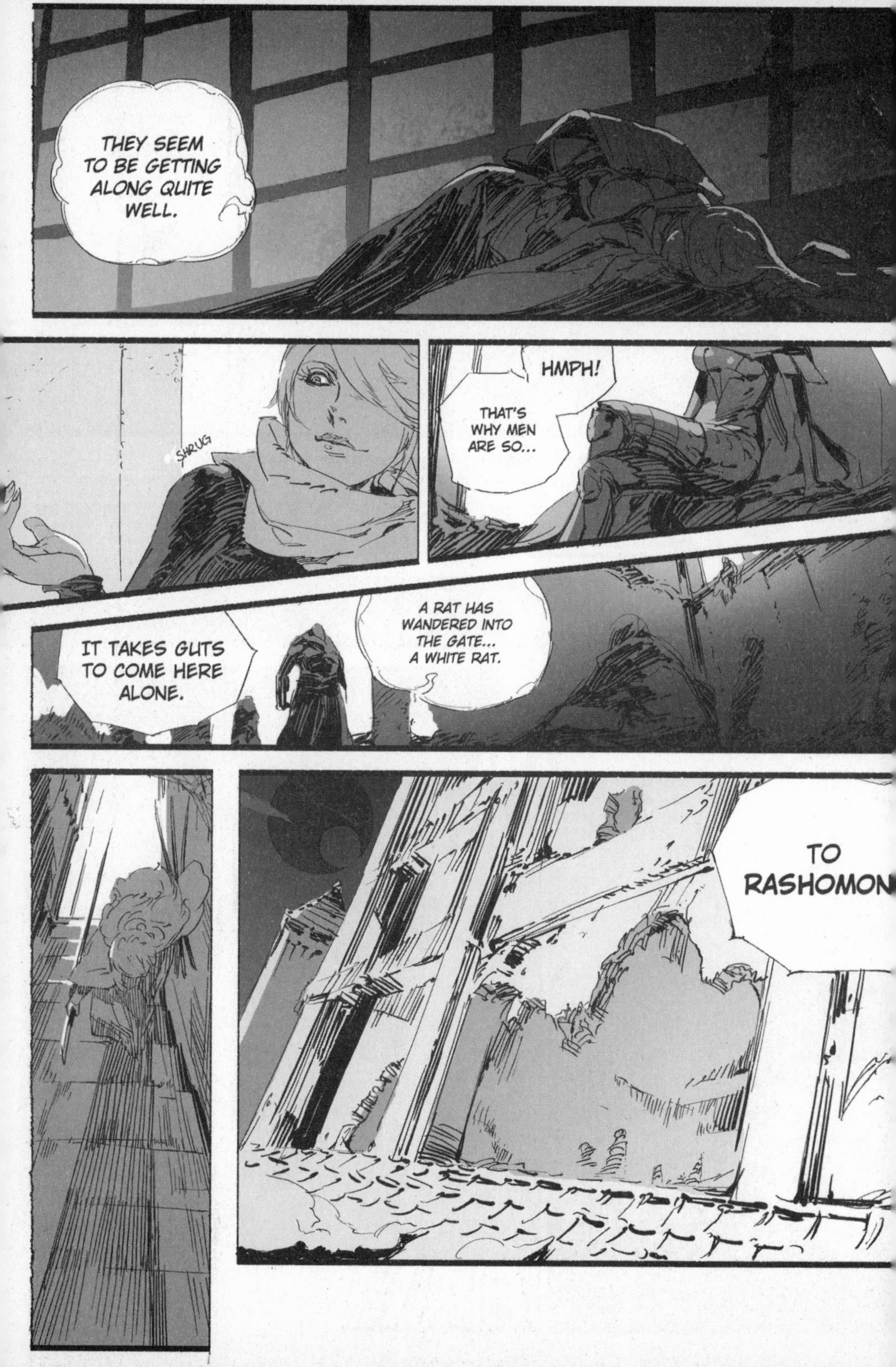
THEY SEEM TO BE GETTING ALONG QUITE WELL.
SHRUG
HMPH!
THAT'S WHY MEN ARE SO...
A RAT HAS WANDERED INTO THE GATE... A WHITE RAT.
IT TAKES GUTS TO COME HERE ALONE.
TO RASHOMON

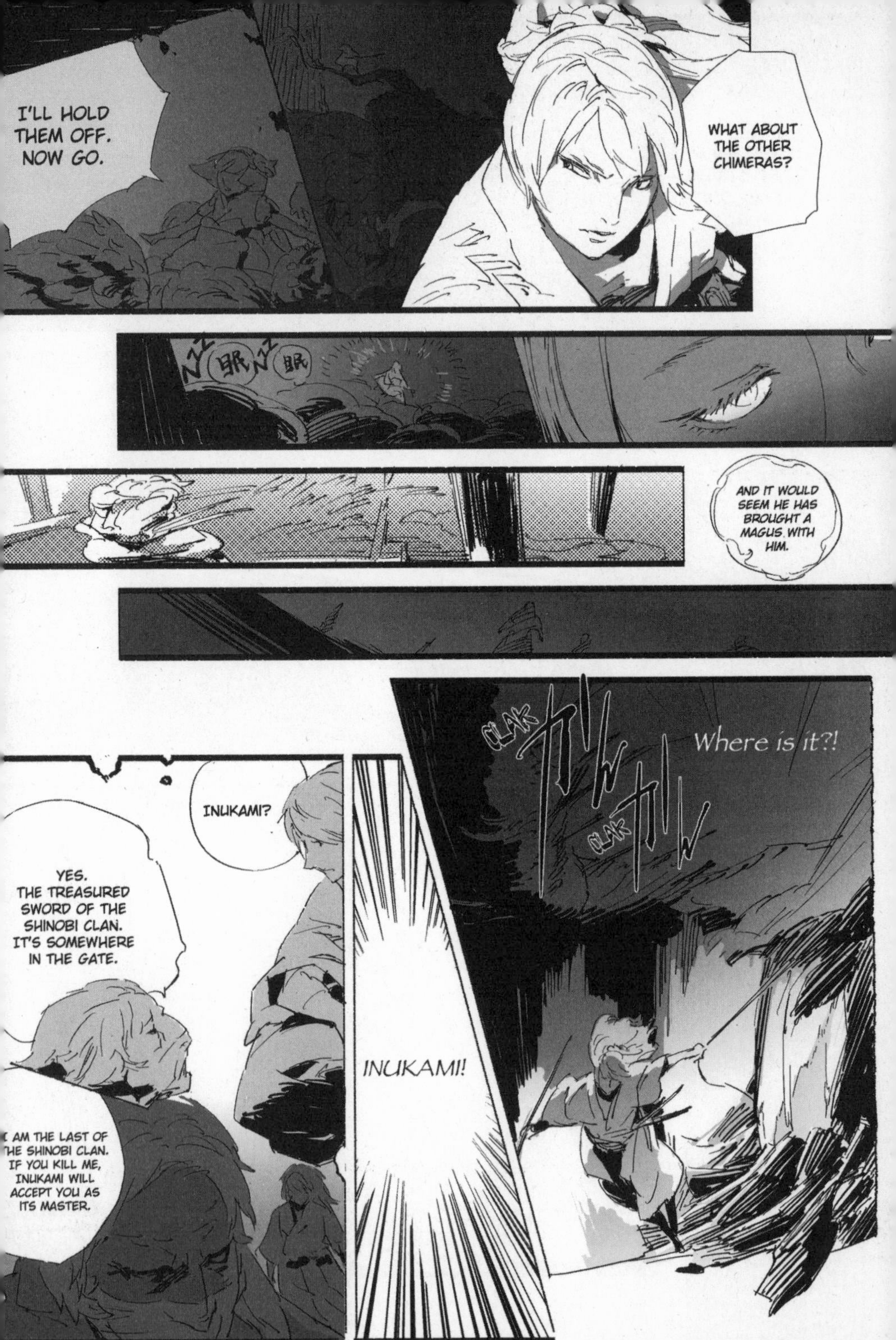
WHAT ABOUT THE OTHER CHIMERAS?
I'LL HOLD THEM OFF. NOW GO.
ZZZ
眠
ZZZ
眠
AND IT WOULD SEEM HE HAS BROUGHT A MAGUS WITH HIM.
CLAK
CLAK
Where is it?!
INUKAMI!
INUKAMI?
YES. THE TREASURED SWORD OF THE SHINOBI CLAN. IT'S SOMEWHERE IN THE GATE.
I AM THE LAST OF THE SHINOBI CLAN. IF YOU KILL ME, INUKAMI WILL ACCEPT YOU AS ITS MASTER.

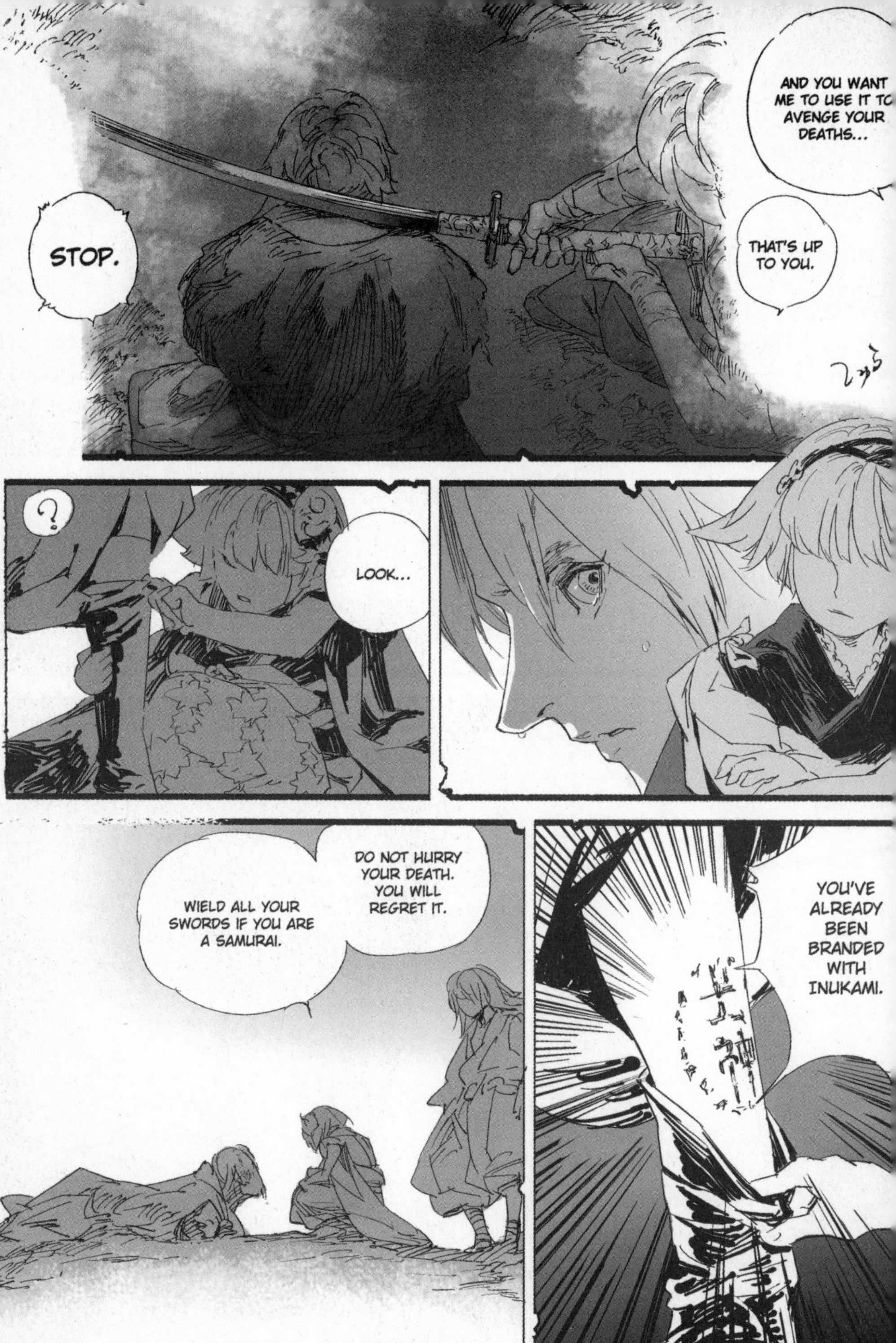
AND YOU WANT ME TO USE IT TO AVENGE YOUR DEATHS...
THAT'S UP TO YOU.
STOP.
?
LOOK...
YOU'VE ALREADY BEEN BRANDED WITH INUKAMI.
DO NOT HURRY YOUR DEATH. YOU WILL REGRET IT.
WIELD ALL YOUR SWORDS IF YOU ARE A SAMURAI.

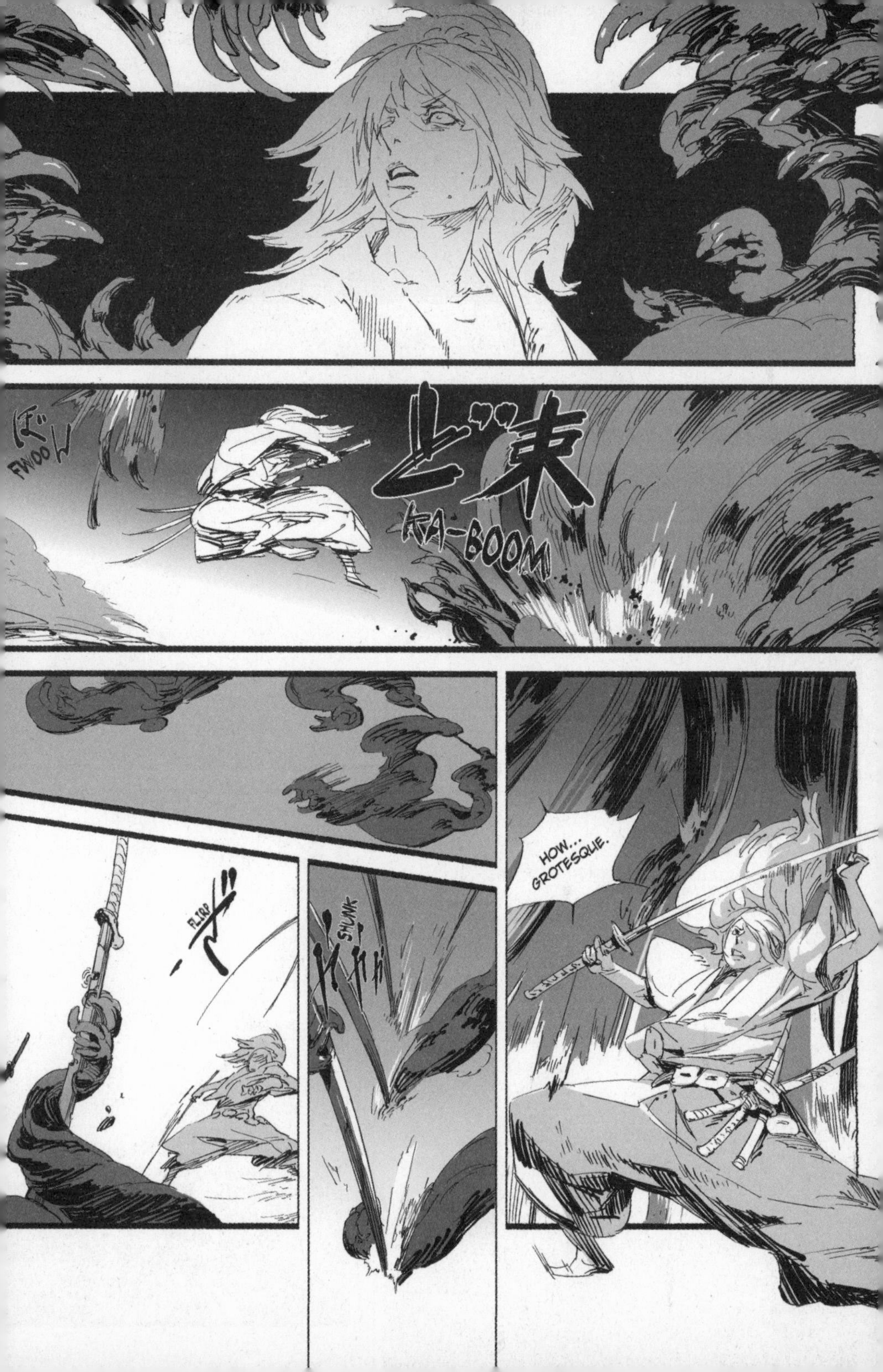

ぼん
FWOOM
ど東
KA-BOOM
HOW... GROTESQUE.
FLIRP
SHUNK

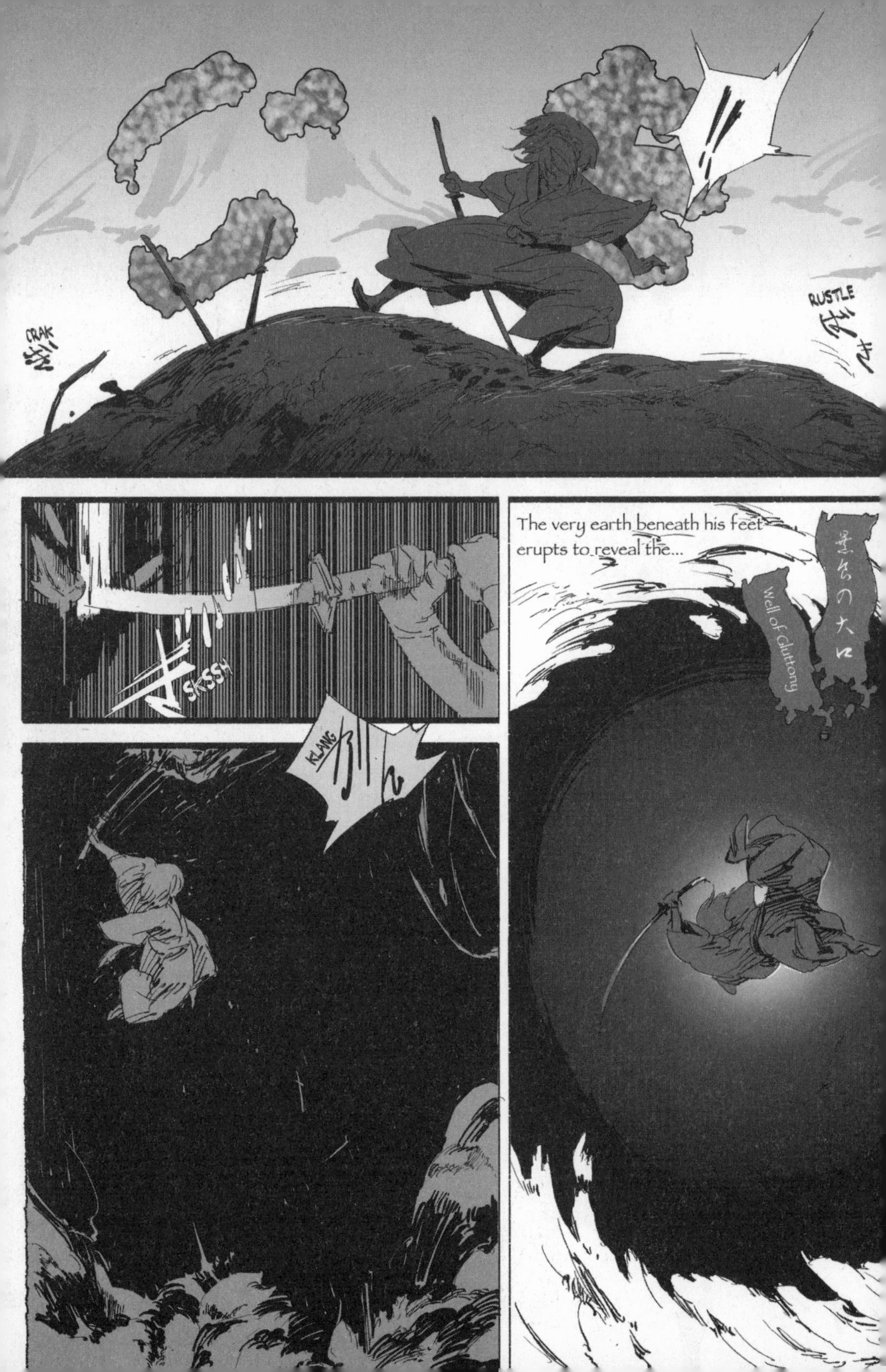
CRAK
RUSTLE
SKSSH
KLANG
The very earth beneath his feet erupts to reveal the...
Well of Gluttony

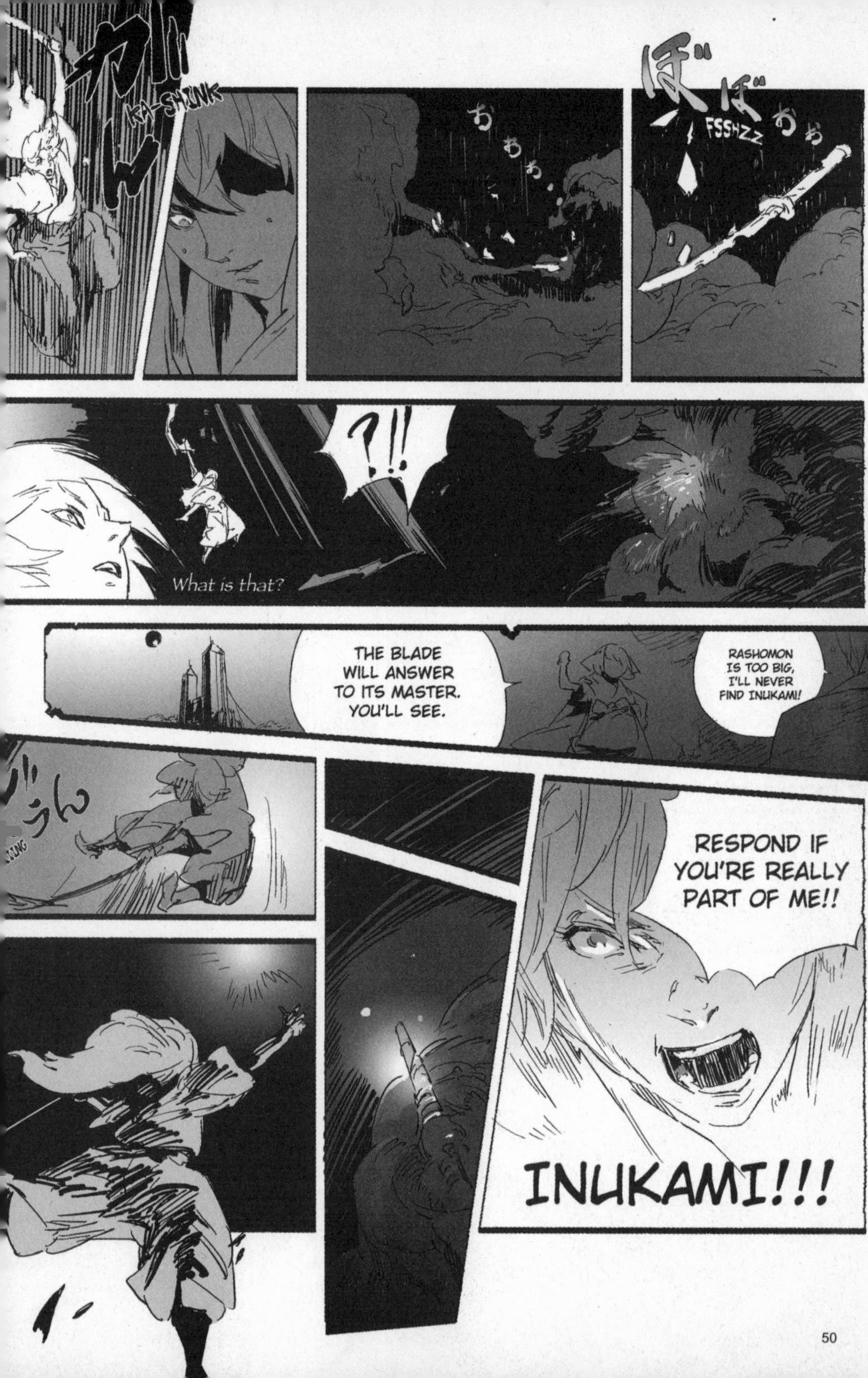
KA-SHINK
FSSHZZ
?!!
What is that?
THE BLADE WILL ANSWER TO ITS MASTER. YOU'LL SEE.
RASHOMON IS TOO BIG, I'LL NEVER FIND INUKAMI!
RESPOND IF YOU'RE REALLY PART OF ME!!
INUKAMI!!!

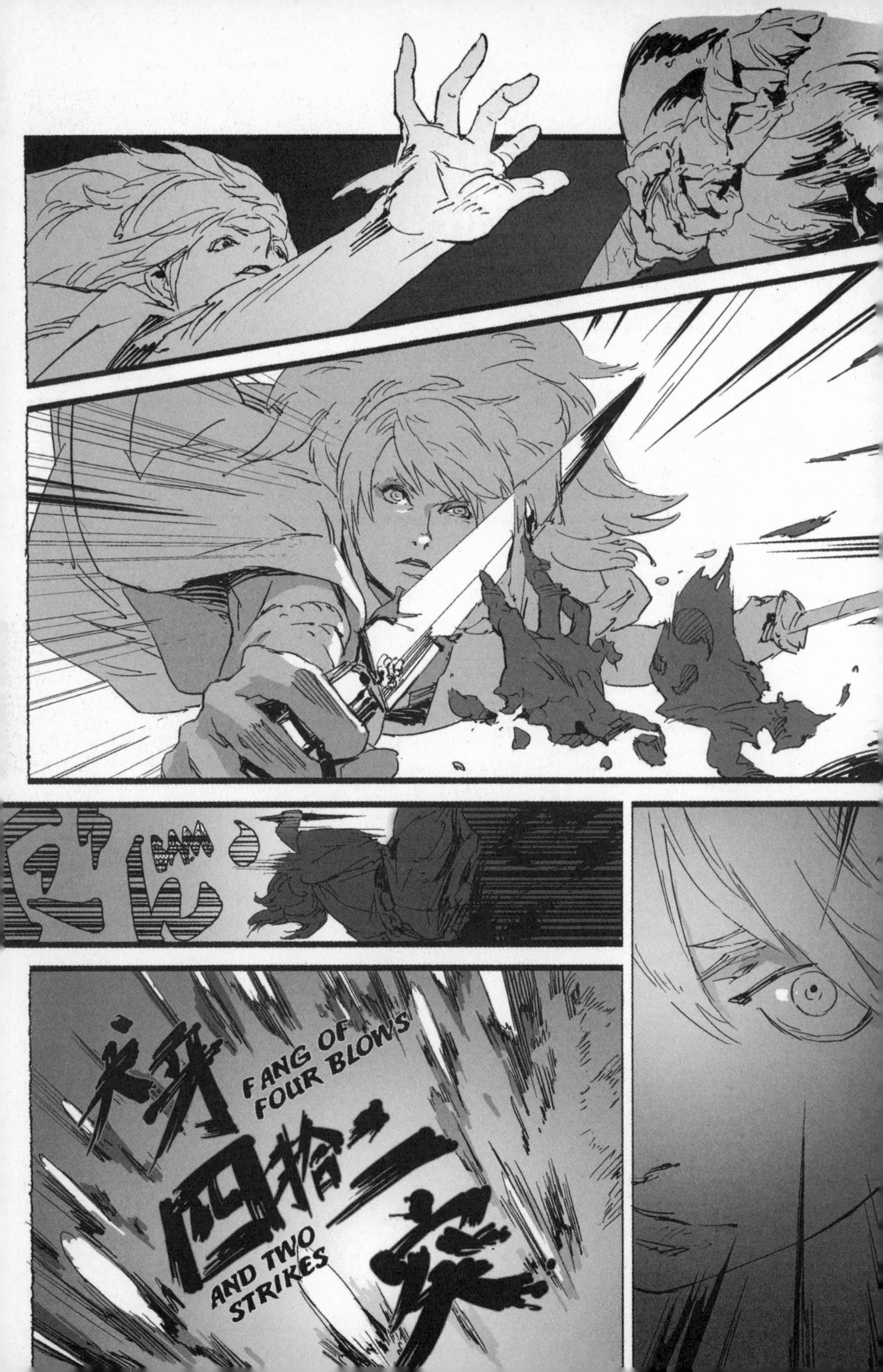
FANG OF FOUR BLOWS
AND TWO STRIKES

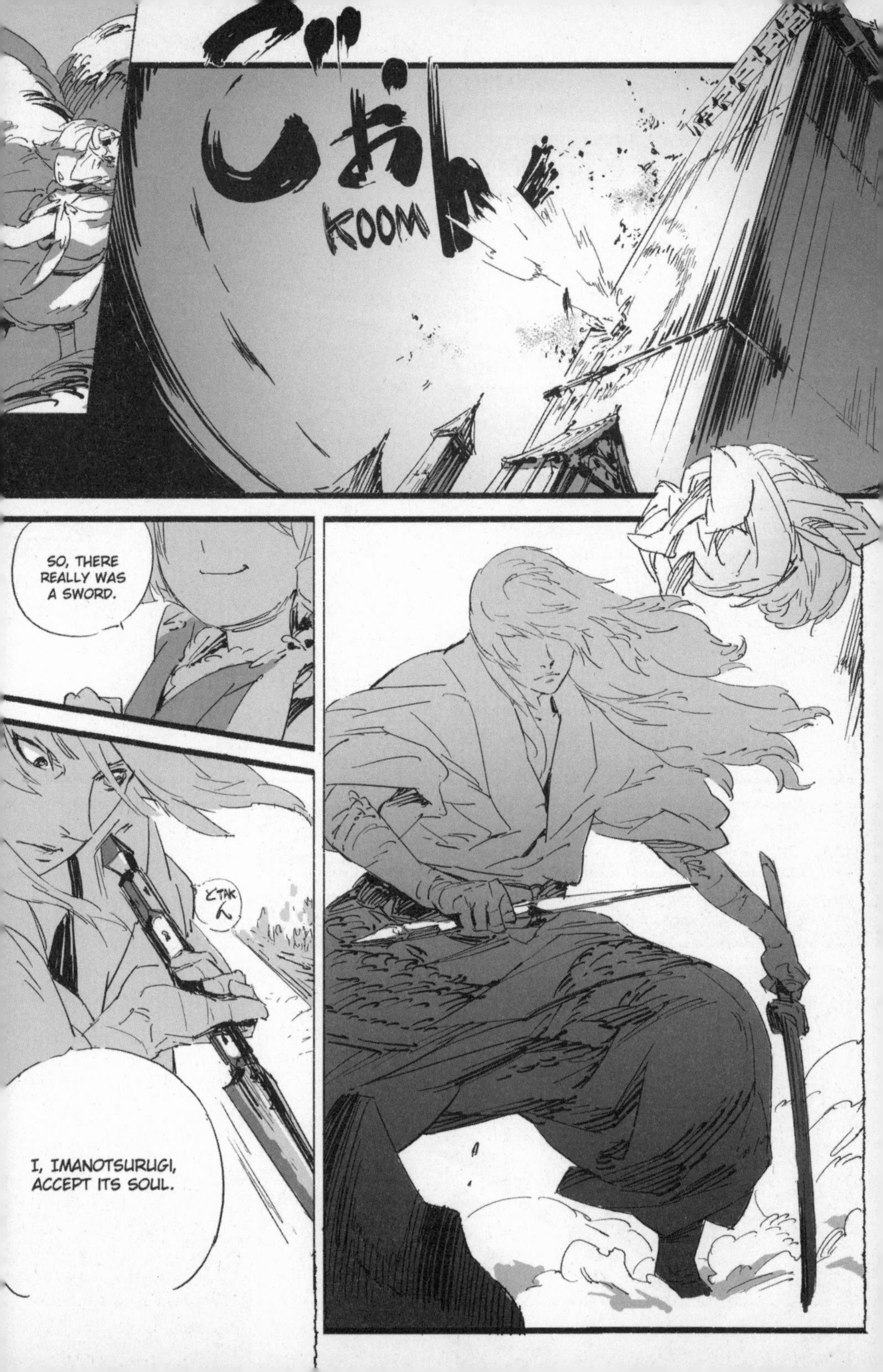
ごおん
KOOM
SO, THERE REALLY WAS A SWORD.
とTAK ん
I, IMANOTSURUGI, ACCEPT ITS SOUL.

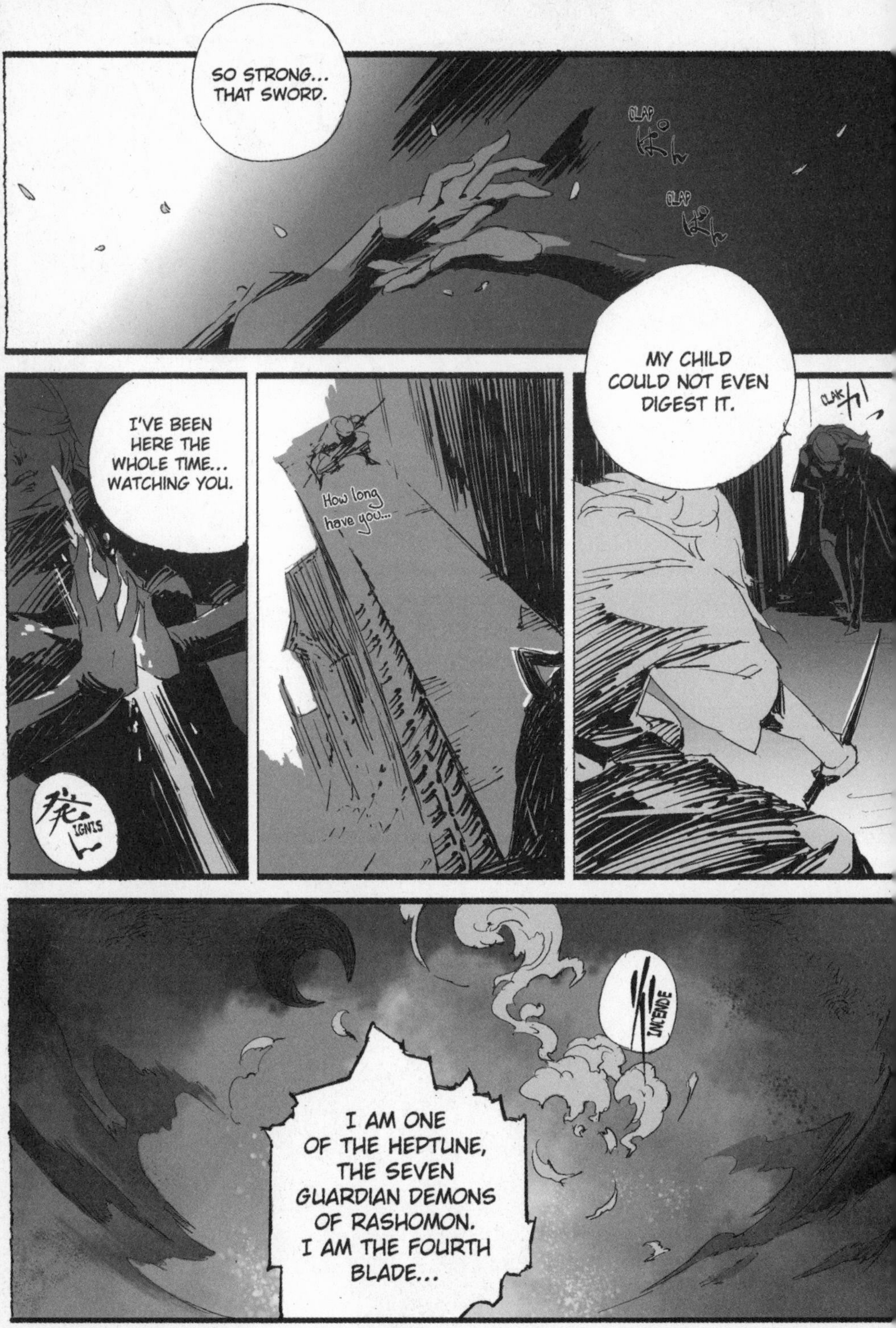
SO STRONG... THAT SWORD.
CLAP ぱん
CLAP ぱん
MY CHILD COULD NOT EVEN DIGEST IT.
I'VE BEEN HERE THE WHOLE TIME... WATCHING YOU.
How long have you...
IGNIS
INCENDE
I AM ONE OF THE HEPTUNE, THE SEVEN GUARDIAN DEMONS OF RASHOMON. I AM THE FOURTH BLADE...

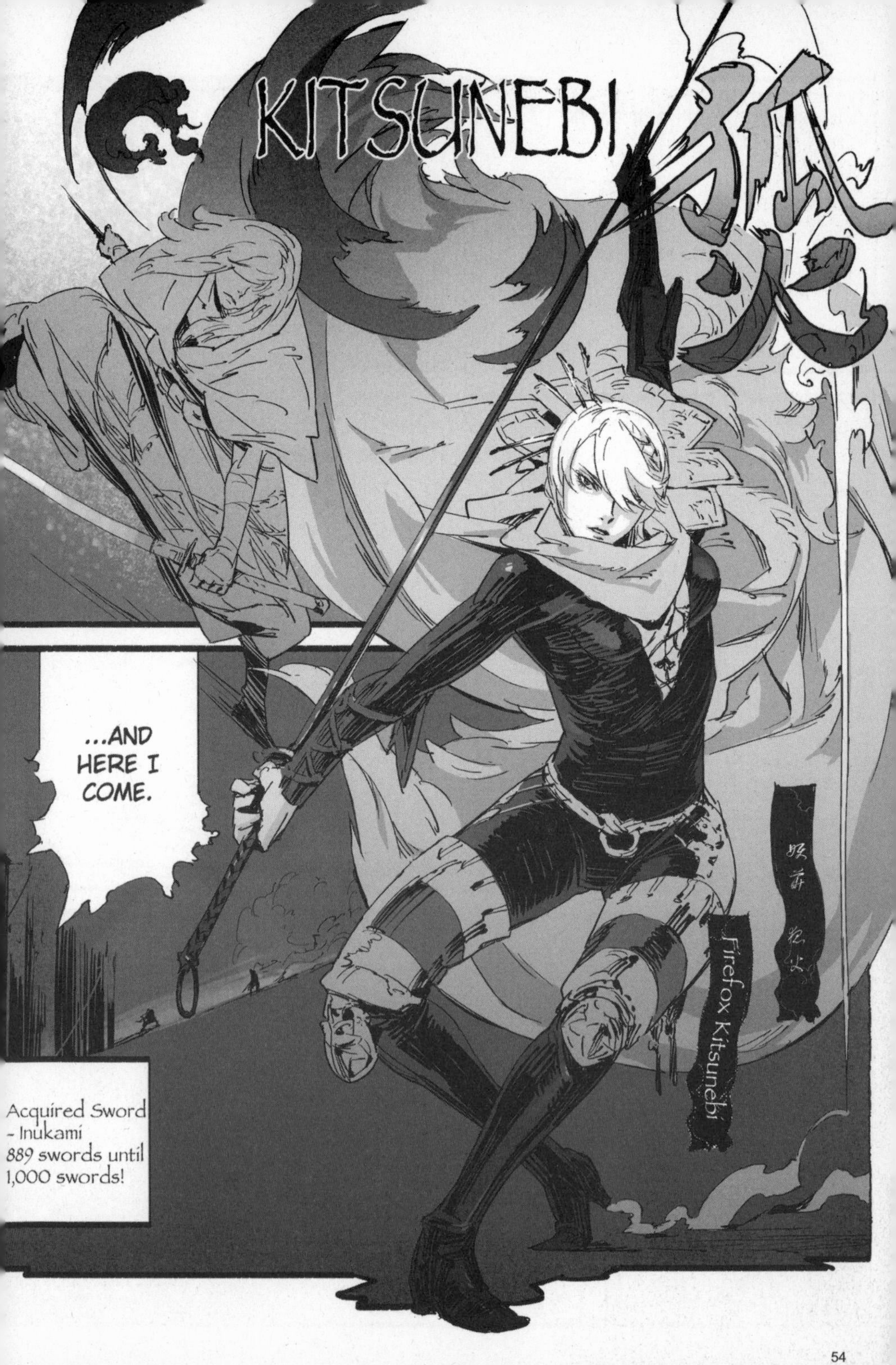
KITSUNEBI
...AND HERE I COME.
Firefox Kitsunebi
Acquired Sword - Inukami
889 swords until 1,000 swords!

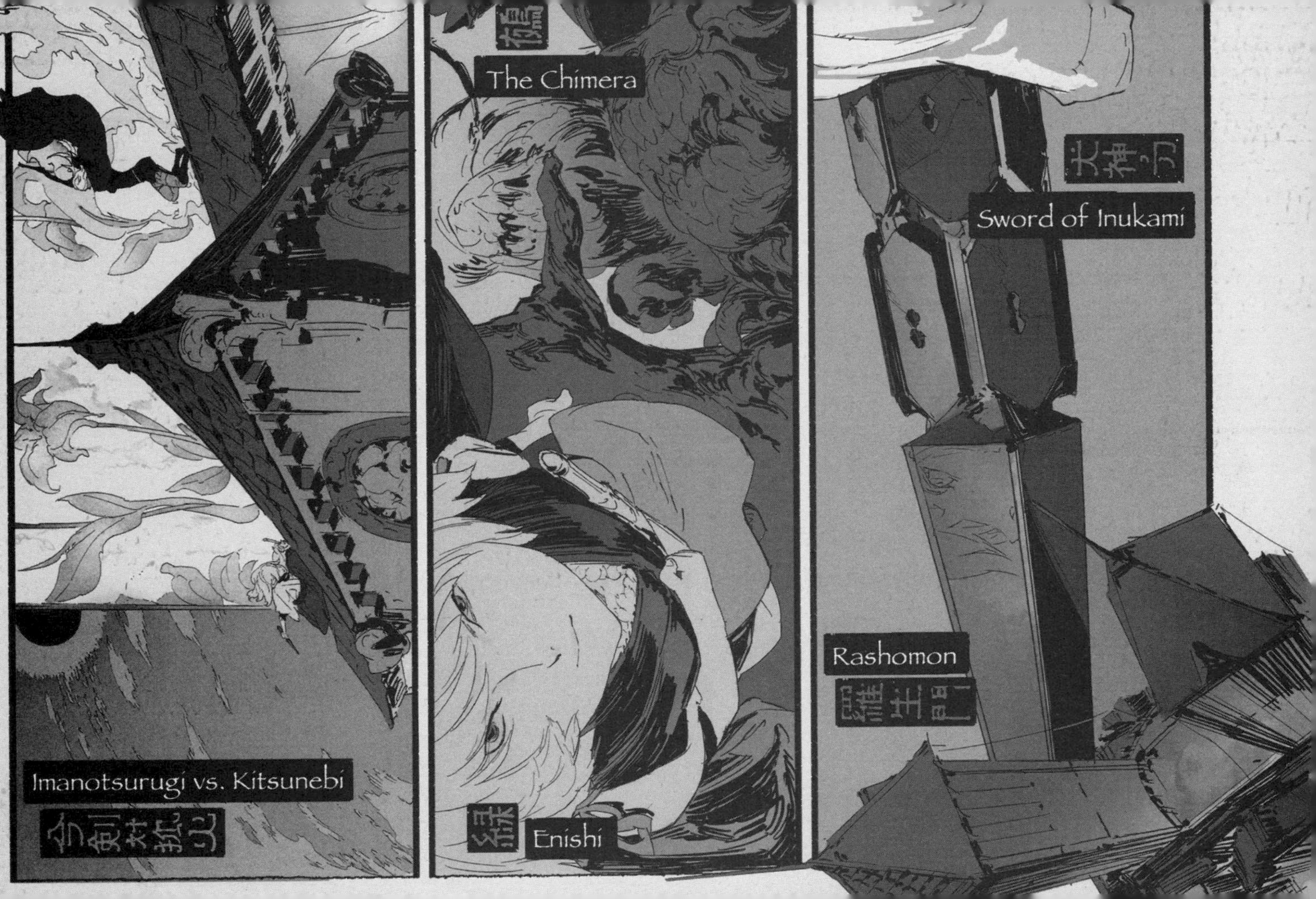

Imanotsurugi vs. Kitsunebi
今剣対狐火
鵺
The Chimera
縁
Enishi
犬神刀
Sword of Inukami
Rashomon
羅生門

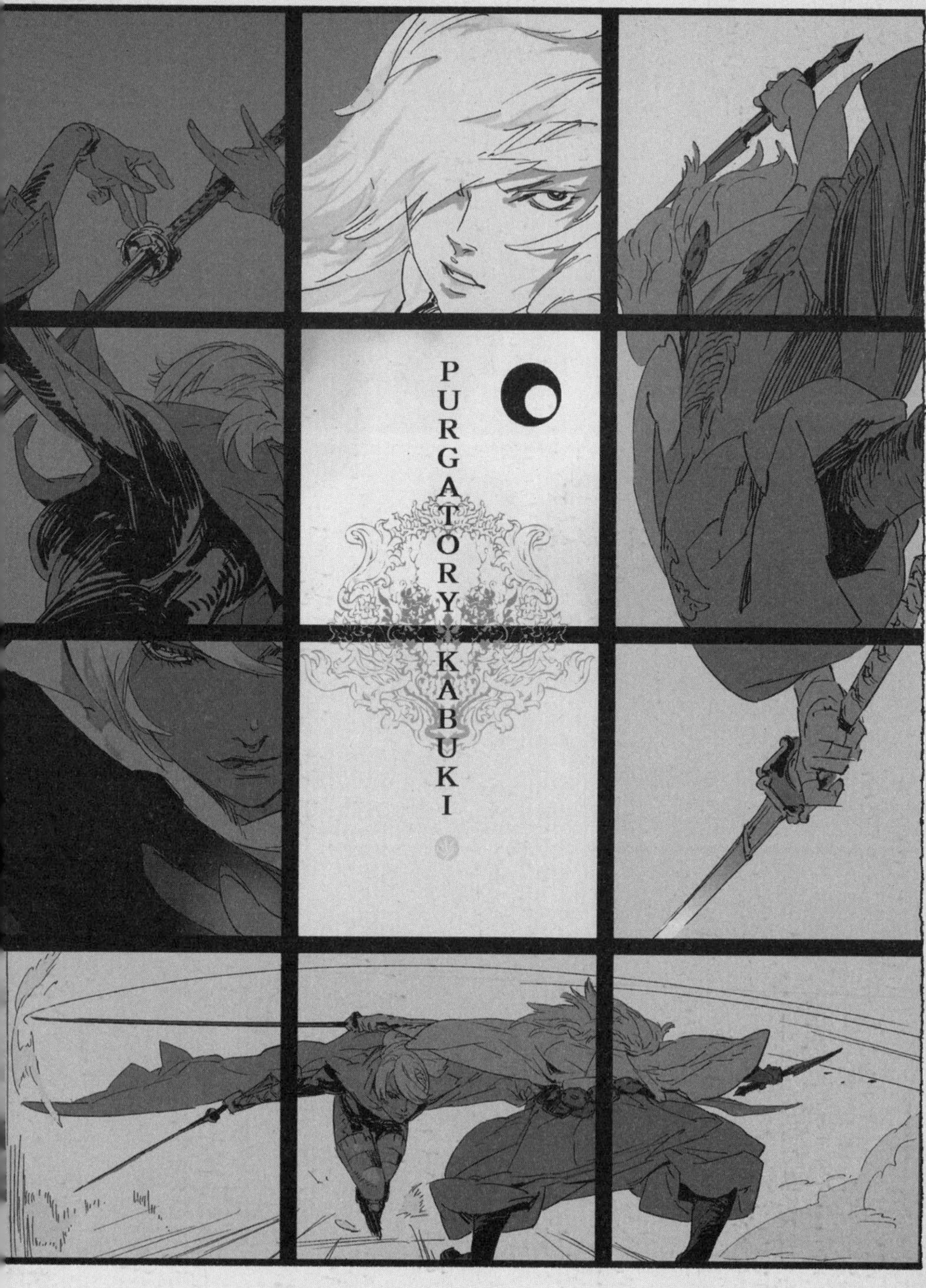
PURGATORY KABUKI

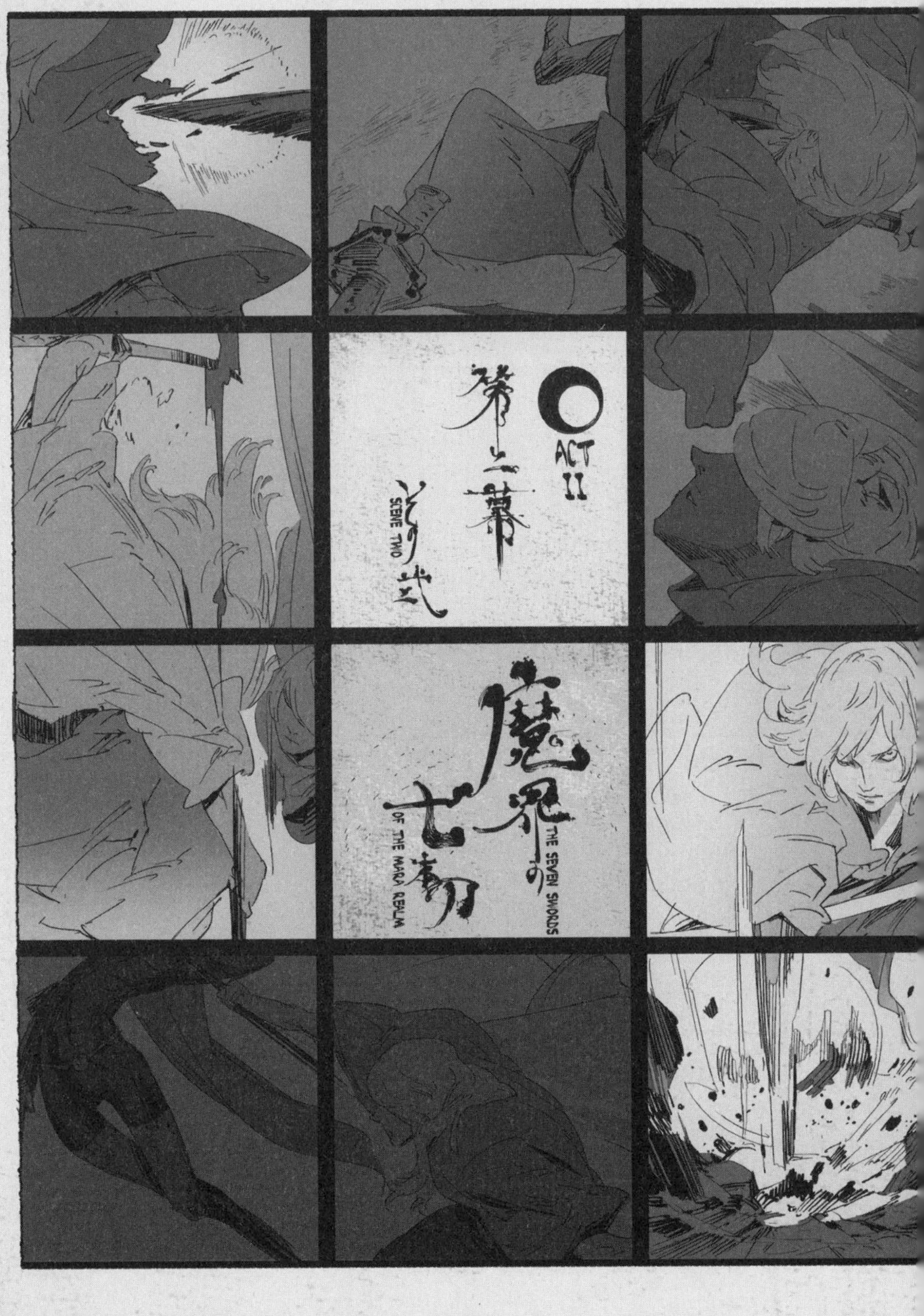
第二幕
ACT II
其の弐
SCENE TWO
魔羅の七剣
THE SEVEN SWORDS
OF THE MARA REALM

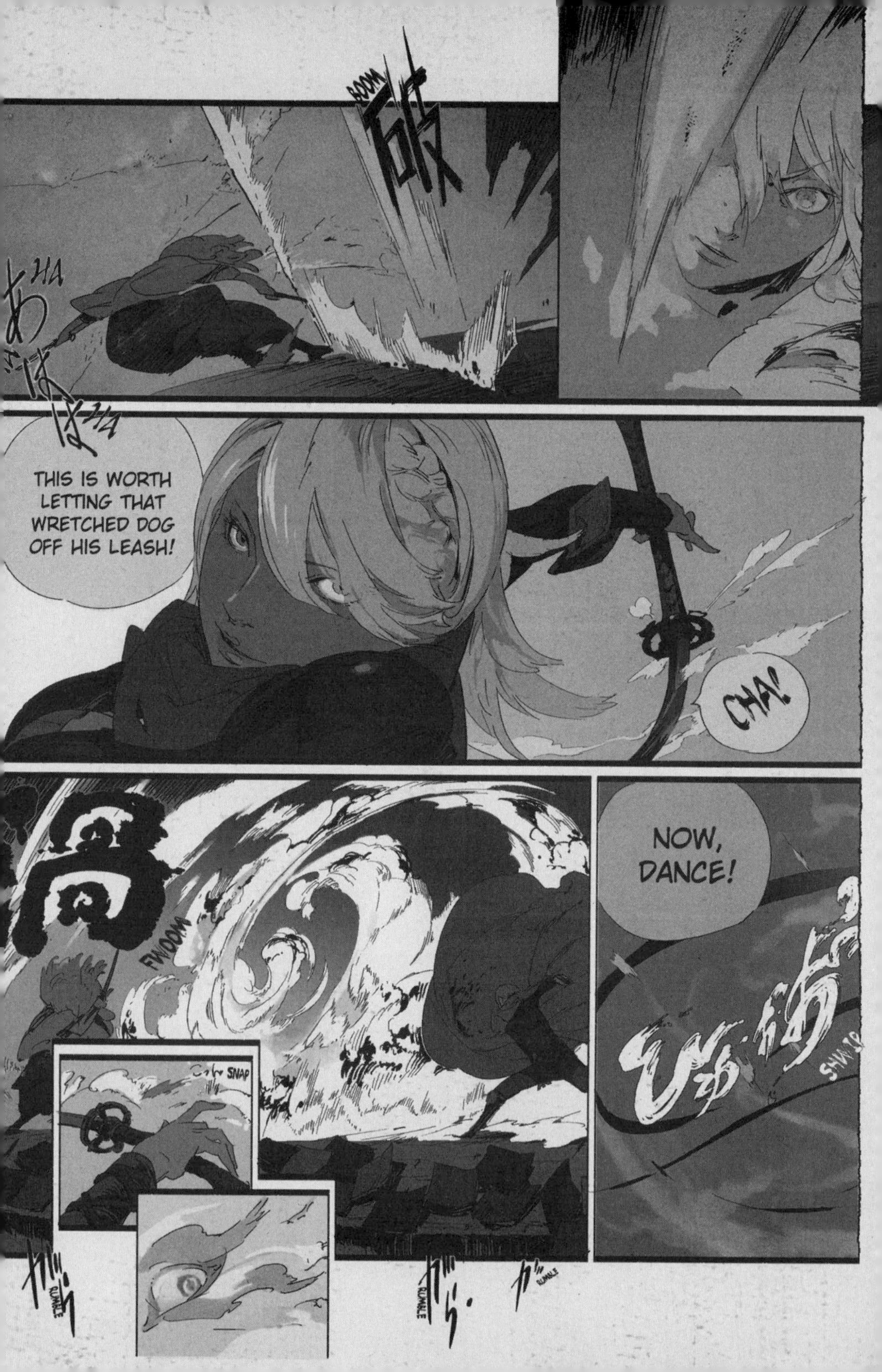
BOOM
HA
HA
THIS IS WORTH LETTING THAT WRETCHED DOG OFF HIS LEASH!
CHA!
NOW, DANCE!
FWOOM
SNAP
SHWIP
RUMBLE
RUMBLE
RUMBLE

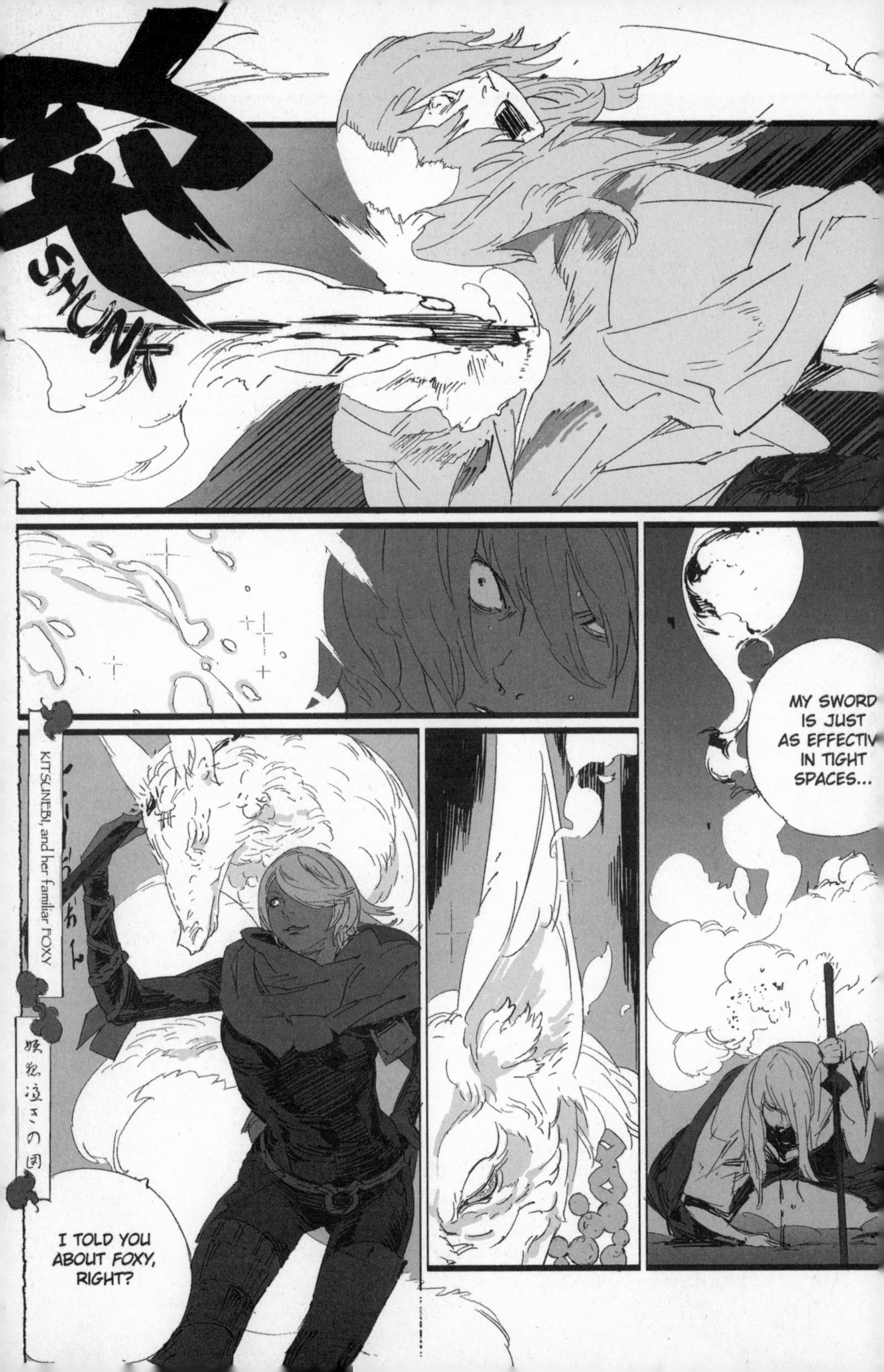
SHUNK
MY SWORD IS JUST AS EFFECTIV IN TIGHT SPACES...
KITSUNEBI, and her familiar FOXY
I TOLD YOU ABOUT FOXY, RIGHT?

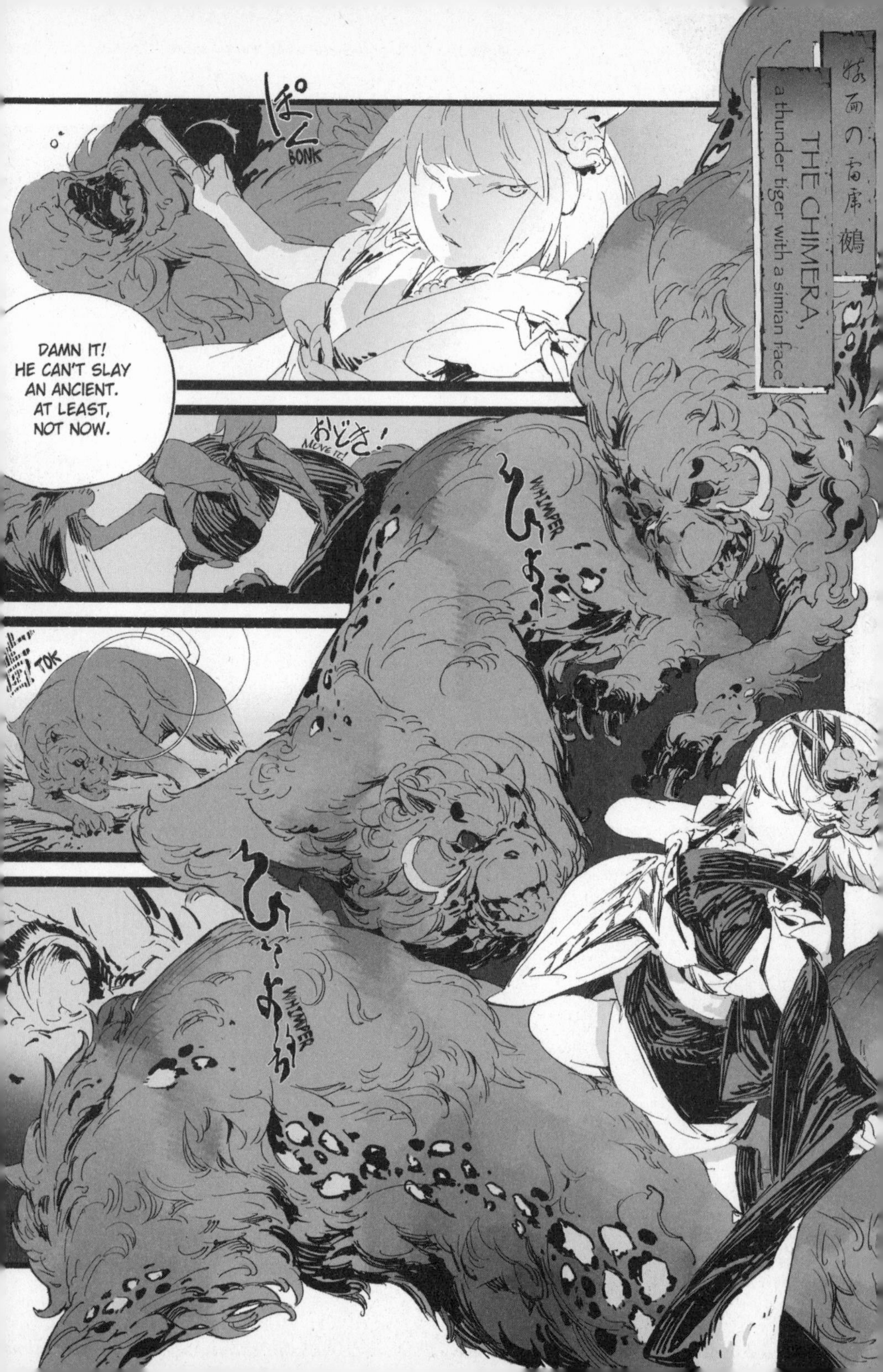
猿面の雷虎鵺
THE CHIMERA,
a thunder tiger with a simian face
ぽく
BONK
DAMN IT! HE CAN'T SLAY AN ANCIENT. AT LEAST, NOT NOW.
おどき!
MOVE IT!
WHIMPER
TOK
WHIMPER

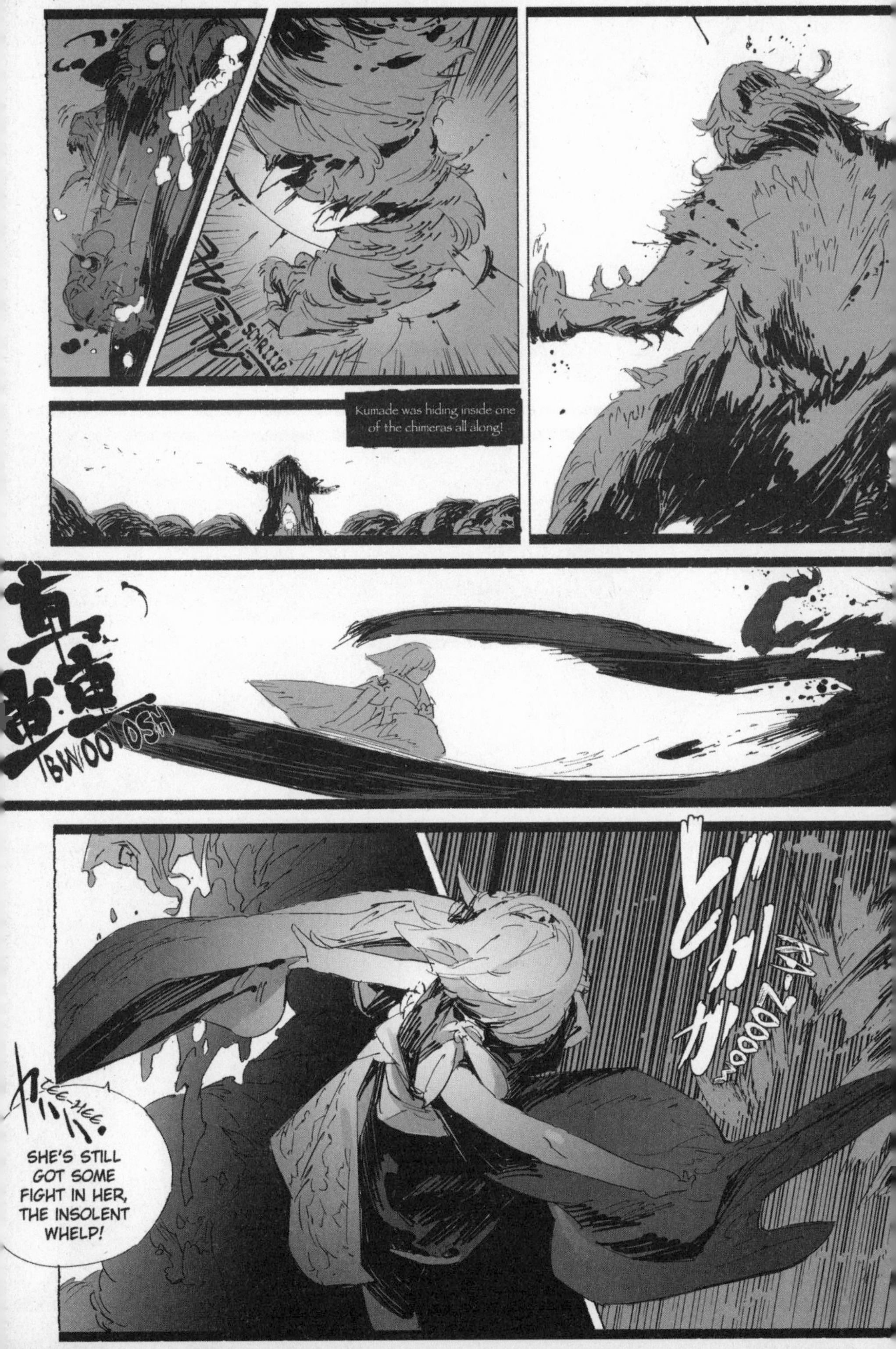
SCHRIIIP
Kumade was hiding inside one of the chimeras all along!
BWOOOOSH
ZOOOOOOM
TEE-HEE.
SHE'S STILL GOT SOME FIGHT IN HER, THE INSOLENT WHELP!

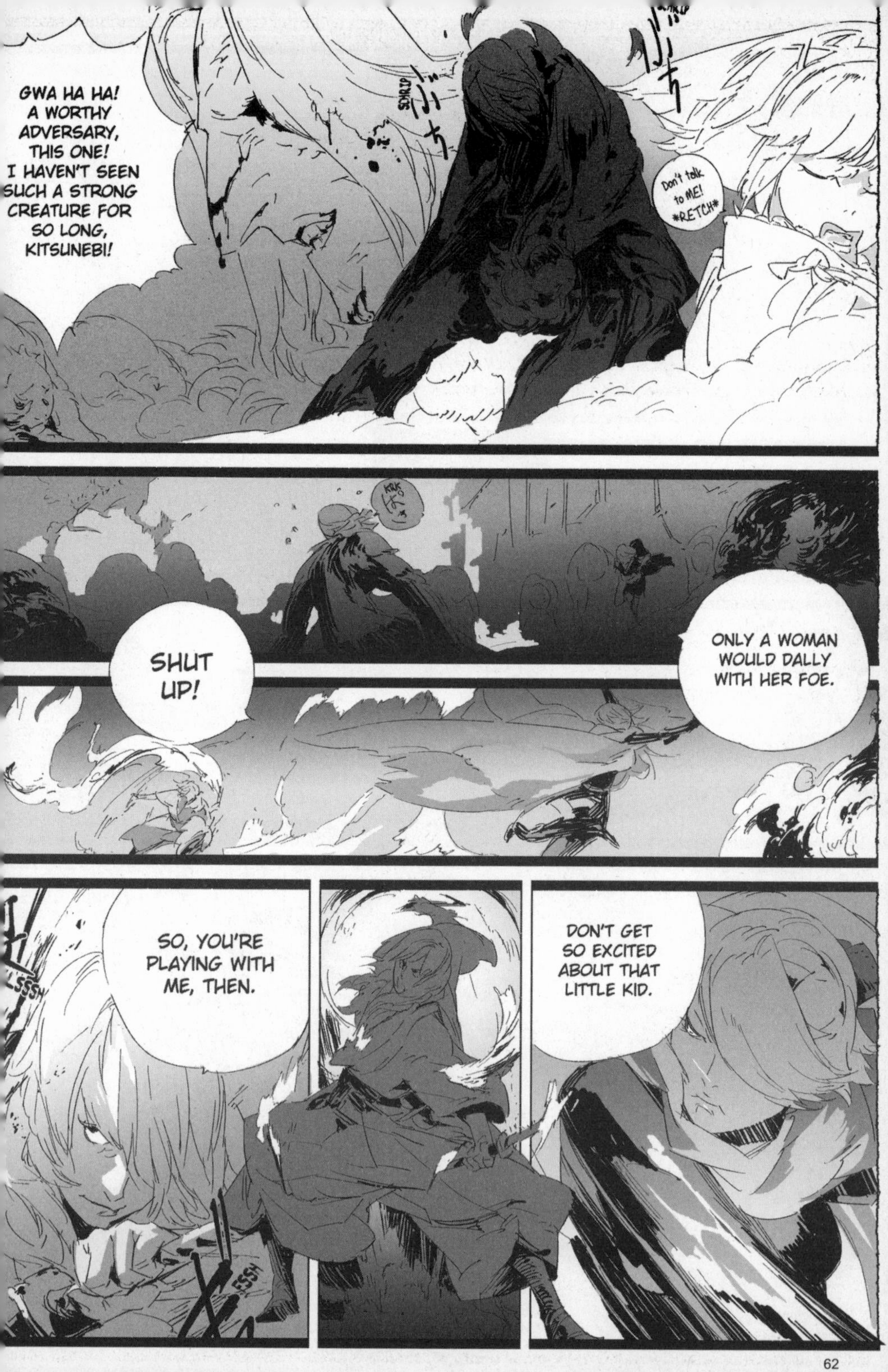
SCHRIP
Don't talk to ME! *RETCH*
GWA HA HA! A WORTHY ADVERSARY, THIS ONE! I HAVEN'T SEEN SUCH A STRONG CREATURE FOR SO LONG, KITSUNEBI!
KRK
ONLY A WOMAN WOULD DALLY WITH HER FOE.
SHUT UP!
DON'T GET SO EXCITED ABOUT THAT LITTLE KID.
SO, YOU'RE PLAYING WITH ME, THEN.
ESSH

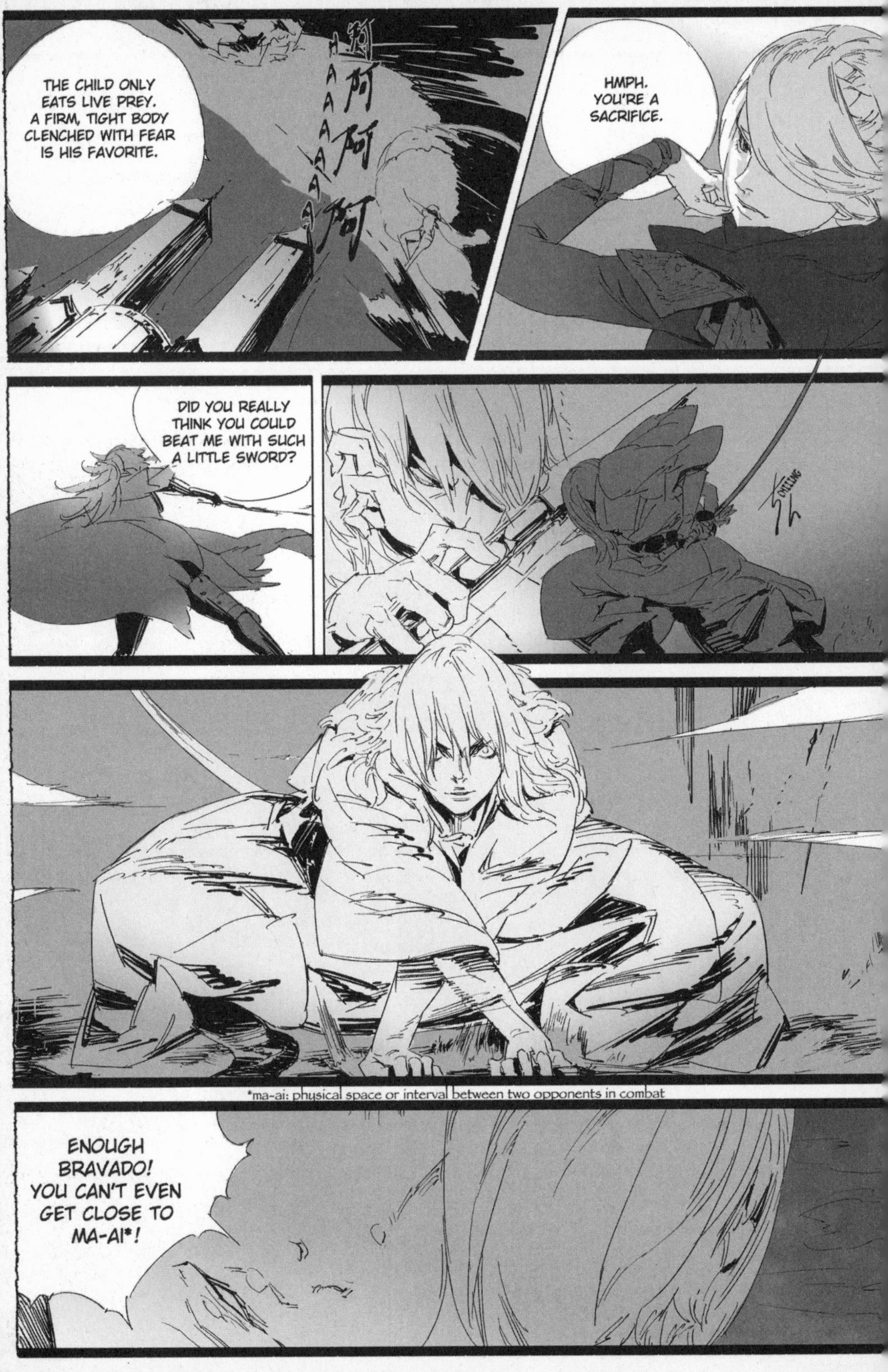
THE CHILD ONLY EATS LIVE PREY. A FIRM, TIGHT BODY CLENCHED WITH FEAR IS HIS FAVORITE.
HAAAAAAA
HMPH. YOU'RE A SACRIFICE.
DID YOU REALLY THINK YOU COULD BEAT ME WITH SUCH A LITTLE SWORD?
SCHIING
ENOUGH BRAVADO! YOU CAN'T EVEN GET CLOSE TO MA-AI*!
*ma-ai: physical space or interval between two opponents in combat

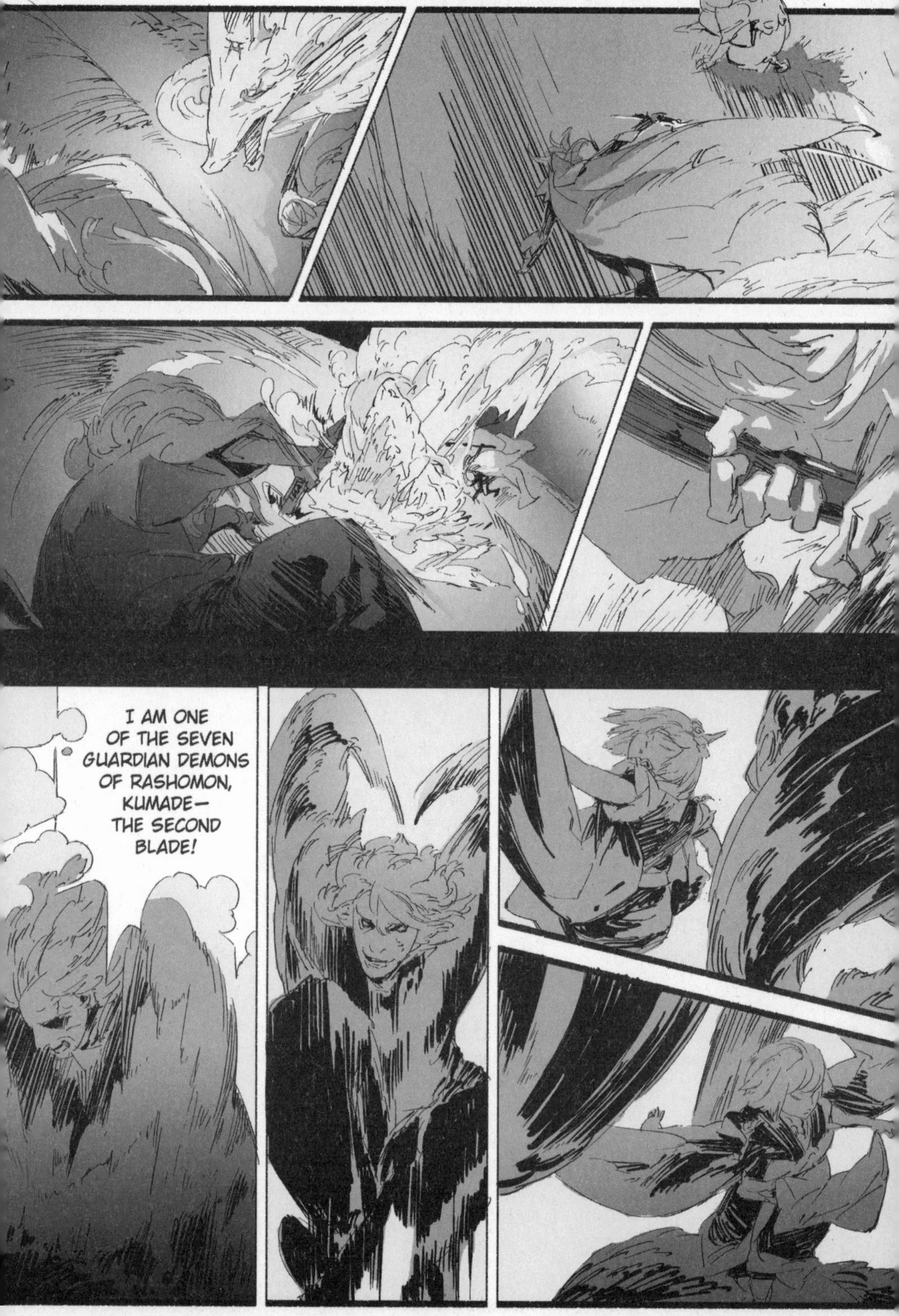
I AM ONE OF THE SEVEN GUARDIAN DEMONS OF RASHOMON, KUMADE— THE SECOND BLADE!

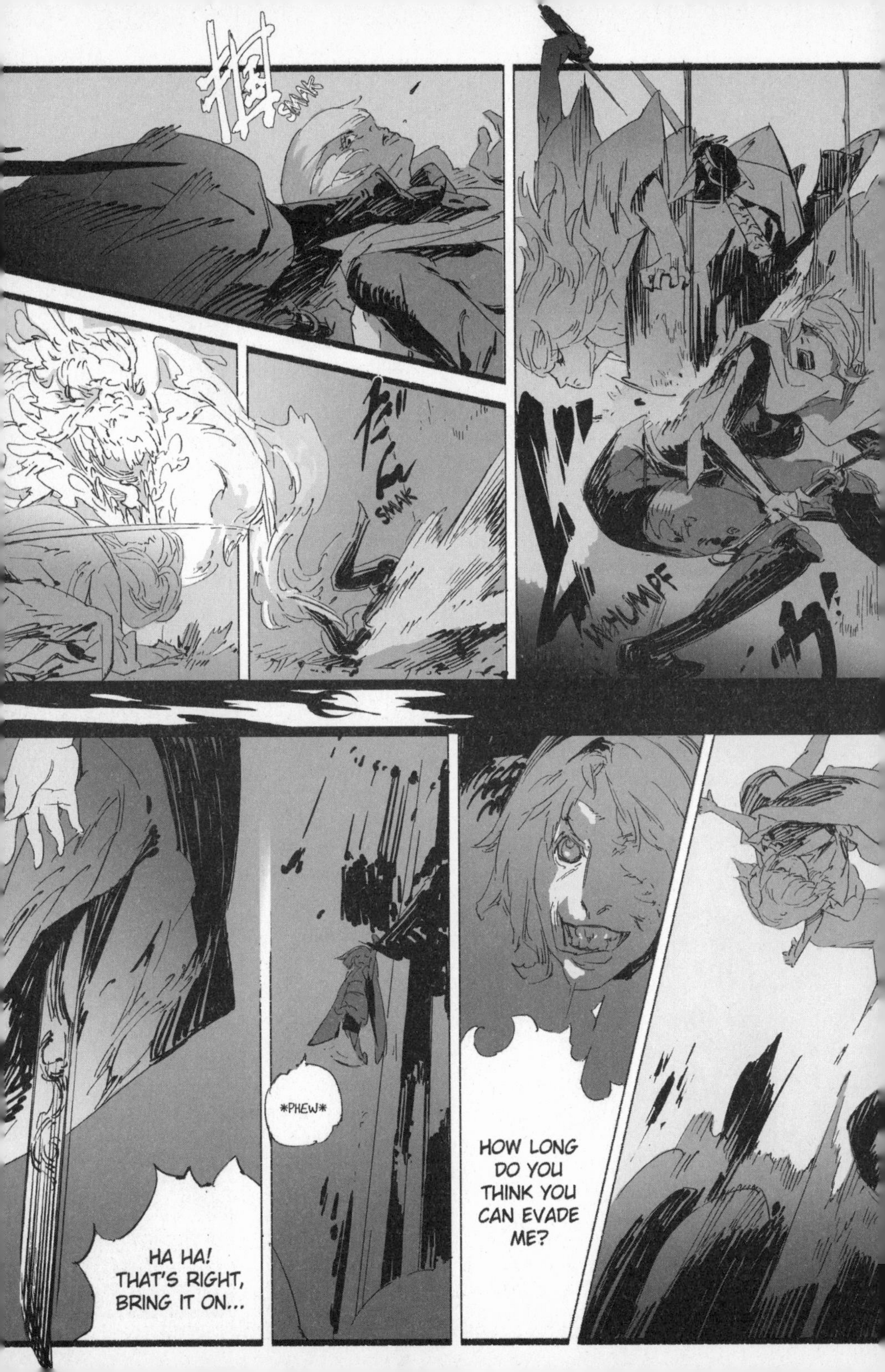

SMAK
WHUMPF
SMAK
HOW LONG DO YOU THINK YOU CAN EVADE ME?
PHEW
HA HA! THAT'S RIGHT, BRING IT ON...

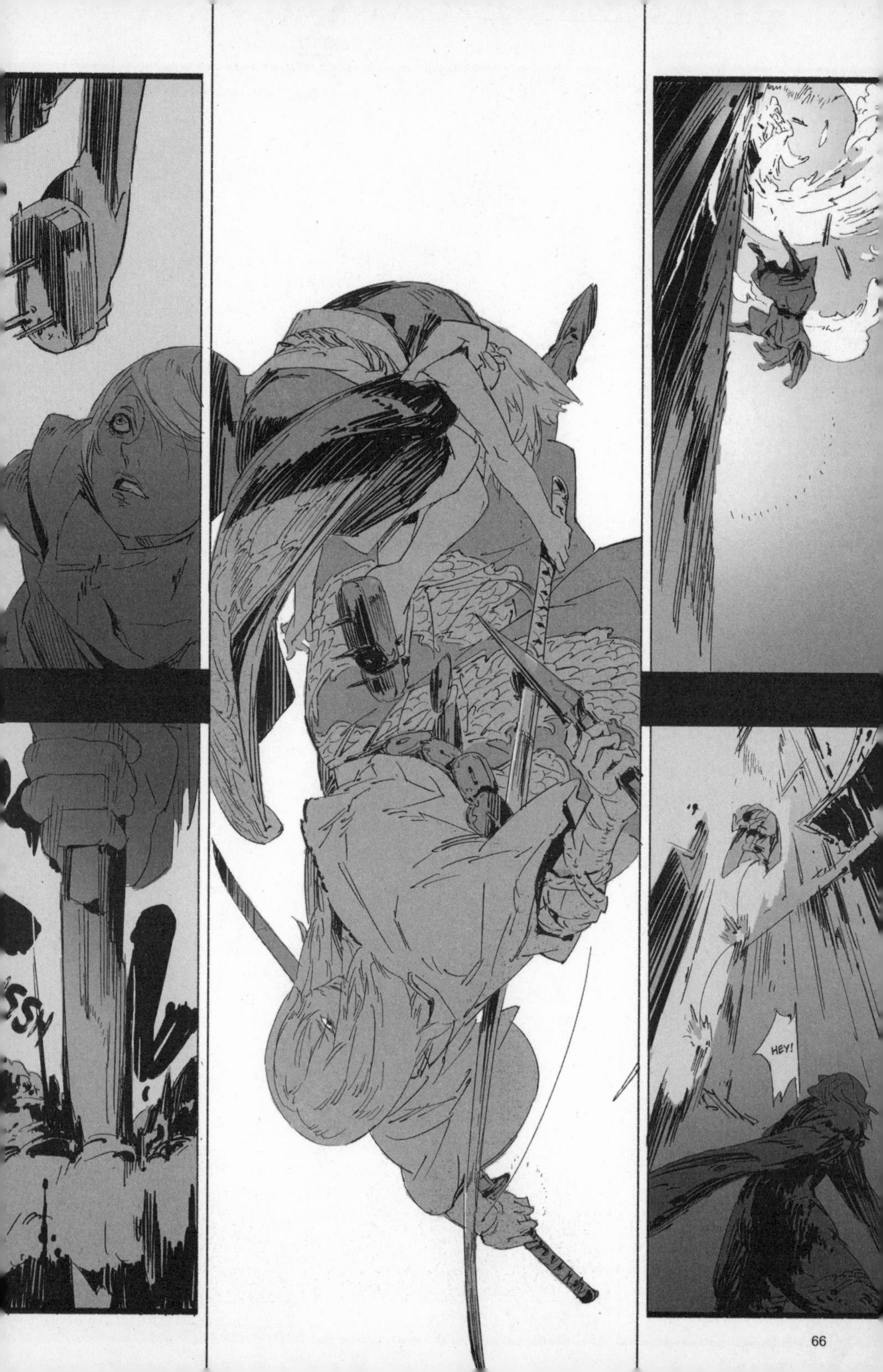
HEY!

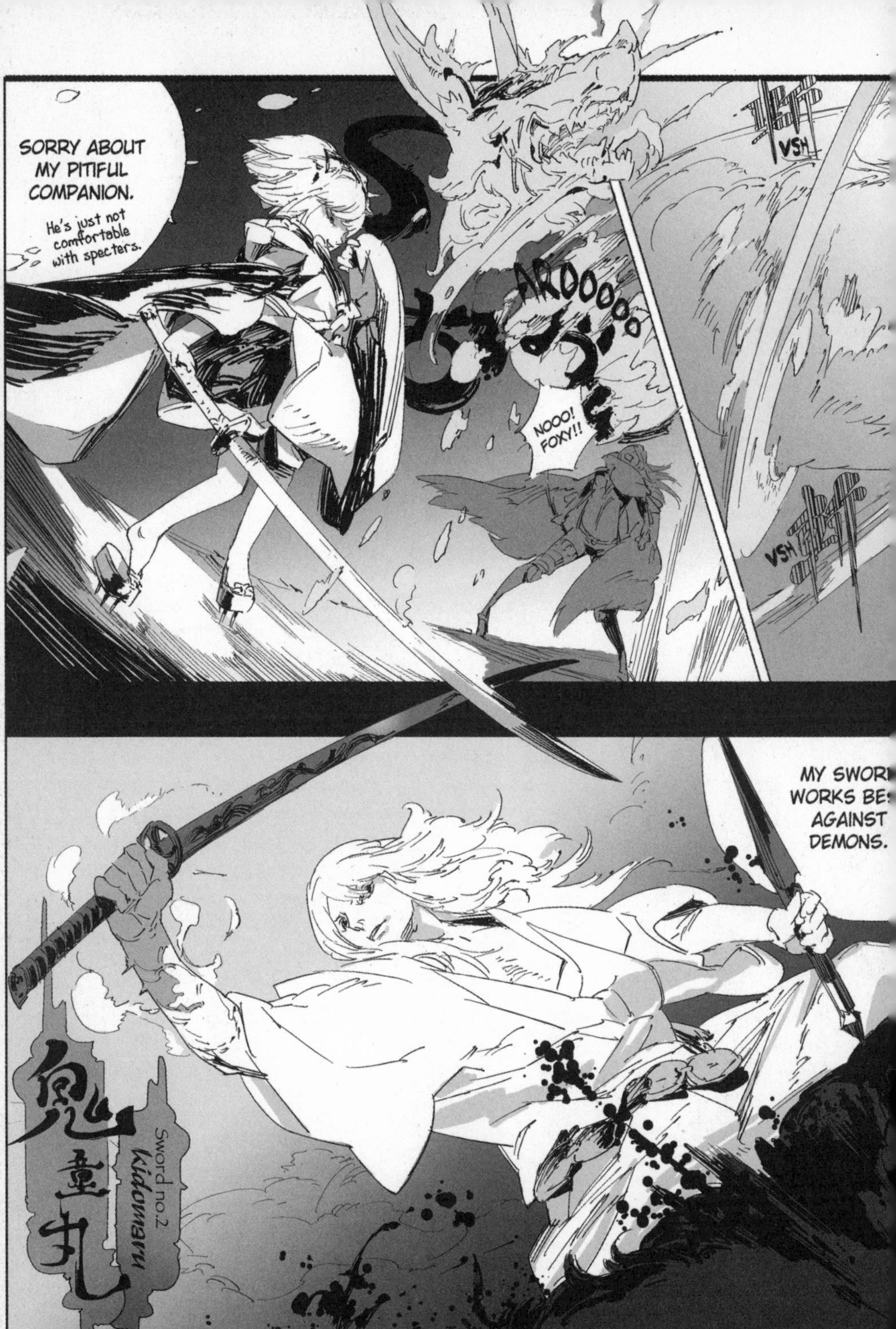
SORRY ABOUT MY PITIFUL COMPANION.
He's just not comfortable with specters.
VSH
AROOOOOO
NOOO! FOXY!!
VSH
MY SWORD WORKS BEST AGAINST DEMONS.
鬼童丸
Sword no.2 Kidomaru

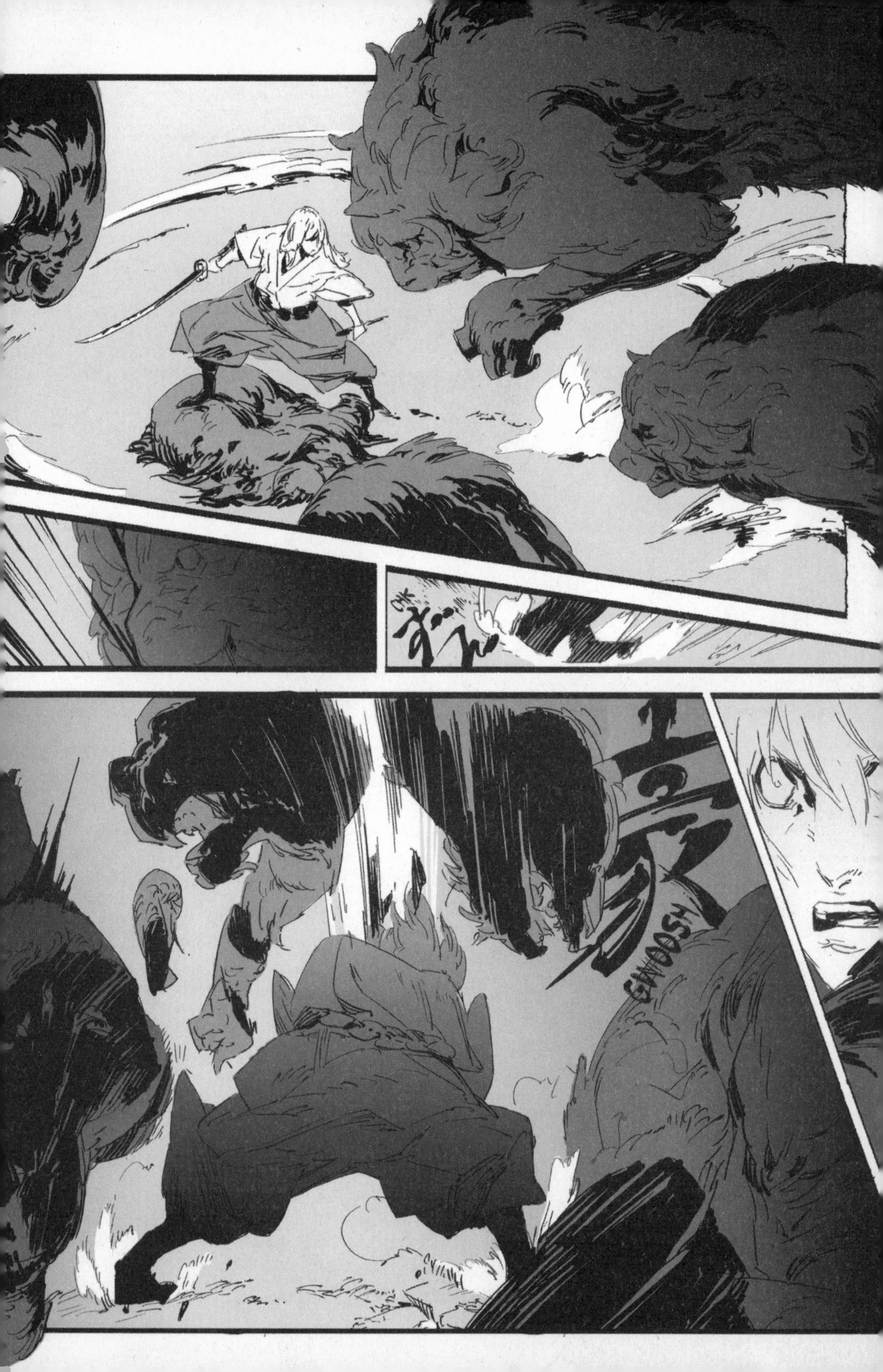
CHK
GWOOSH

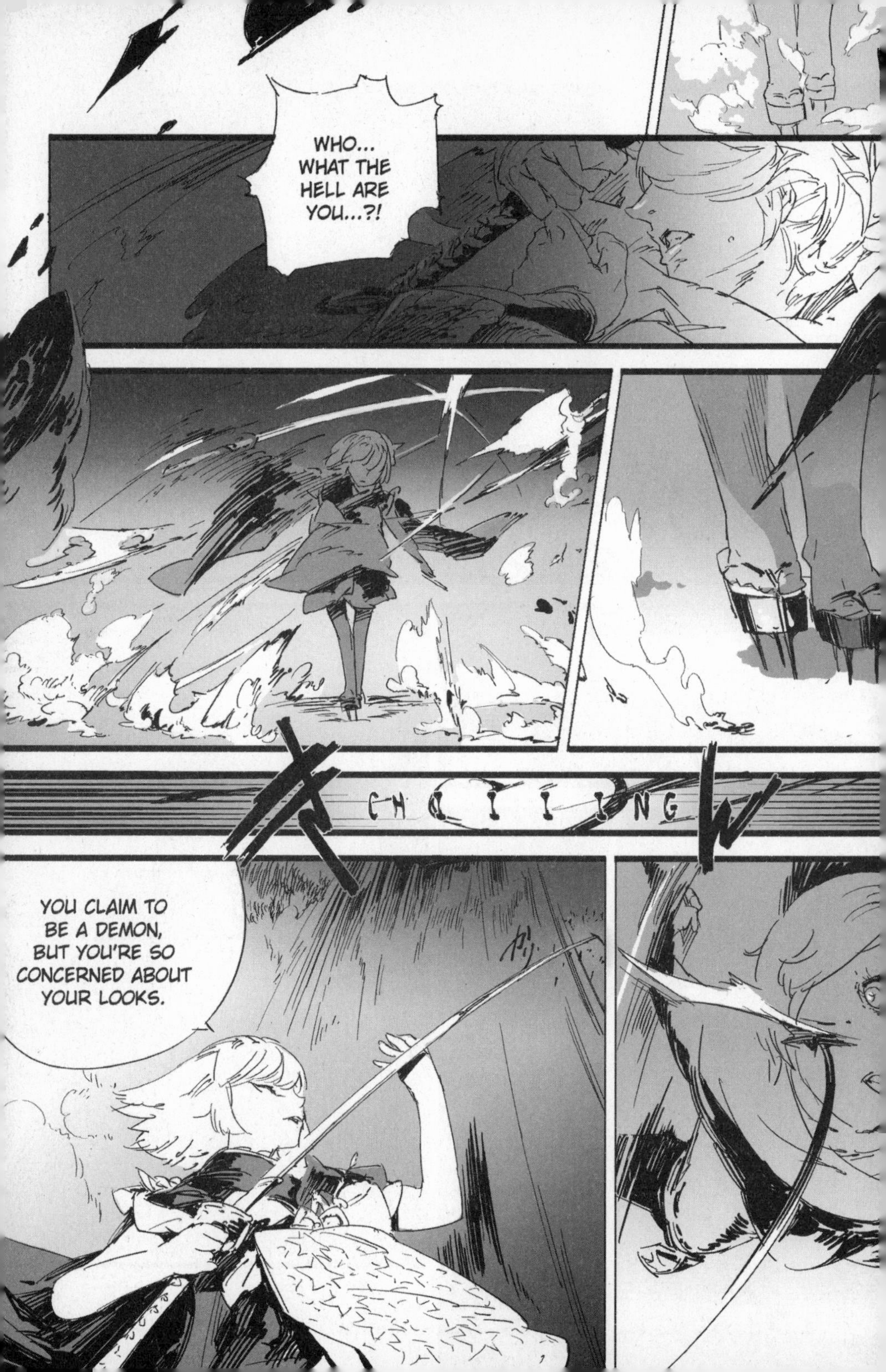
WHO... WHAT THE HELL ARE YOU...?!
CHIIING
YOU CLAIM TO BE A DEMON, BUT YOU'RE SO CONCERNED ABOUT YOUR LOOKS.

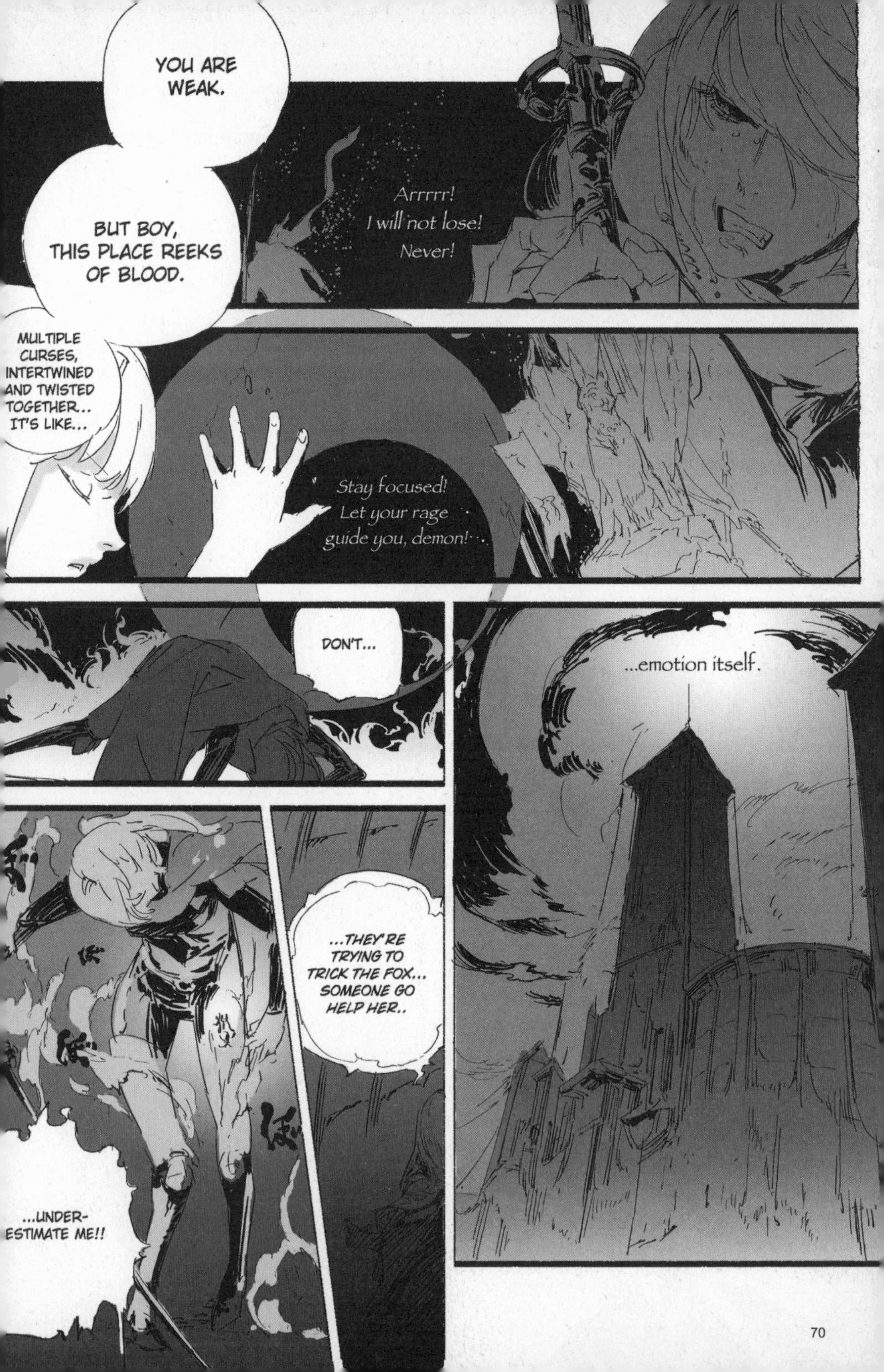
YOU ARE WEAK.
BUT BOY, THIS PLACE REEKS OF BLOOD.
Arrrrr! I will not lose! Never!
MULTIPLE CURSES, INTERTWINED AND TWISTED TOGETHER... IT'S LIKE...
Stay focused! Let your rage guide you, demon!
DON'T...
...emotion itself.
...THEY'RE TRYING TO TRICK THE FOX... SOMEONE GO HELP HER..
...UNDER-ESTIMATE ME!!

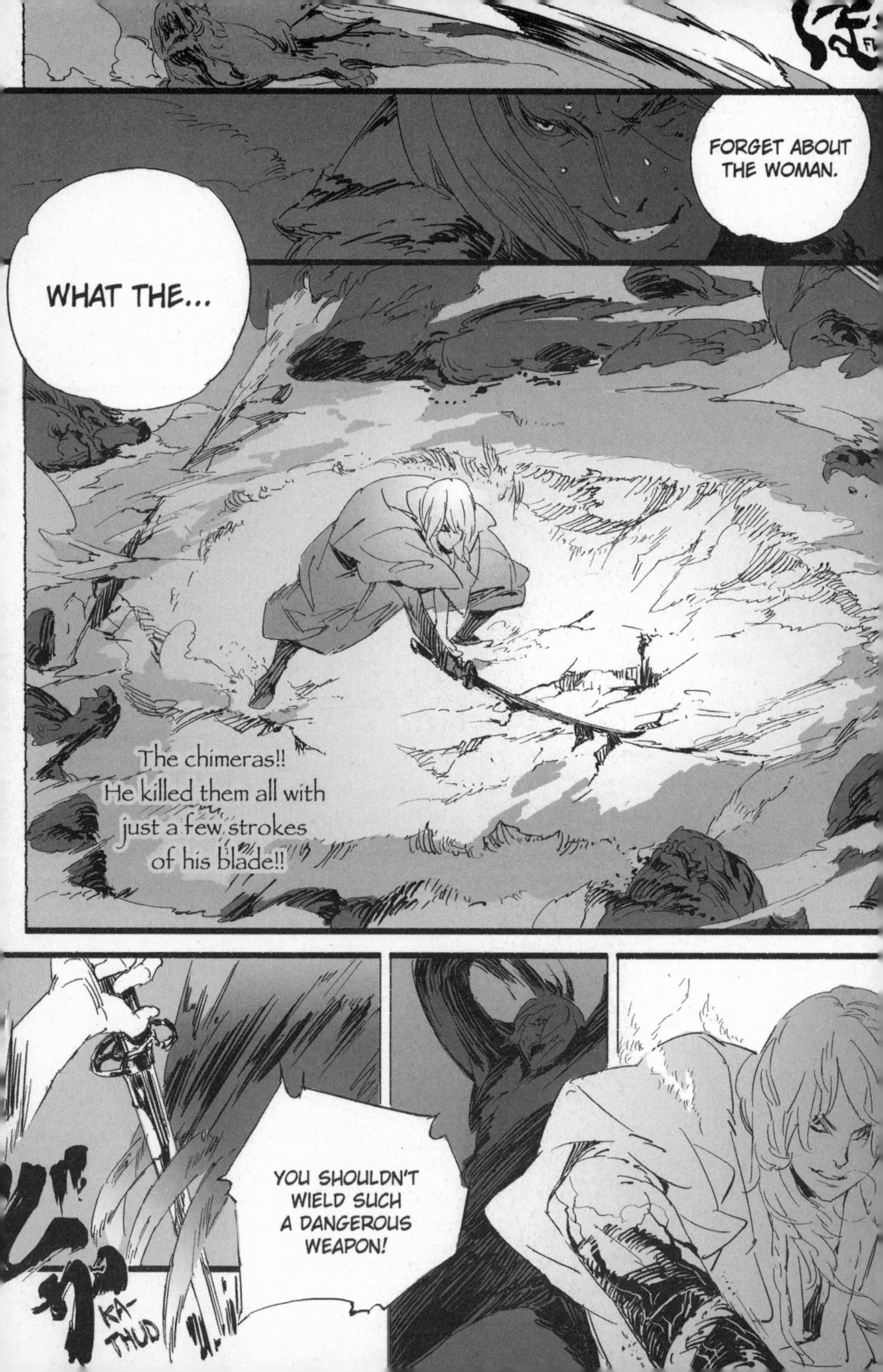
FORGET ABOUT THE WOMAN.
WHAT THE...
The chimeras!! He killed them all with just a few strokes of his blade!!
YOU SHOULDN'T WIELD SUCH A DANGEROUS WEAPON!
KA-THUD

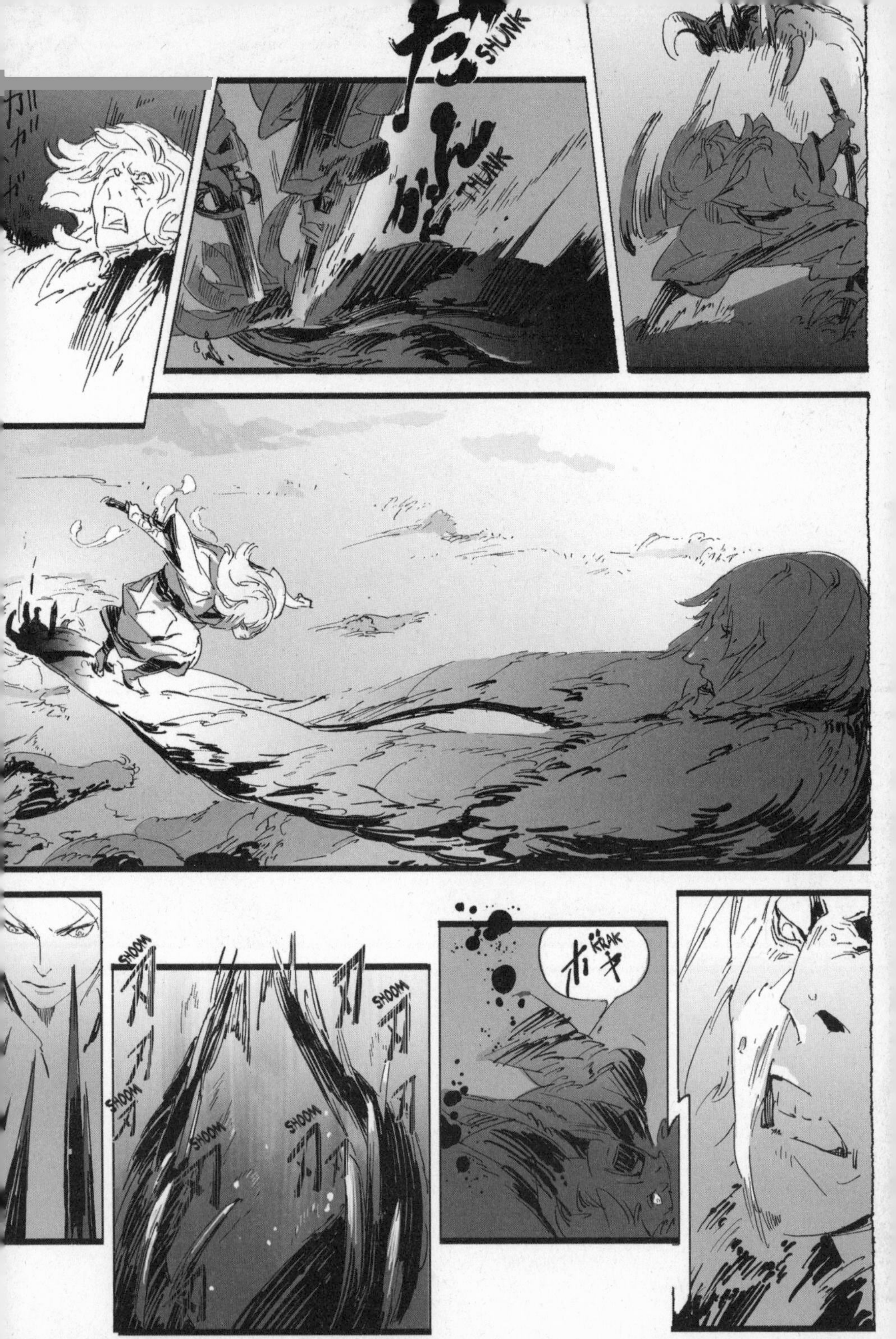

ガガガ
だん SHUNK
がん THUNK
SHOOM
SHOOM
SHOOM
SHOOM
SHOOM
ガキ KRAK

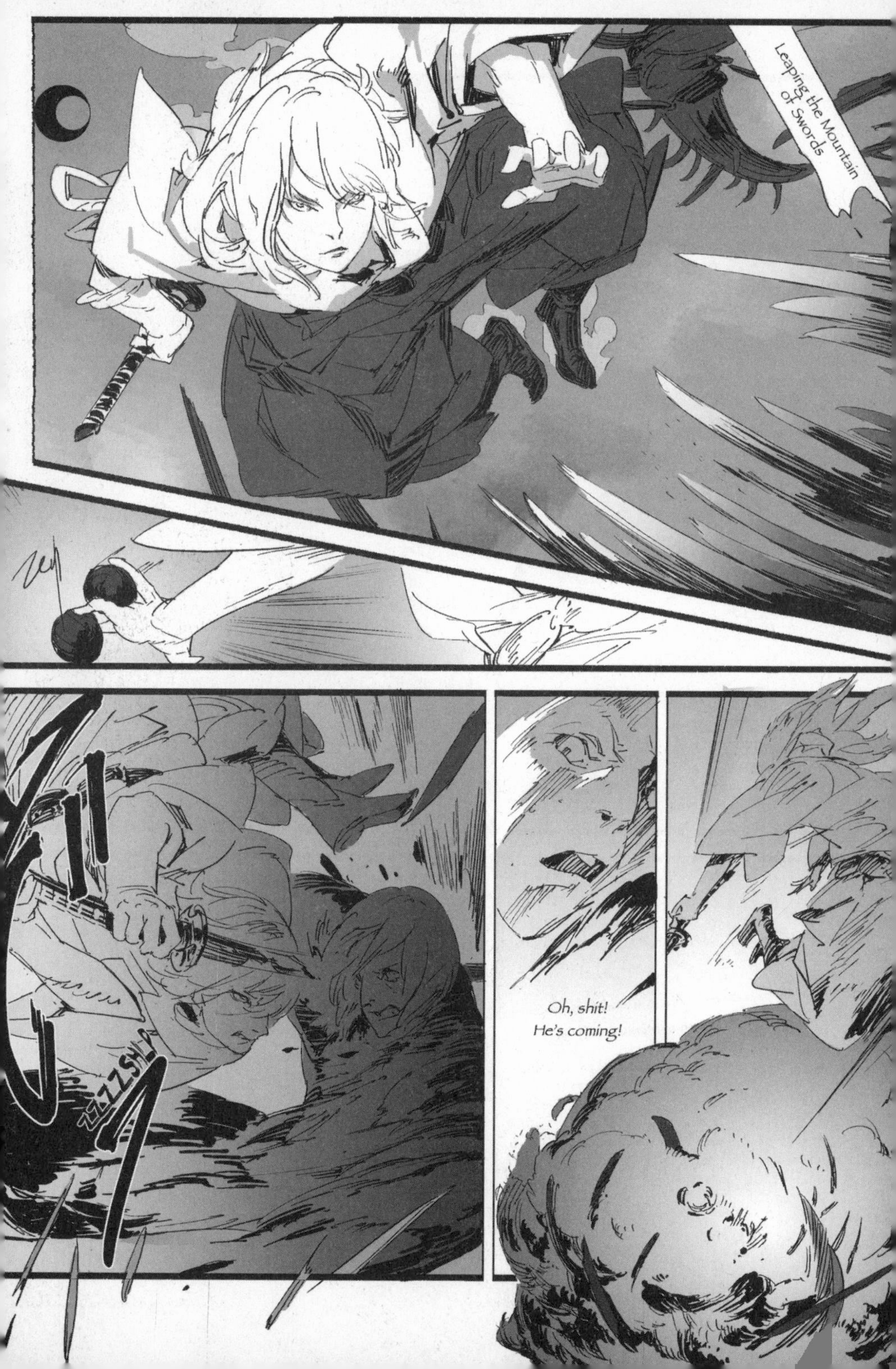
Leaping the Mountain of Swords
ZZZZSHP
Oh, shit!
He's coming!

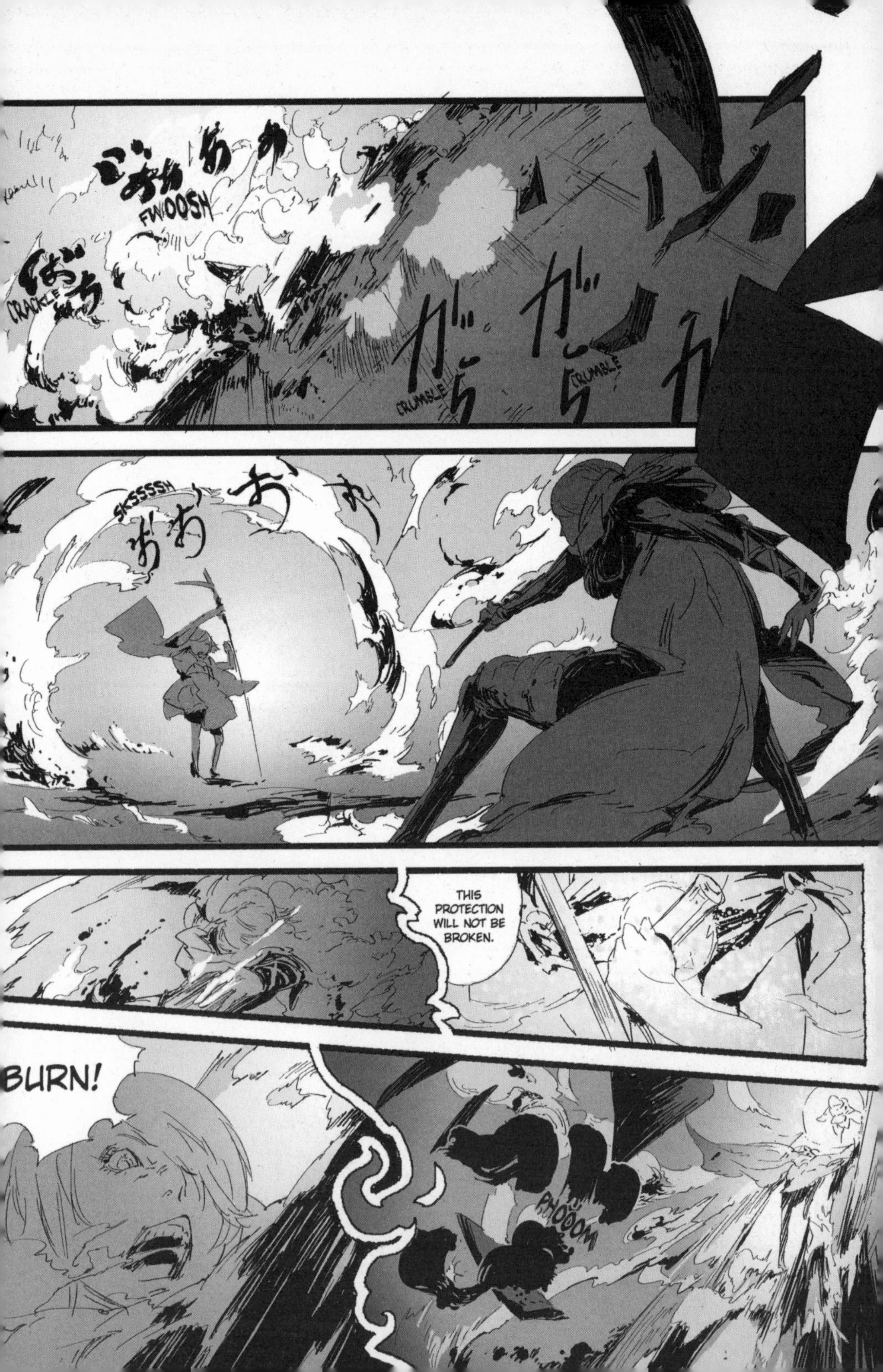
FWOOSH
CRACKLE
CRUMBLE
CRUMBLE
SKSSSSH
THIS PROTECTION WILL NOT BE BROKEN.
BURN!
PHOOOM

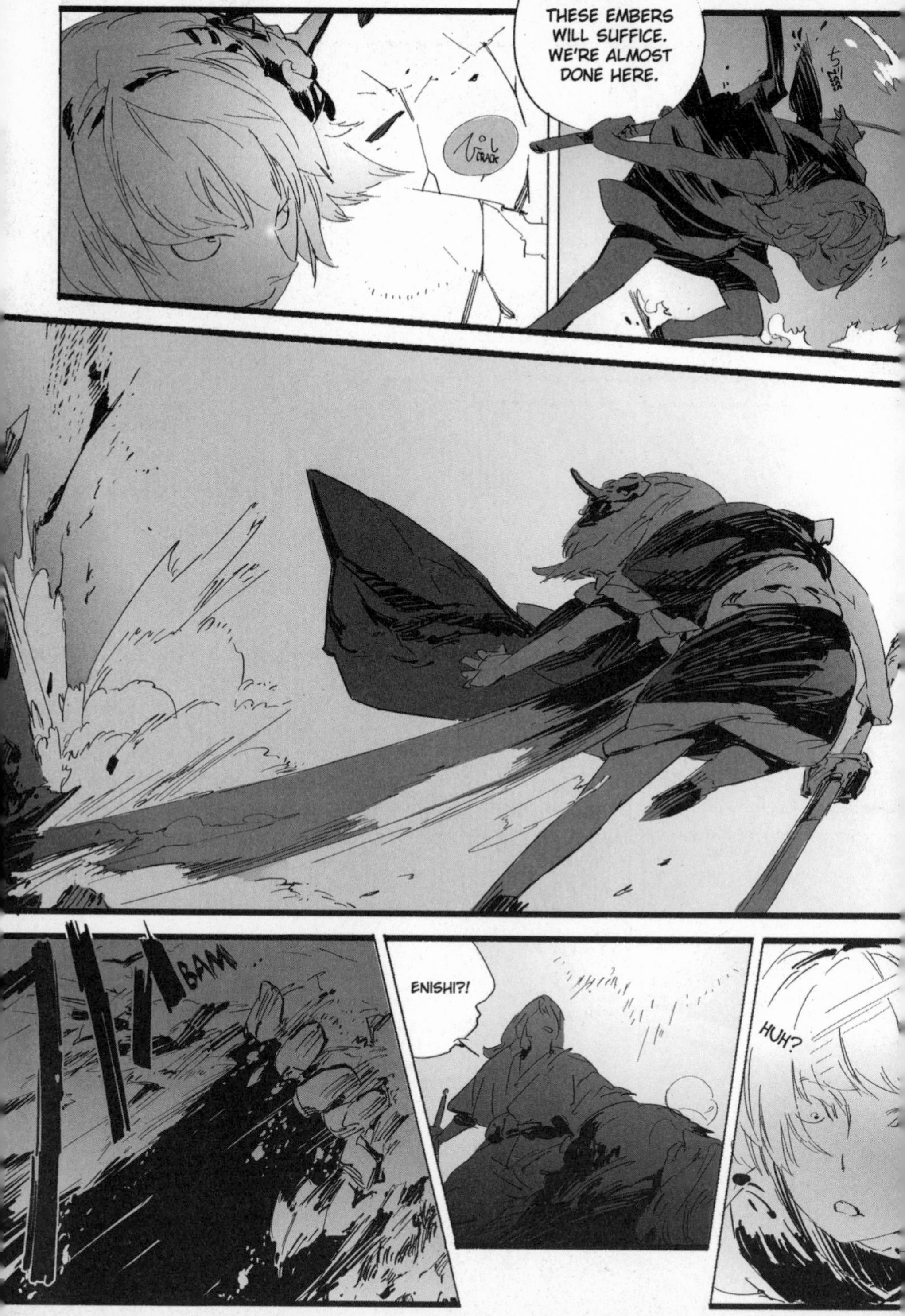
THESE EMBERS WILL SUFFICE. WE'RE ALMOST DONE HERE.
CRACK
BAM
ENISHI?!
HUH?

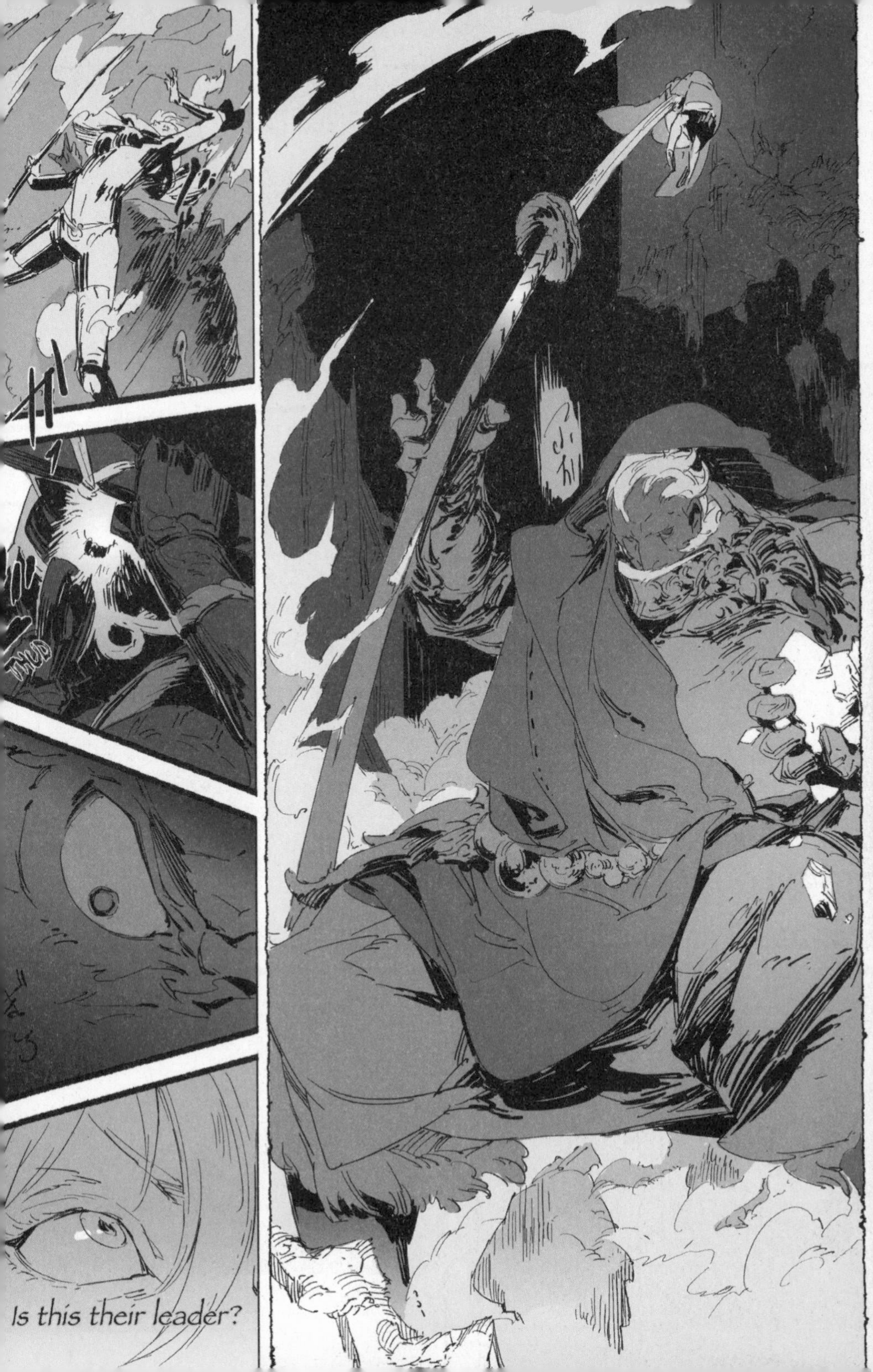
THUD
Is this their leader?

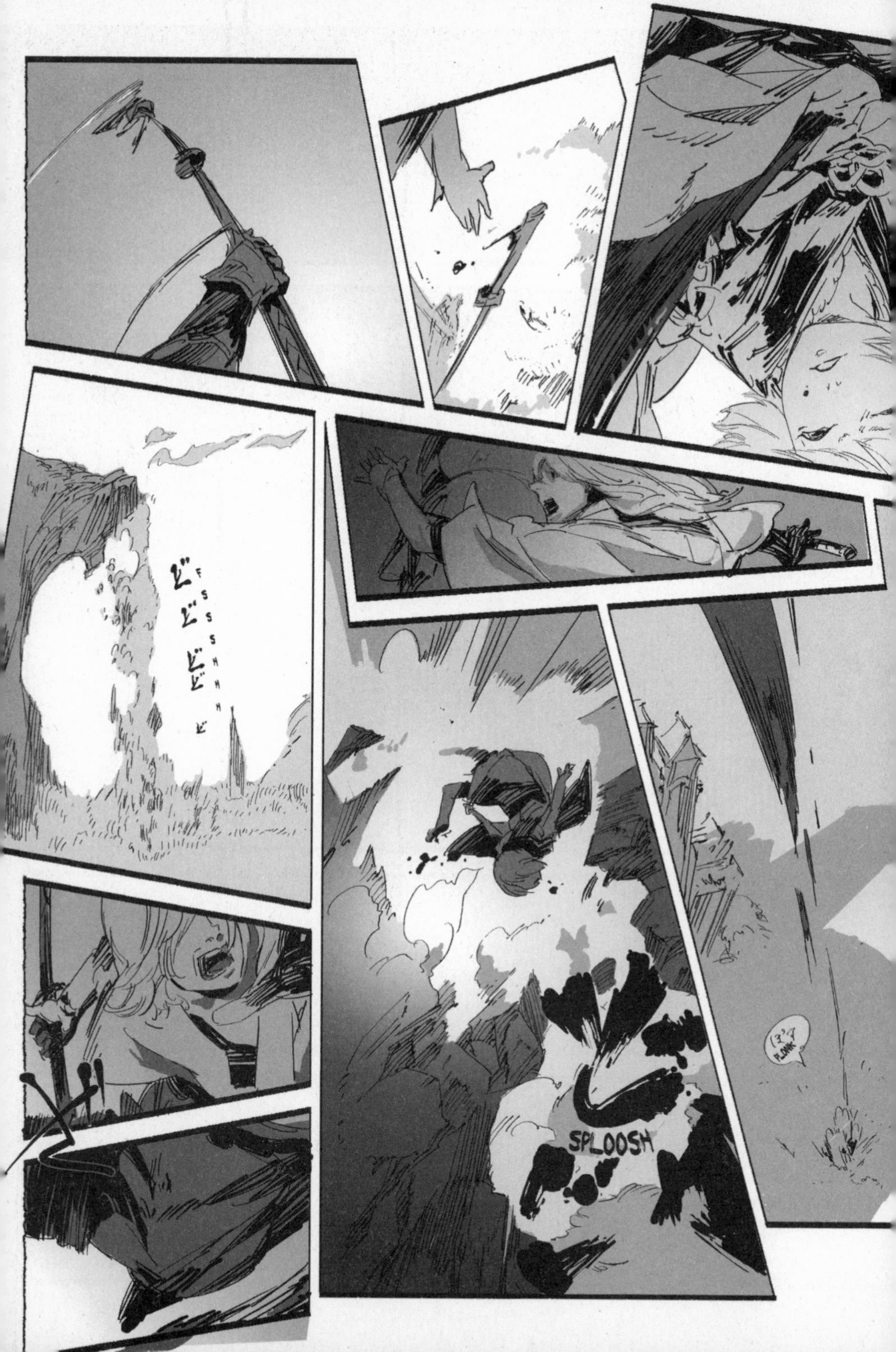
ドドドドド
FSSSHHH
SPLOOSH
ぽつ
PLONK

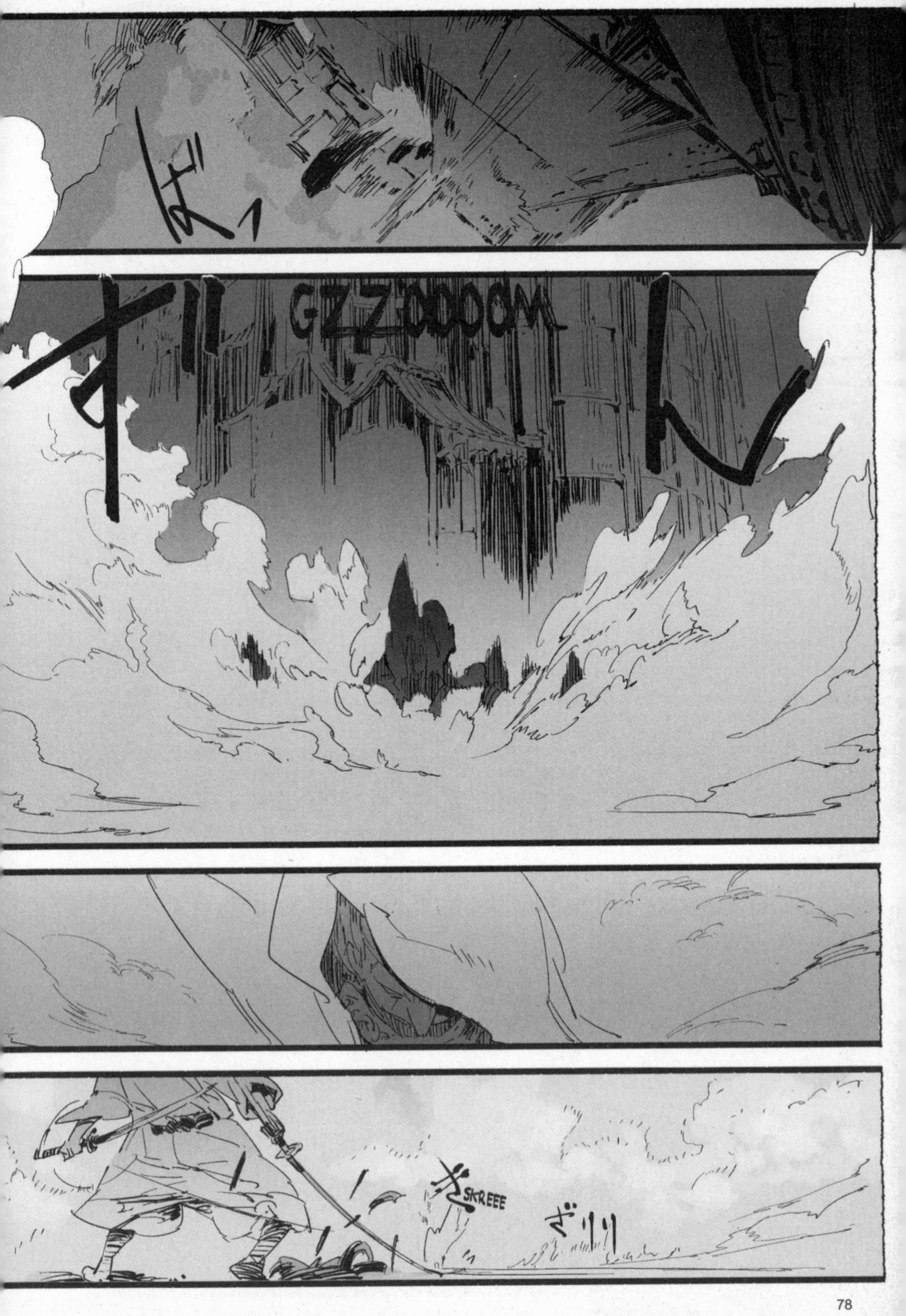
GZZOOOOM
SKREEE

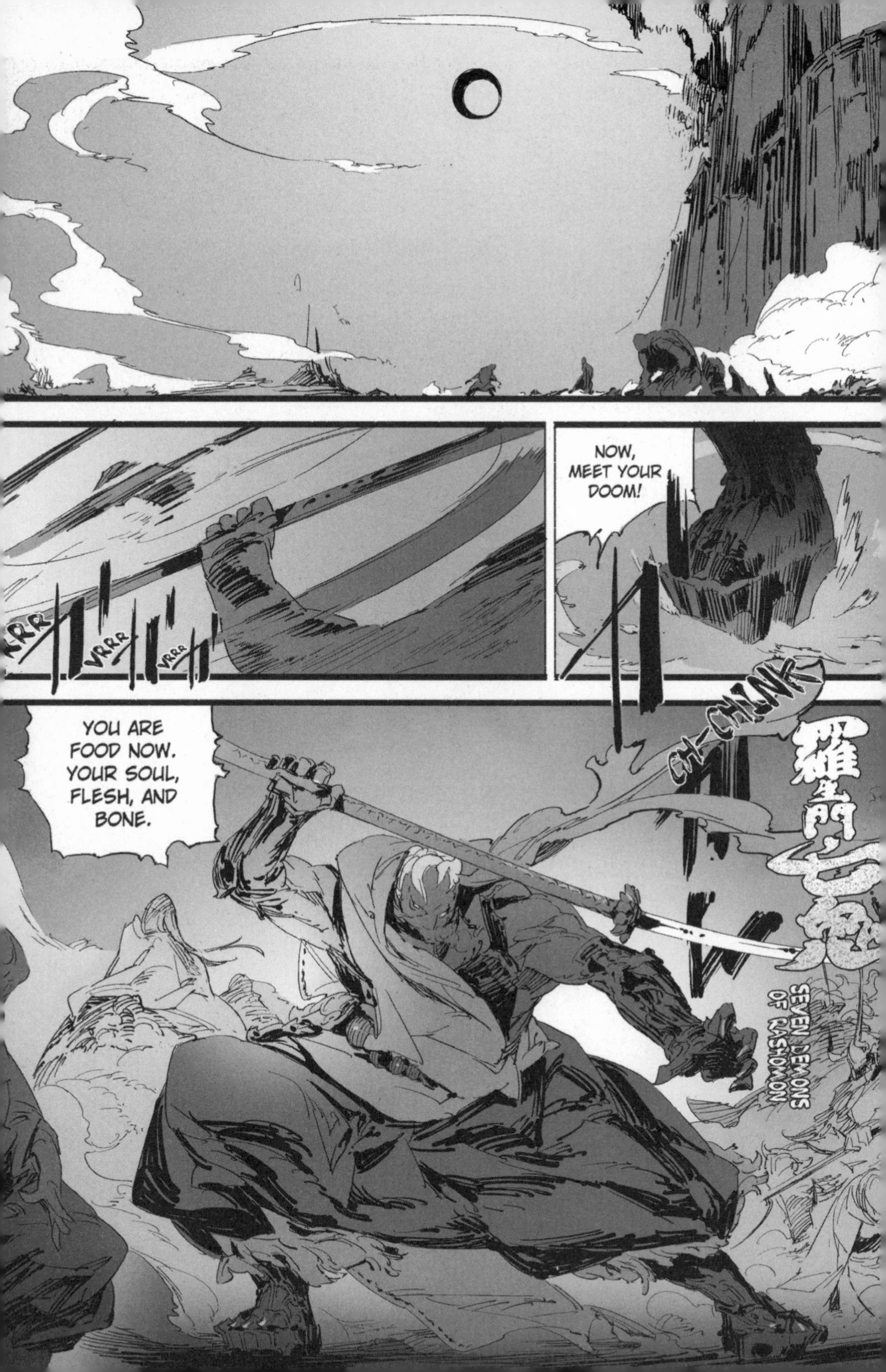
VRRR
VRRR
VRRR
NOW, MEET YOUR DOOM!
CH-CHUNK
YOU ARE FOOD NOW. YOUR SOUL, FLESH, AND BONE.
羅門
SEVEN DEMONS OF RASHOMON

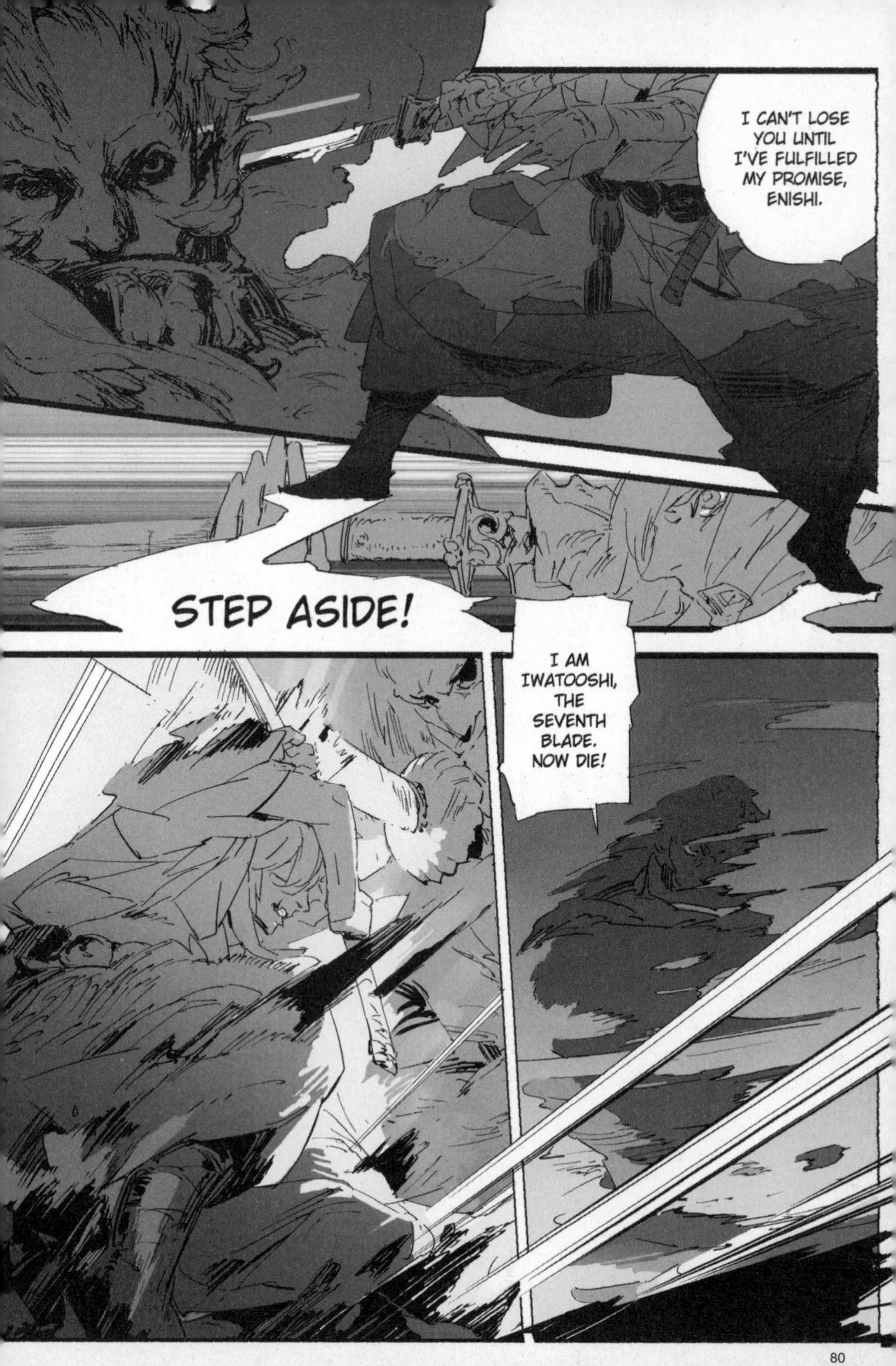
I CAN'T LOSE YOU UNTIL I'VE FULFILLED MY PROMISE, ENISHI.
STEP ASIDE!
I AM IWATOOSHI, THE SEVENTH BLADE. NOW DIE!

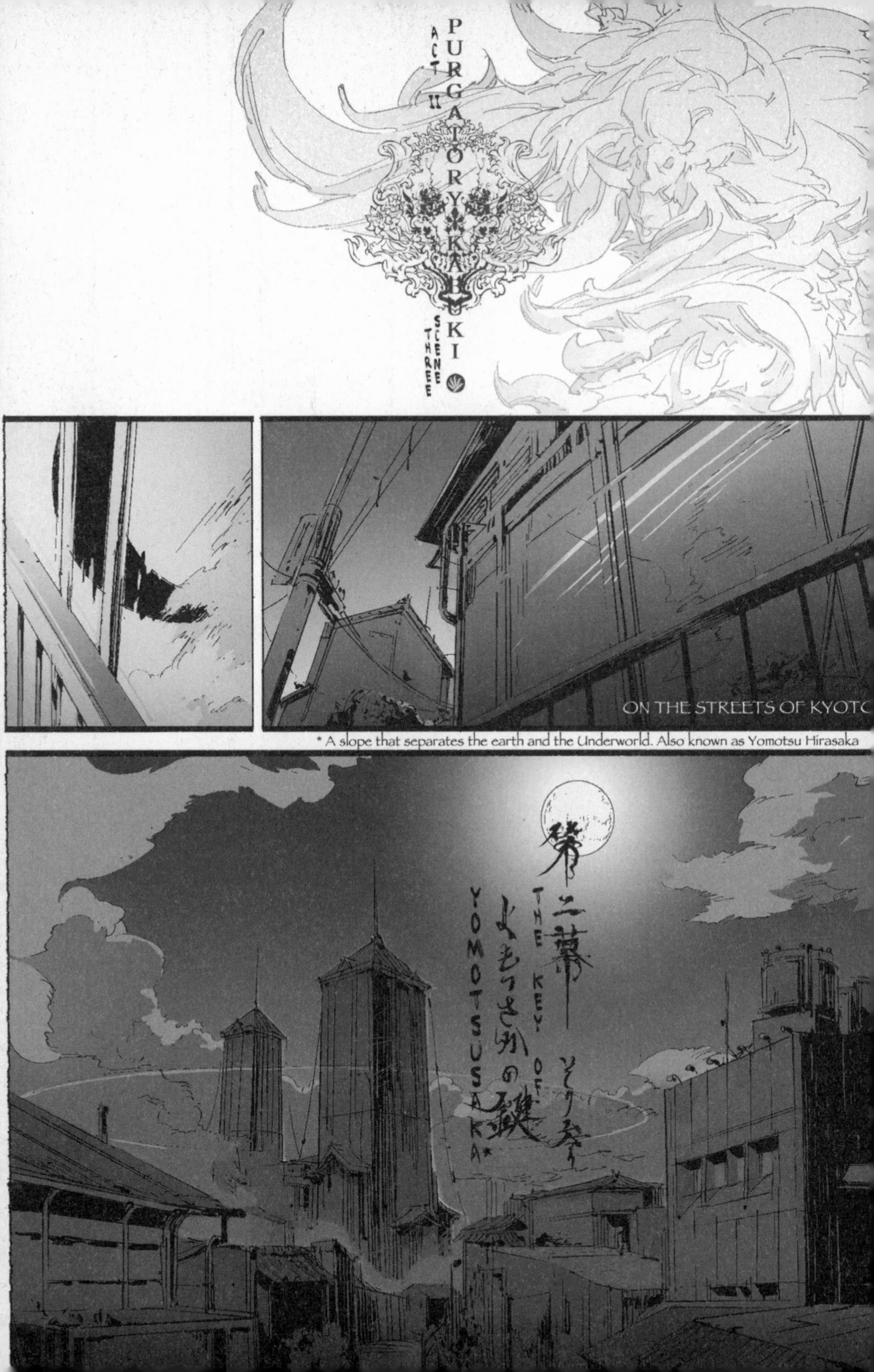
PURGATORY KABUKI
ACT II SCENE THREE
ON THE STREETS OF KYOTO
THE KEY OF YOMOTSUSAKA*
* A slope that separates the earth and the Underworld. Also known as Yomotsu Hirasaka

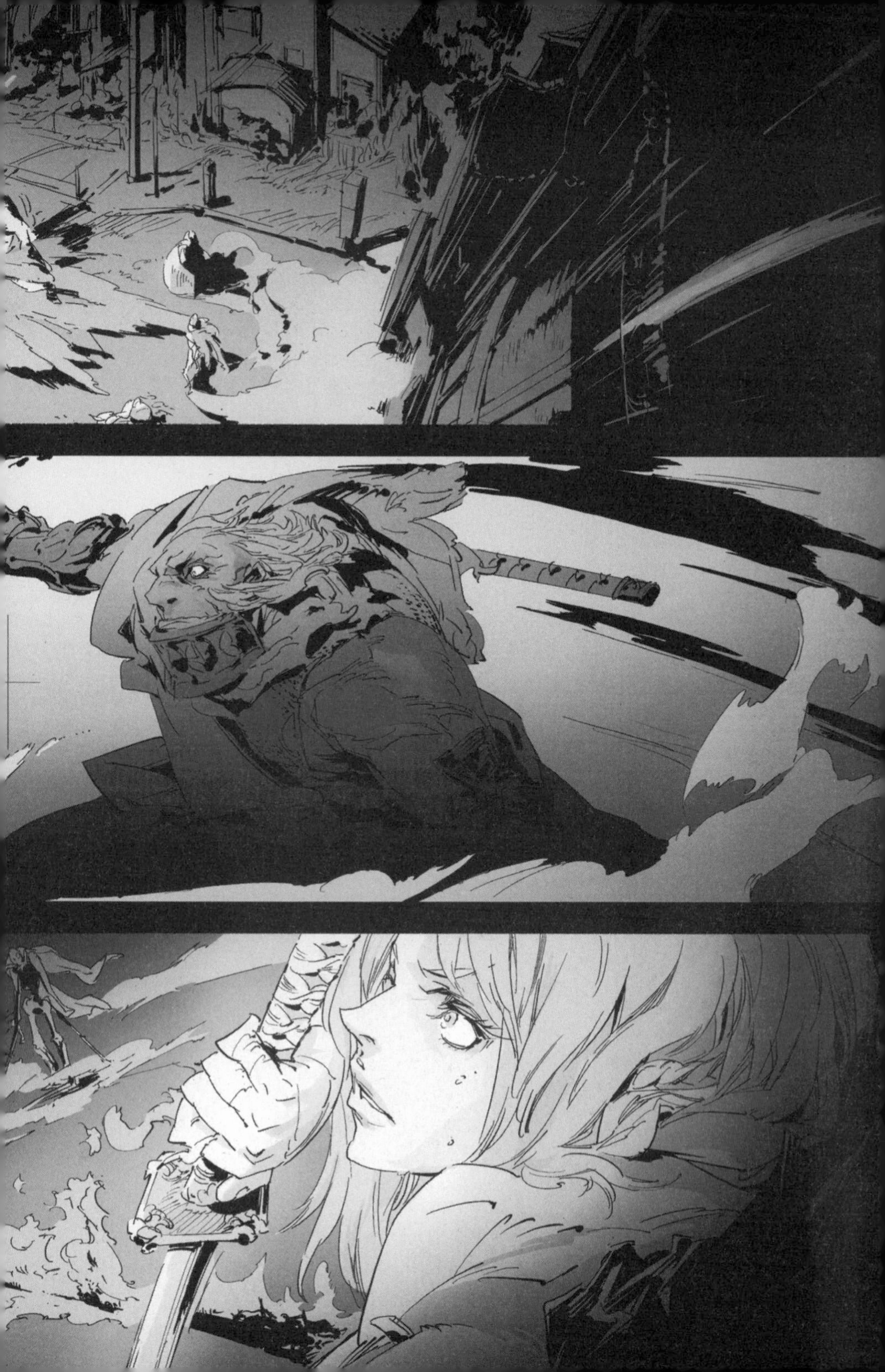

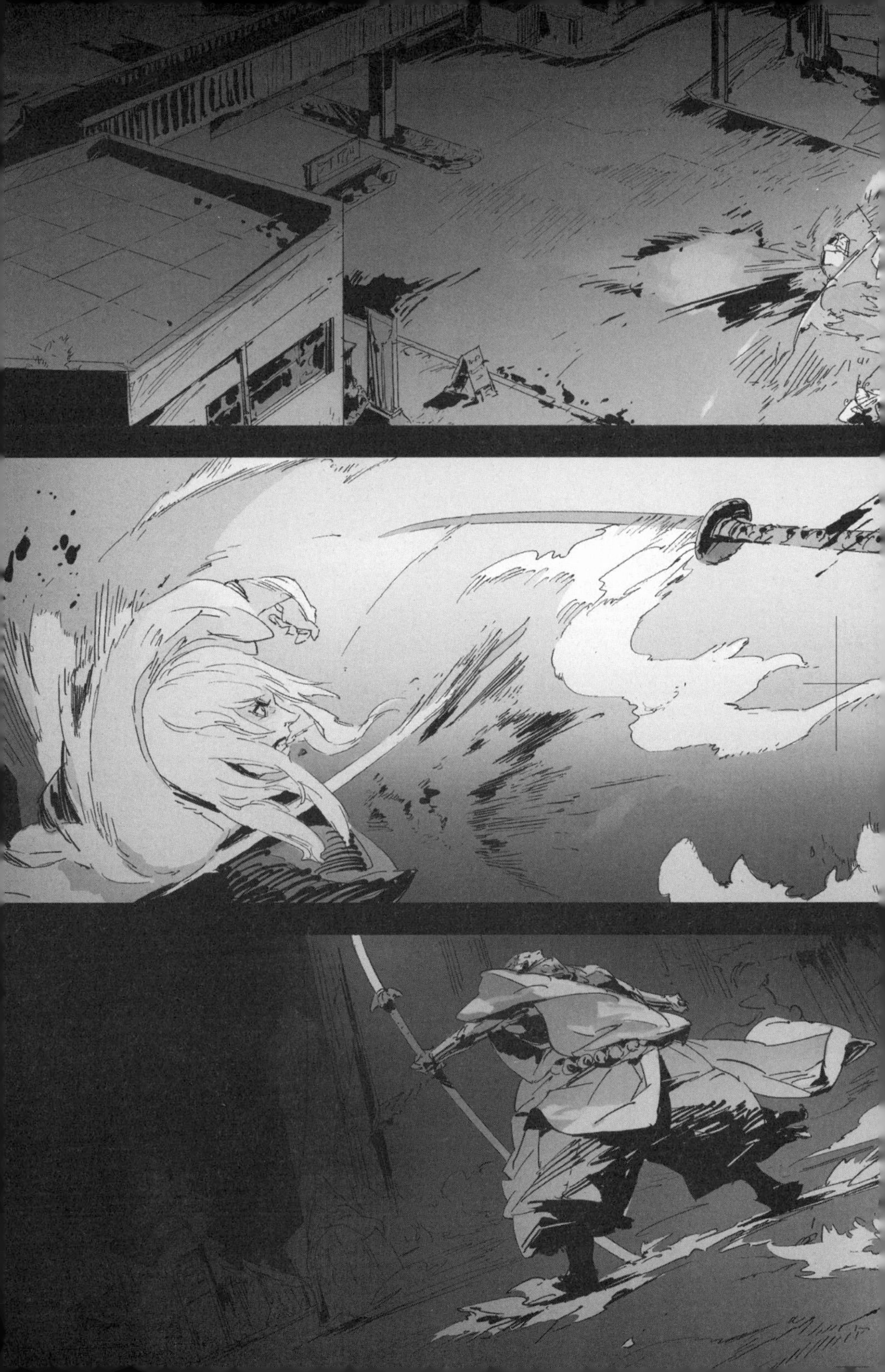

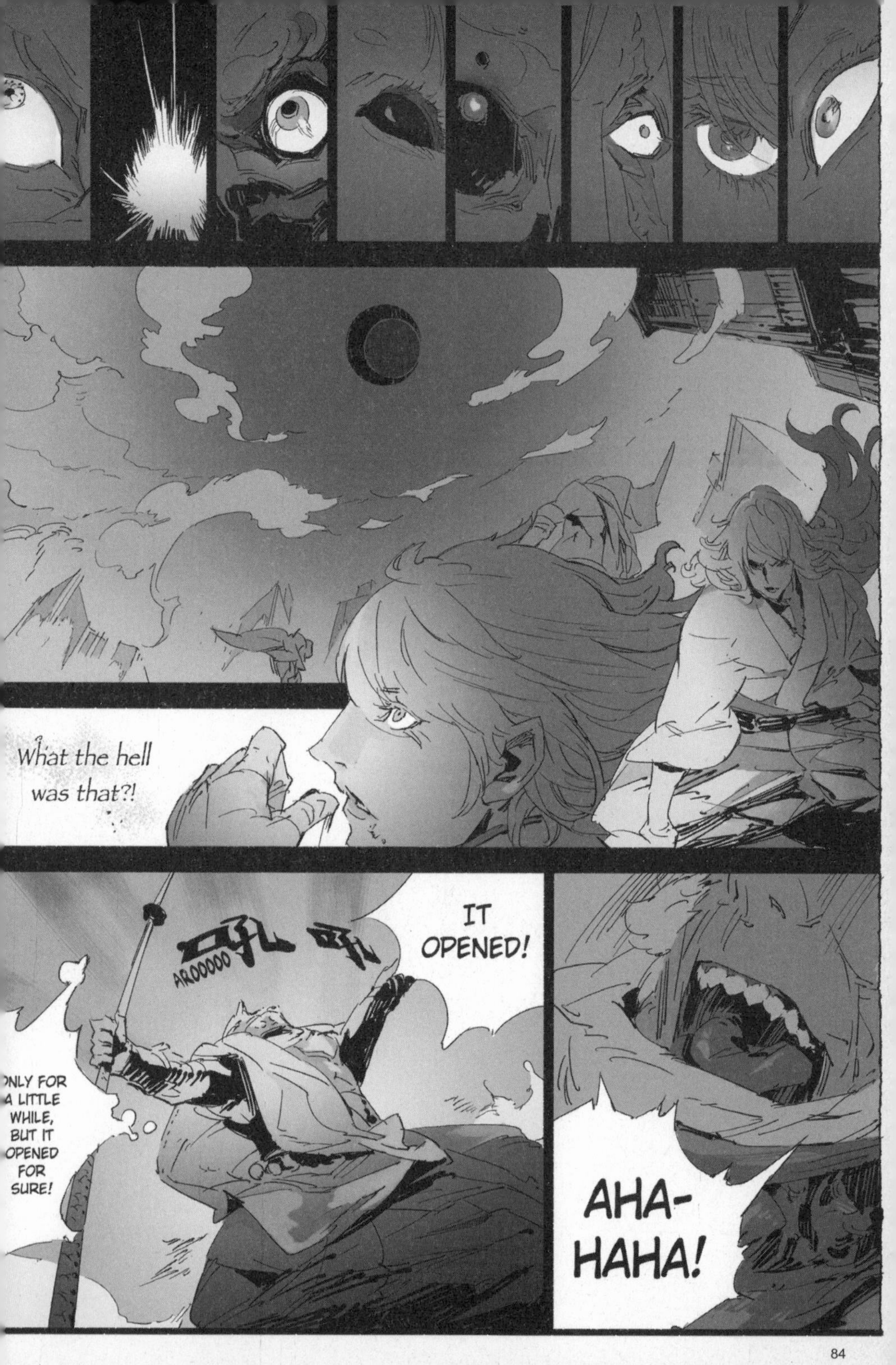
What the hell was that?!
AROOOOO
IT OPENED!
ONLY FOR A LITTLE WHILE, BUT IT OPENED FOR SURE!
AHA-HAHA!

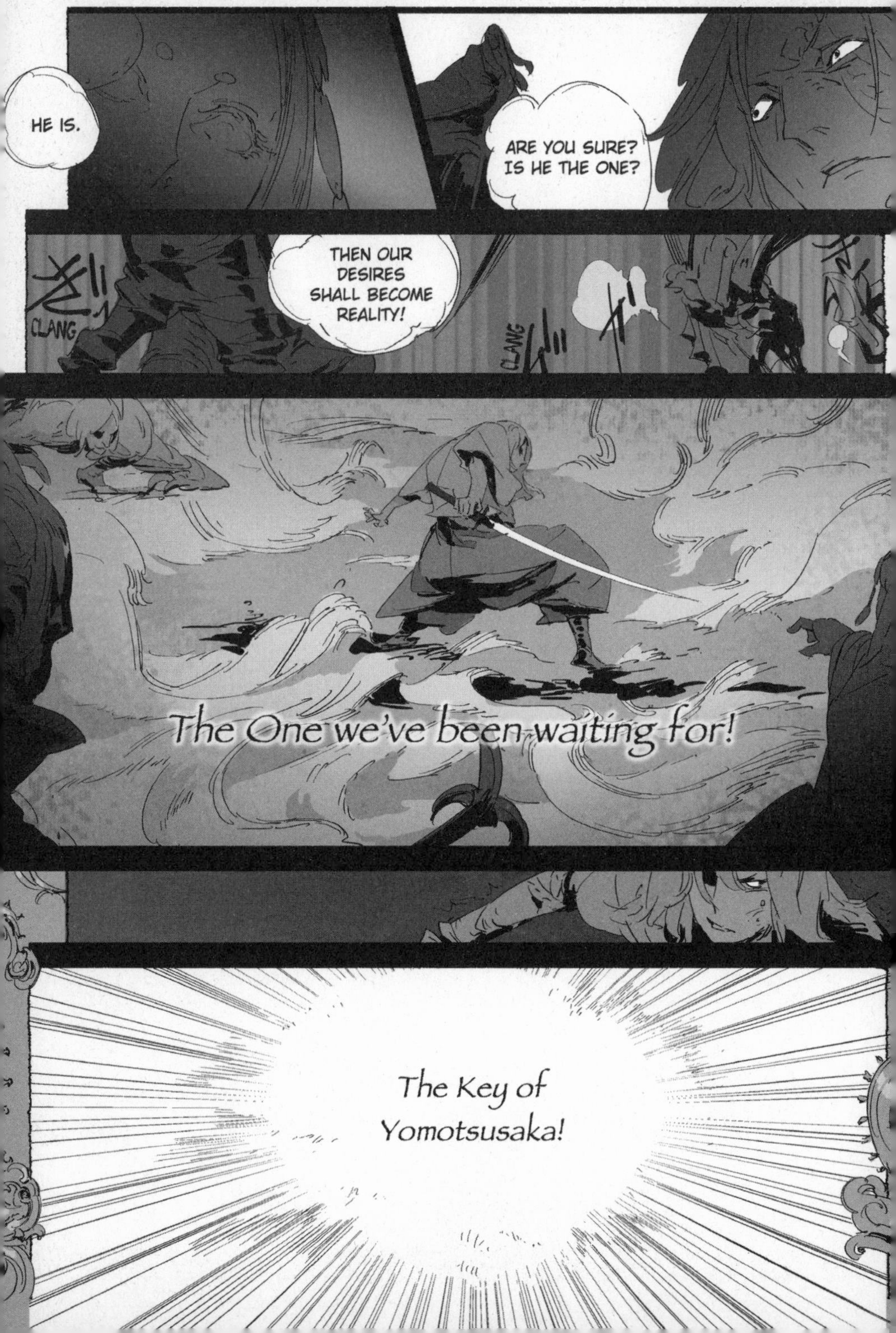
ARE YOU SURE? IS HE THE ONE?
HE IS.
THEN OUR DESIRES SHALL BECOME REALITY!
CLANG
CLANG
The One we've been waiting for!
The Key of Yomotsusaka!

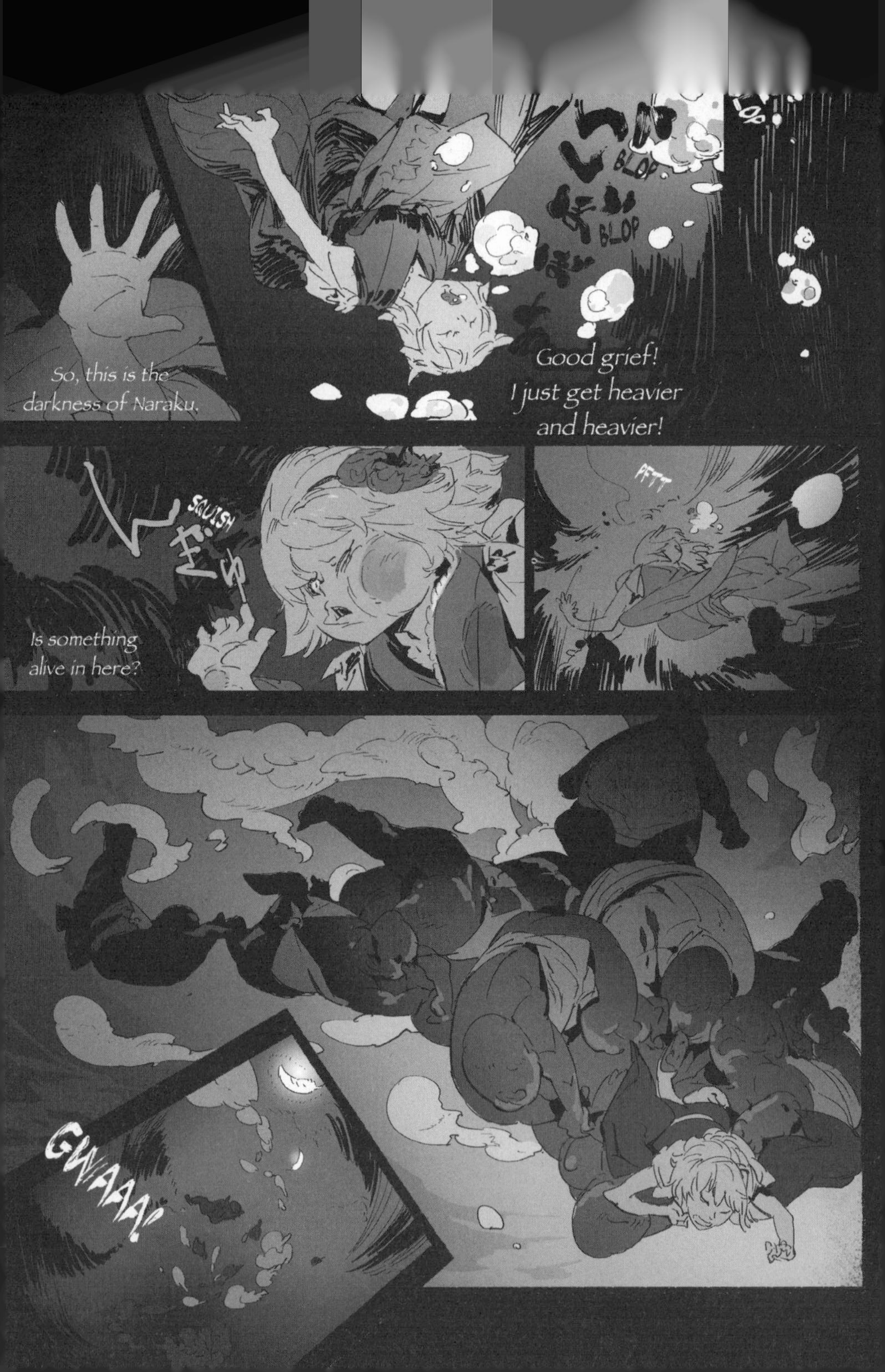
BLOP
BLOP
BLOP
So, this is the darkness of Naraku.
Good grief! I just get heavier and heavier!
SQUISH
Is something alive in here?
PFTT
GWAAA!

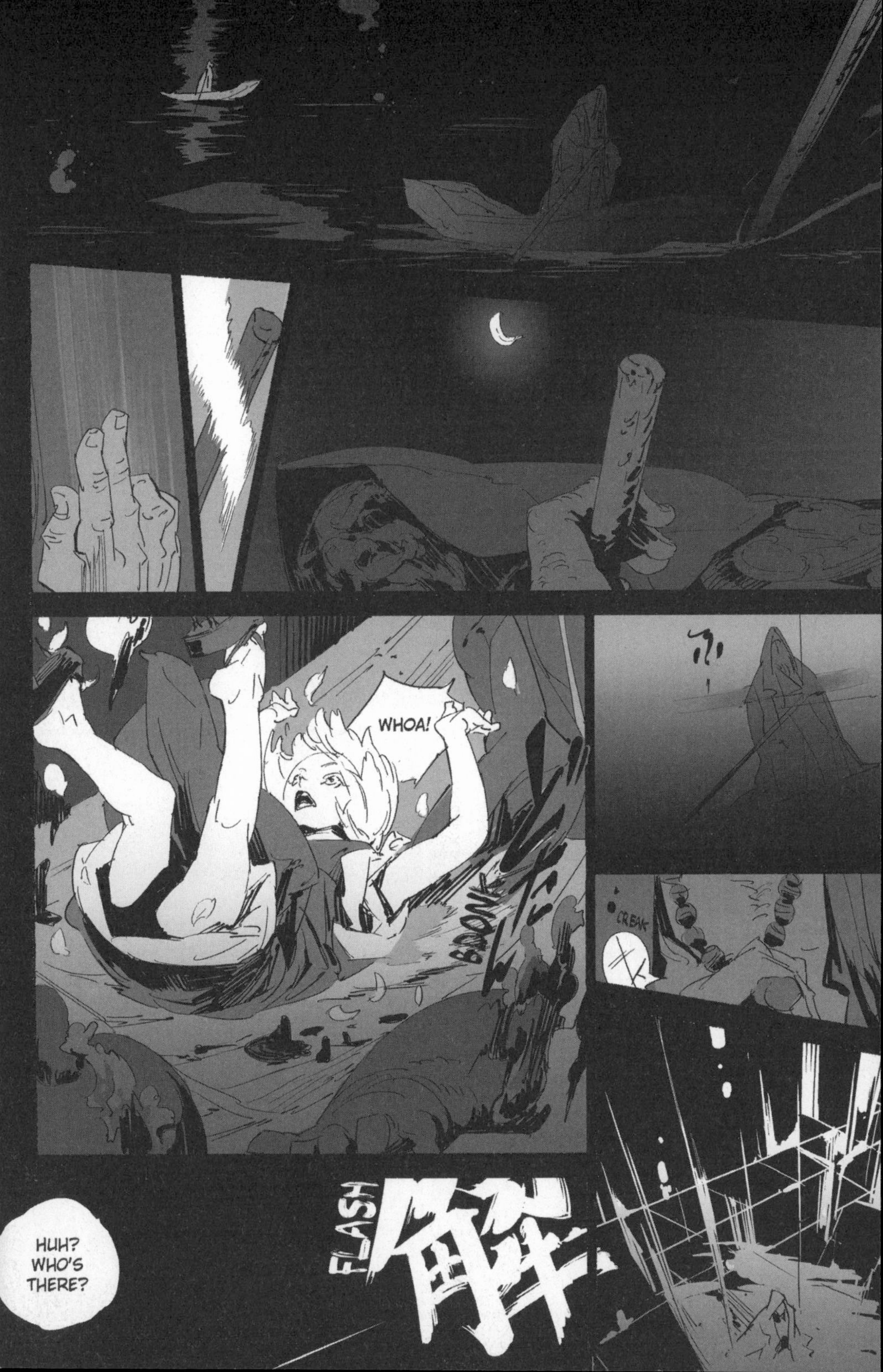
WHOA!
BADONK
CREAK
FLASH
HUH? WHO'S THERE?

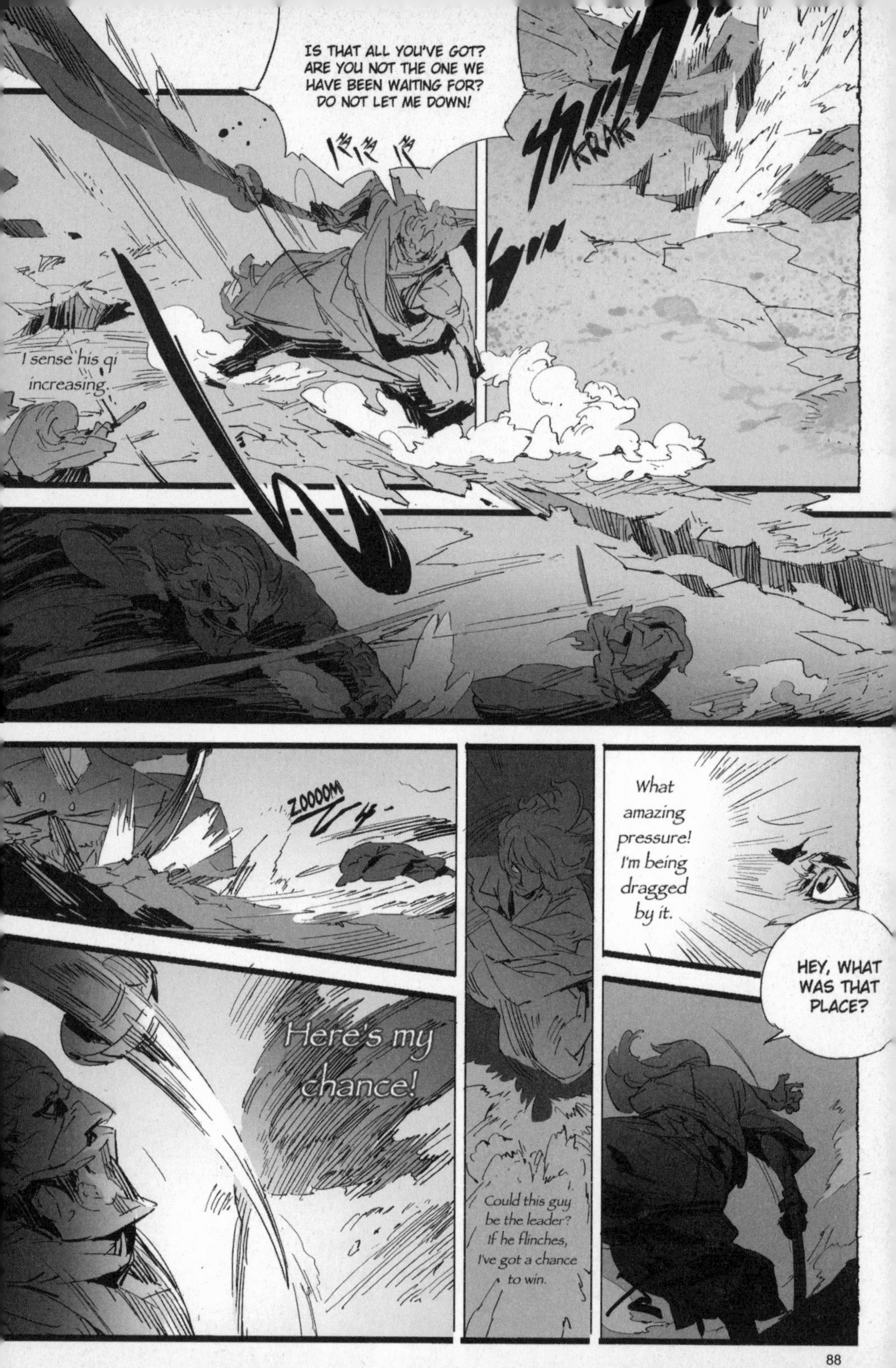

IS THAT ALL YOU'VE GOT? ARE YOU NOT THE ONE WE HAVE BEEN WAITING FOR? DO NOT LET ME DOWN!
KRAK
I sense his qi increasing.
ZOOOOM
What amazing pressure! I'm being dragged by it.
HEY, WHAT WAS THAT PLACE?
Here's my chance!
Could this guy be the leader? If he flinches, I've got a chance to win.

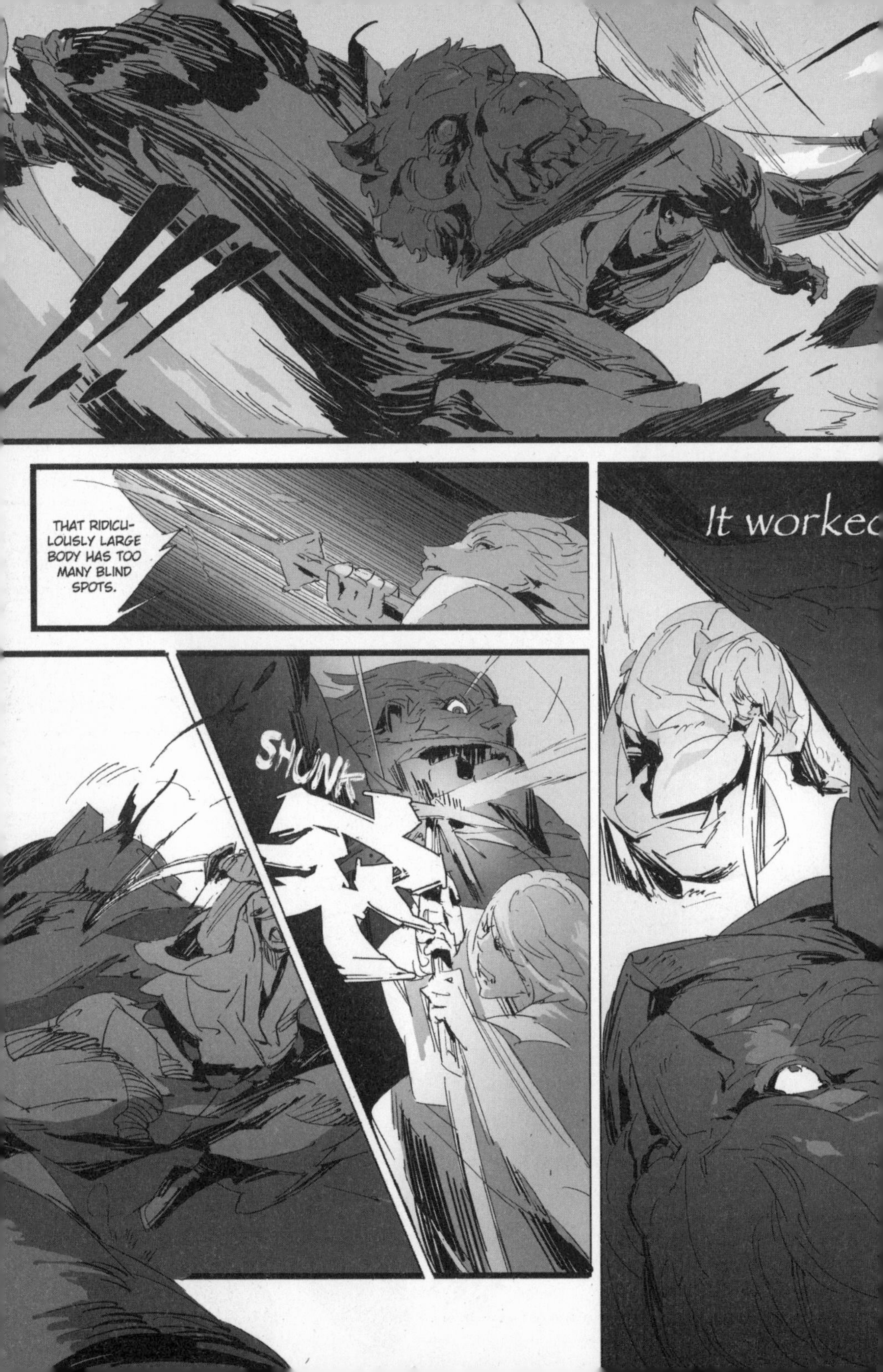
THAT RIDICU-LOUSLY LARGE BODY HAS TOO MANY BLIND SPOTS.
It workec
SHUNK

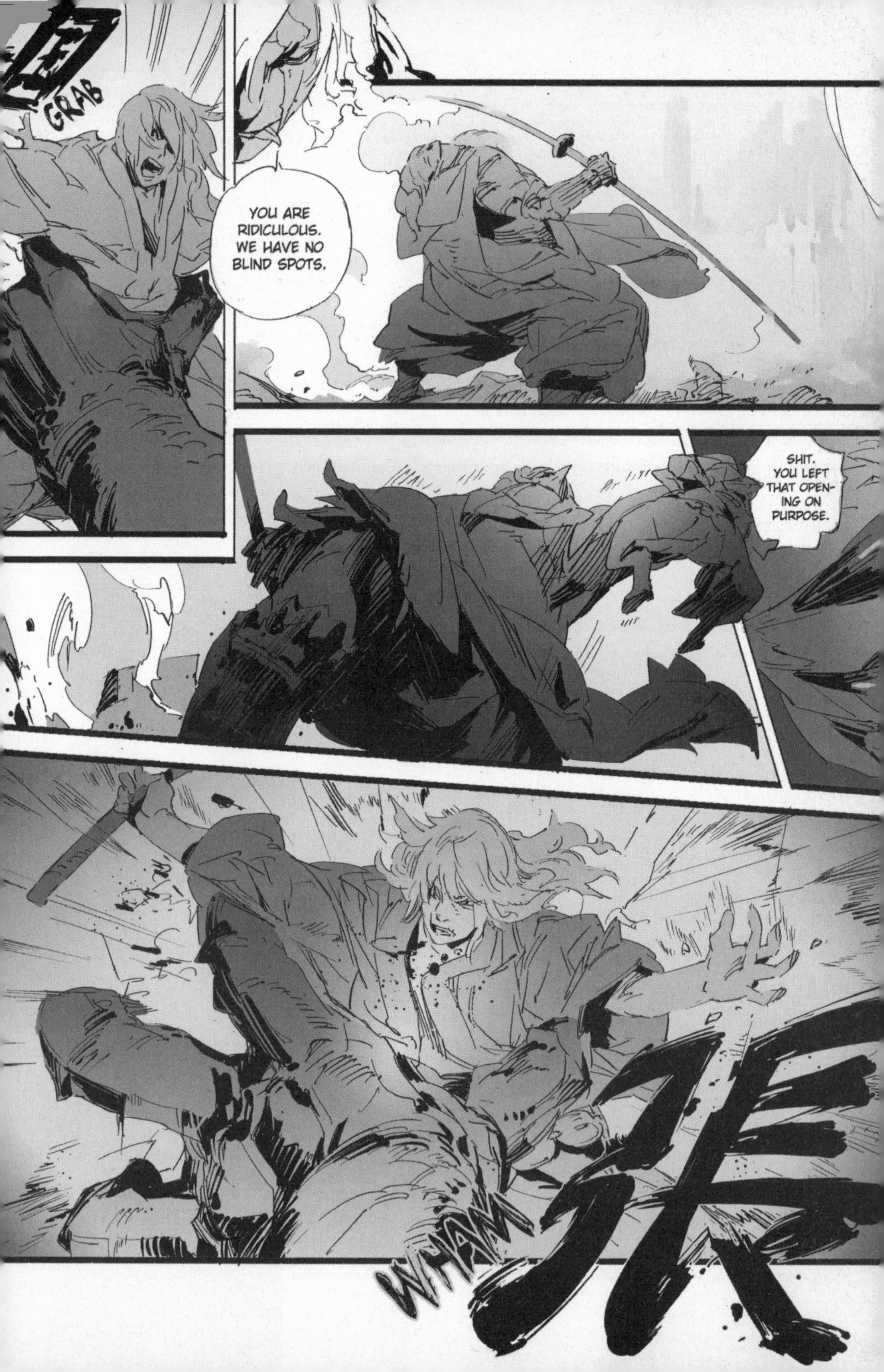
GRAB
YOU ARE RIDICULOUS. WE HAVE NO BLIND SPOTS.
SHIT. YOU LEFT THAT OPENING ON PURPOSE.
WHAM

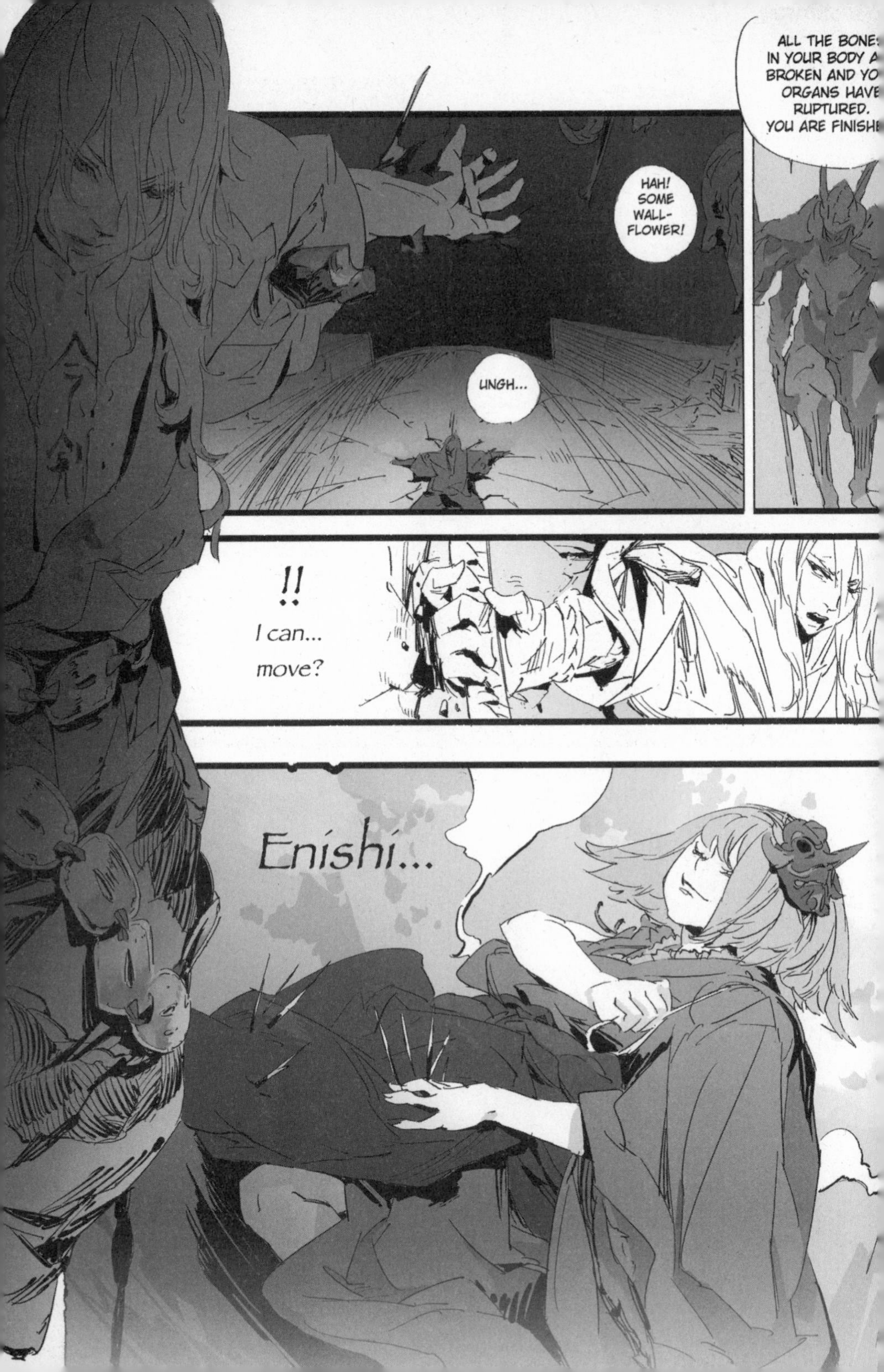

ALL THE BONE
IN YOUR BODY A
BROKEN AND YO
ORGANS HAVE
RUPTURED.
YOU ARE FINISH
HAH! SOME WALL-FLOWER!
UNGH...
!!
I can... move?
Enishi...

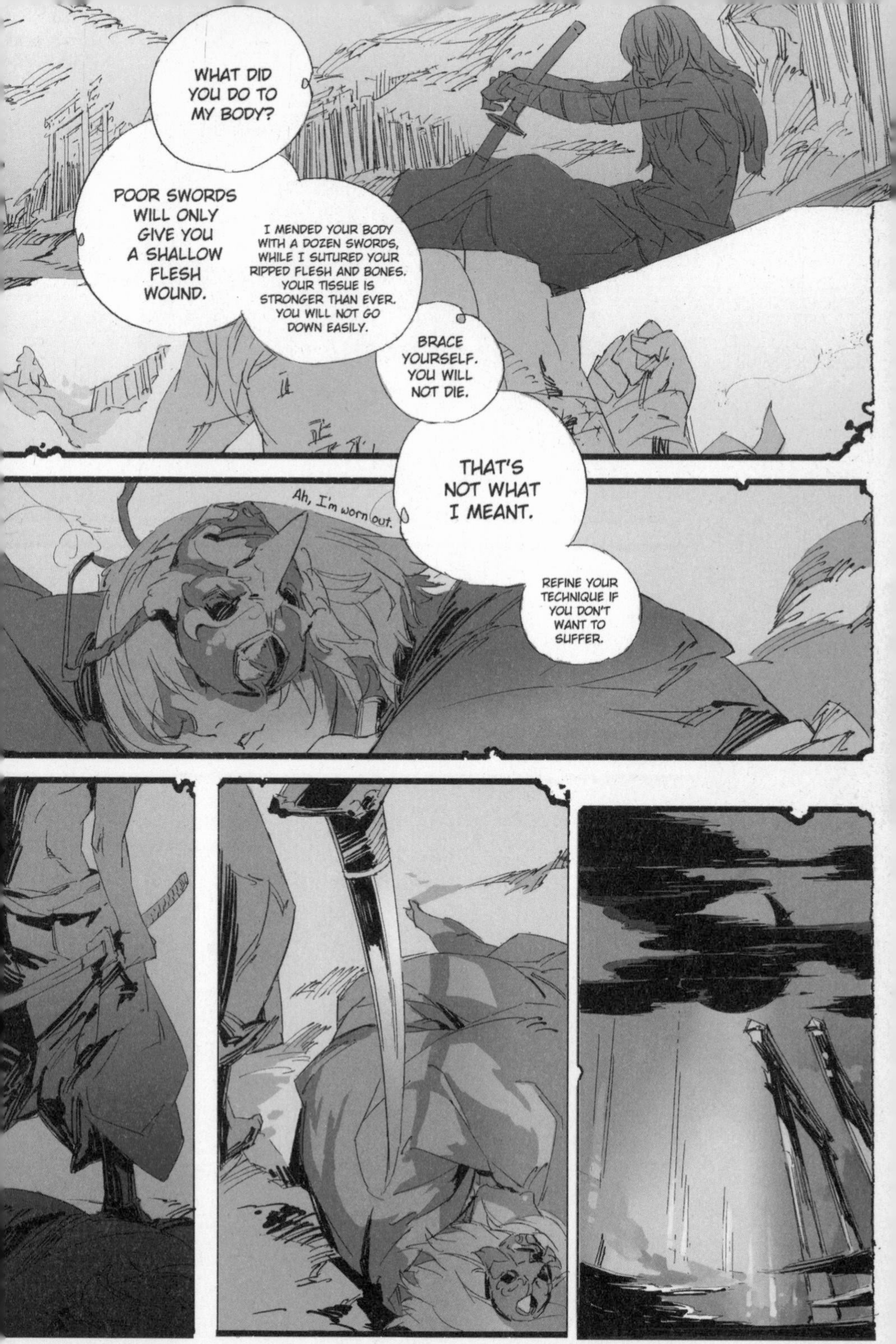
WHAT DID YOU DO TO MY BODY?
POOR SWORDS WILL ONLY GIVE YOU A SHALLOW FLESH WOUND.
I MENDED YOUR BODY WITH A DOZEN SWORDS, WHILE I SUTURED YOUR RIPPED FLESH AND BONES. YOUR TISSUE IS STRONGER THAN EVER. YOU WILL NOT GO DOWN EASILY.
BRACE YOURSELF. YOU WILL NOT DIE.
THAT'S NOT WHAT I MEANT.
Ah, I'm worn out.
REFINE YOUR TECHNIQUE IF YOU DON'T WANT TO SUFFER.

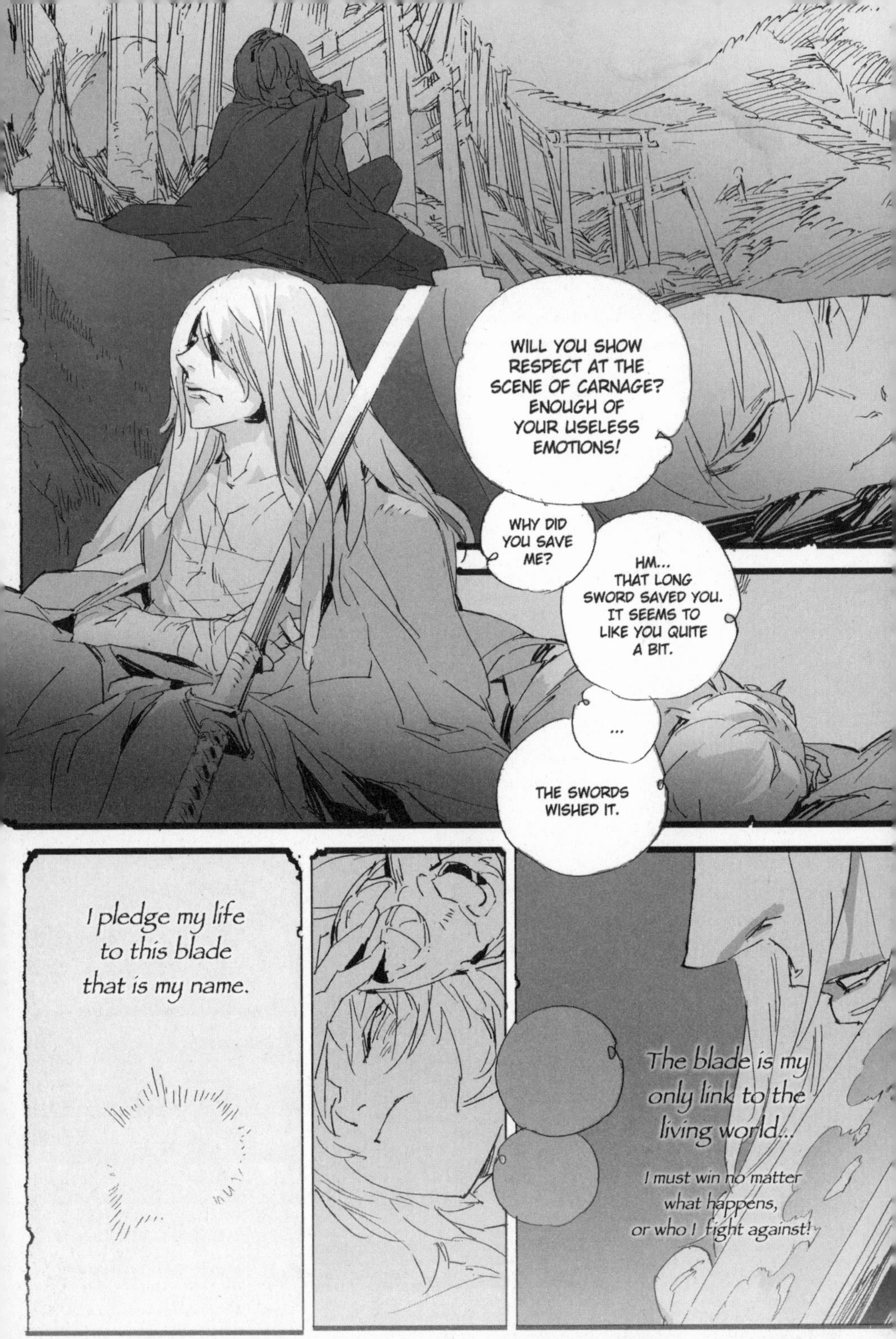
WILL YOU SHOW RESPECT AT THE SCENE OF CARNAGE? ENOUGH OF YOUR USELESS EMOTIONS!
WHY DID YOU SAVE ME?
HM... THAT LONG SWORD SAVED YOU. IT SEEMS TO LIKE YOU QUITE A BIT.
...
THE SWORDS WISHED IT.
I pledge my life to this blade that is my name.
The blade is my only link to the living world...
I must win no matter what happens, or who I fight against!

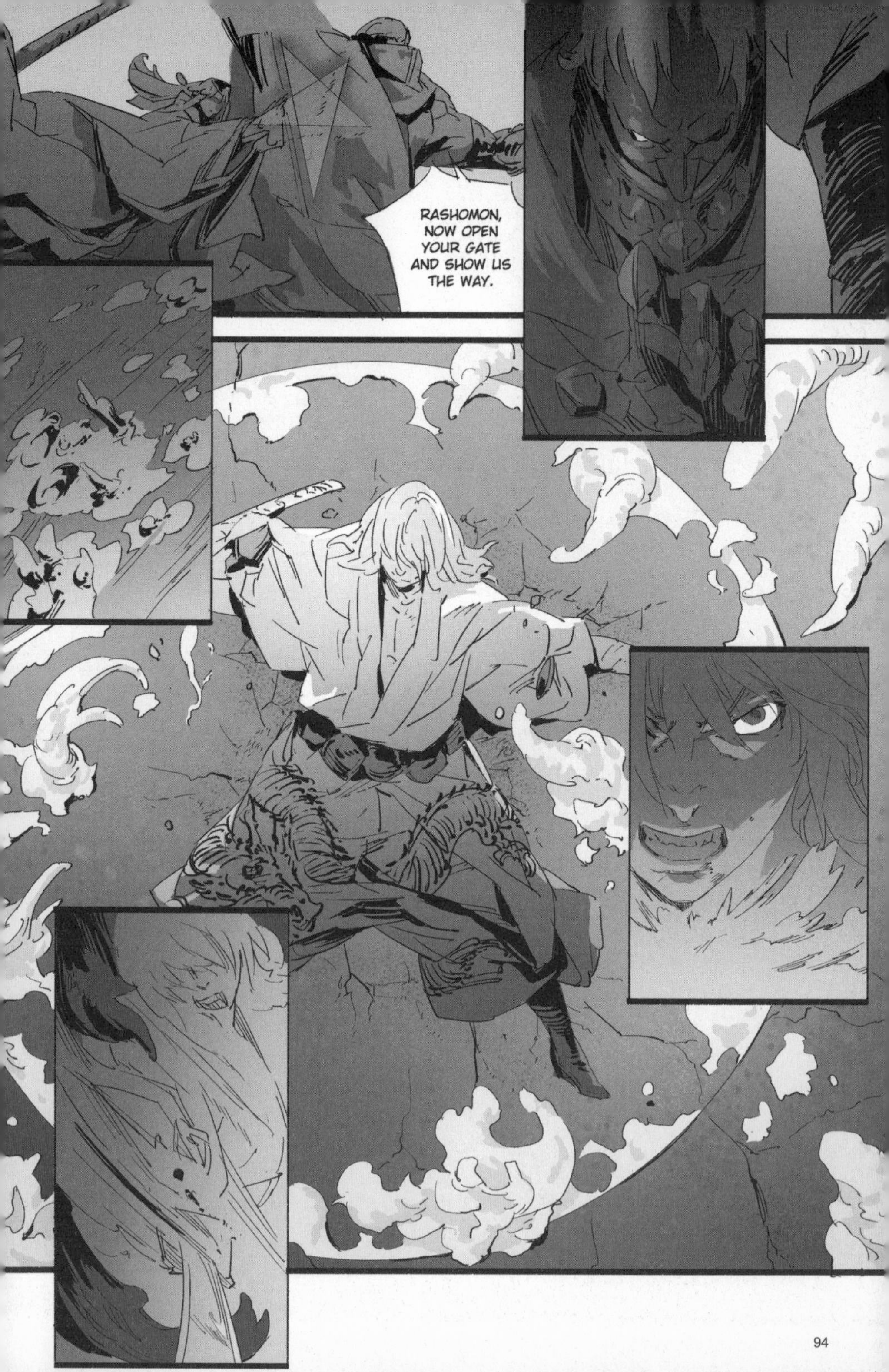
RASHOMON, NOW OPEN YOUR GATE AND SHOW US THE WAY.

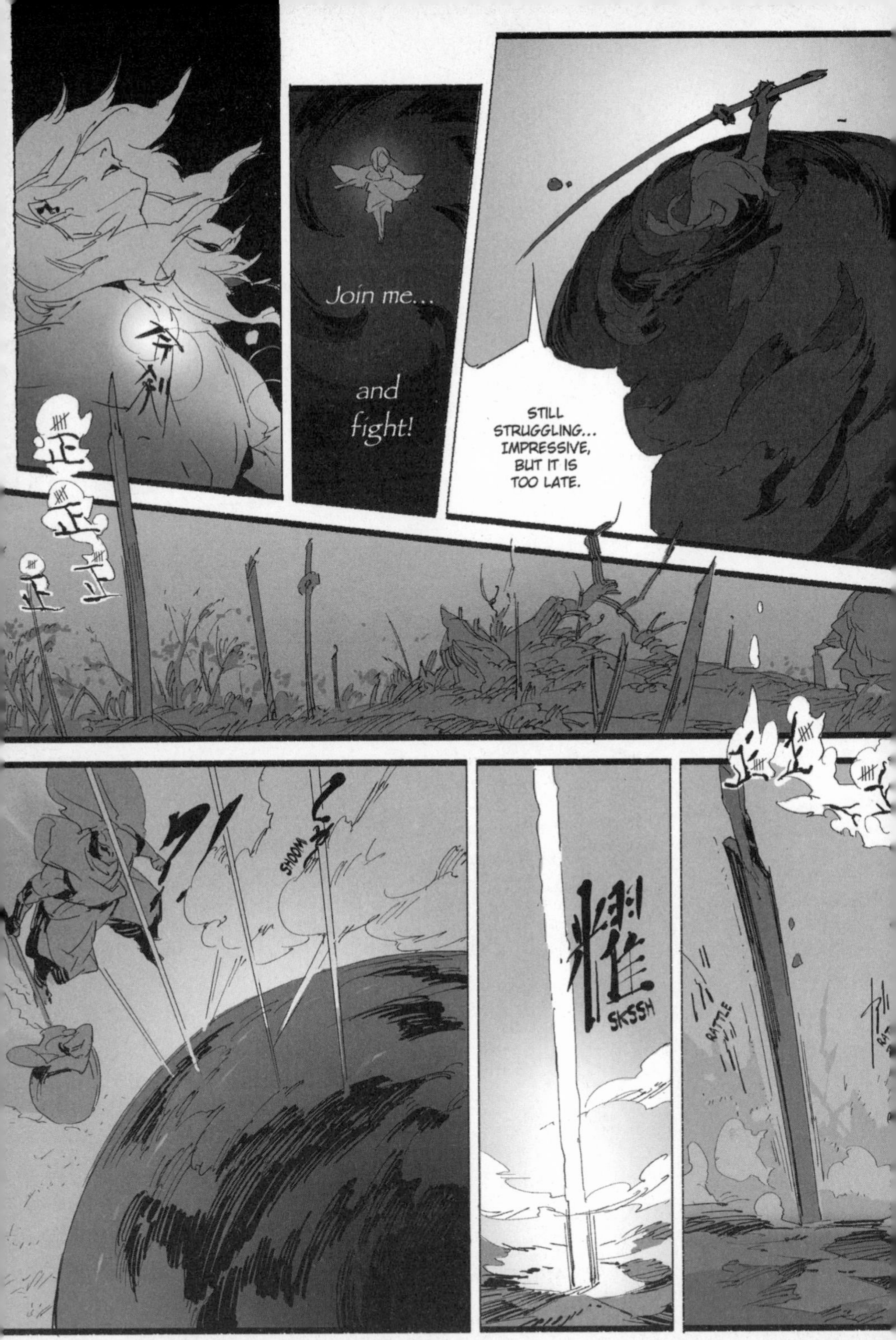

Join me...
and fight!
STILL STRUGGLING... IMPRESSIVE, BUT IT IS TOO LATE.
SHOOM
SKSSH
RATTLE

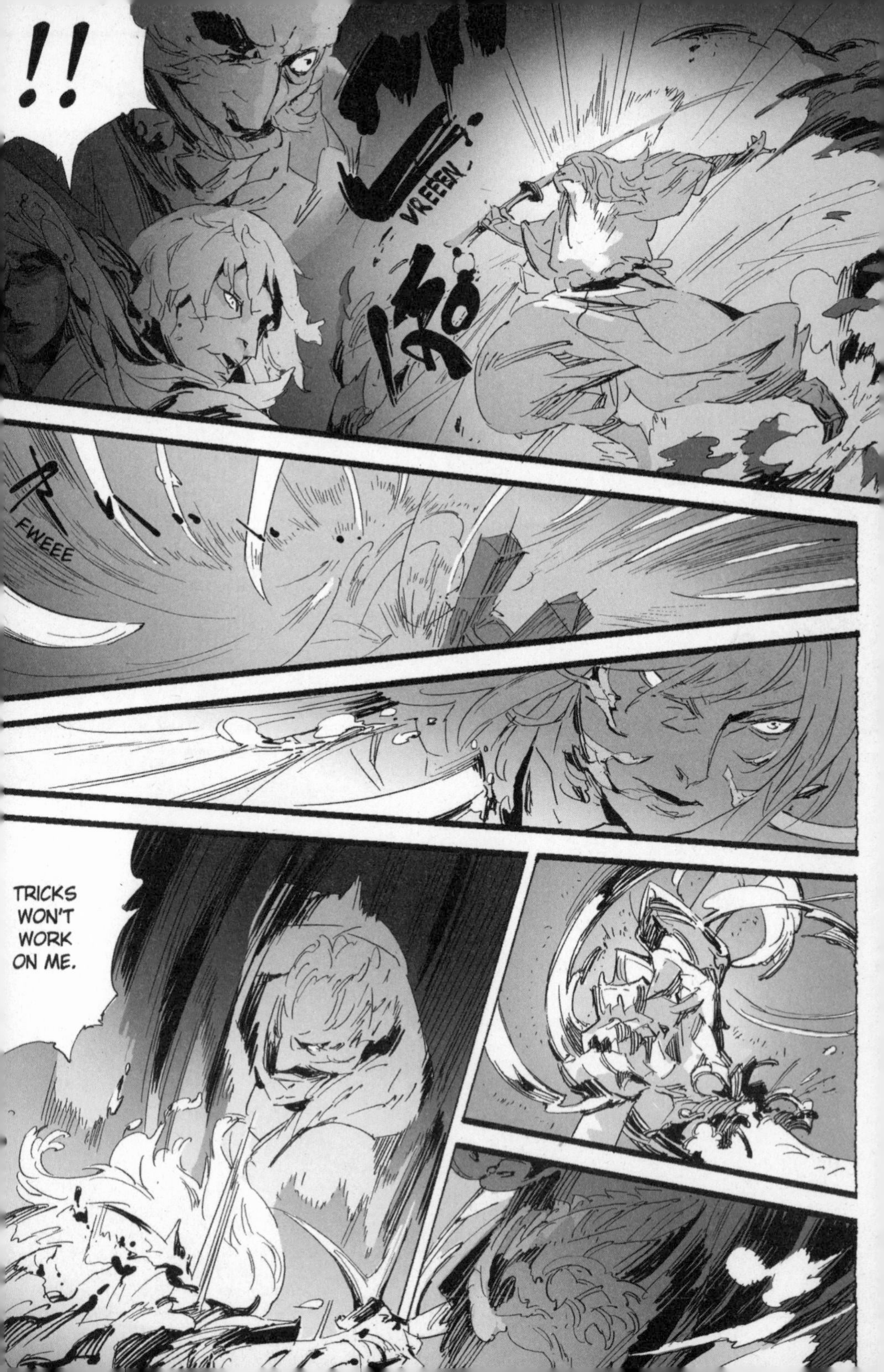
!!
VREEEN
FWEEEE
TRICKS WON'T WORK ON ME.

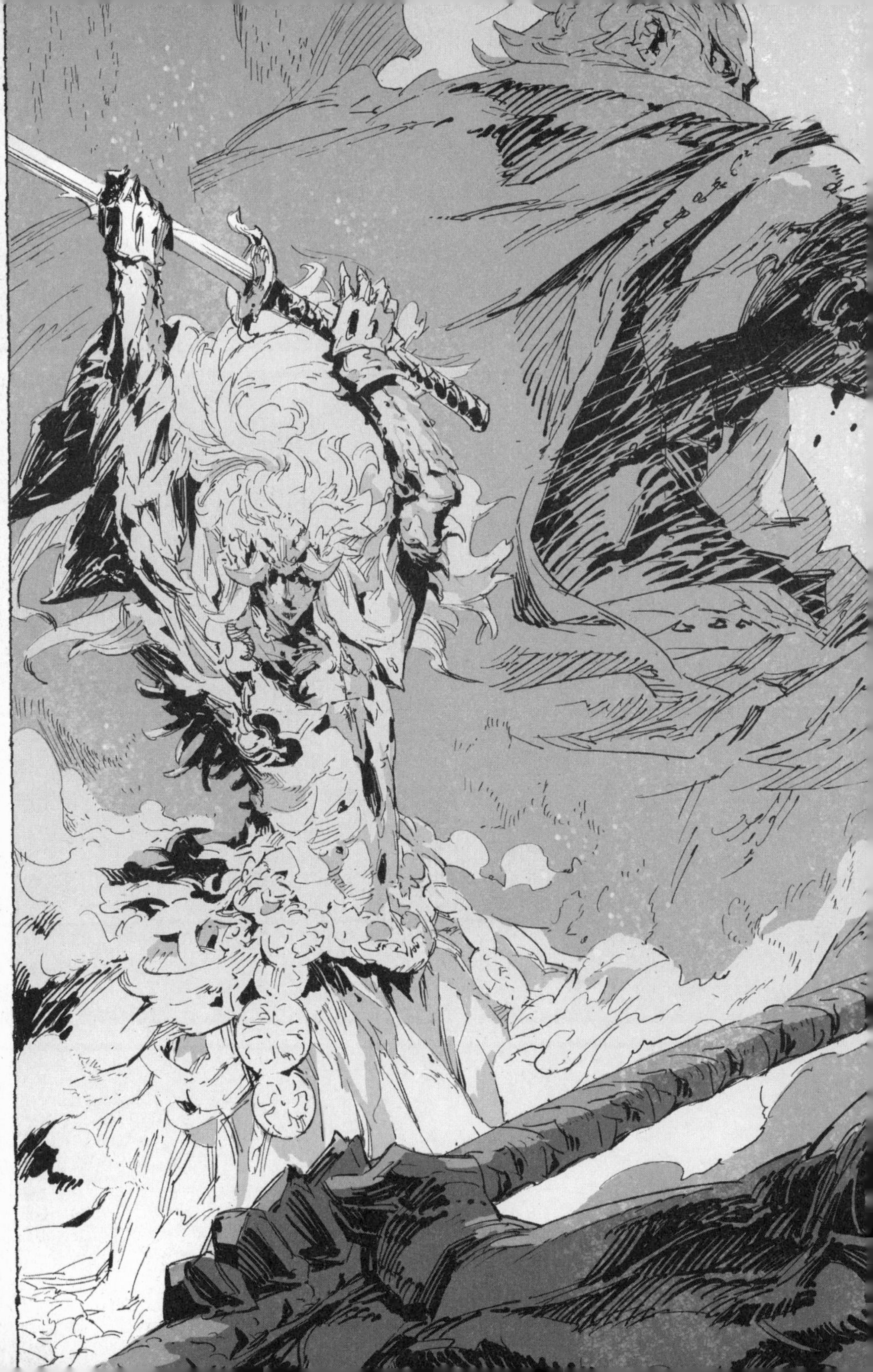

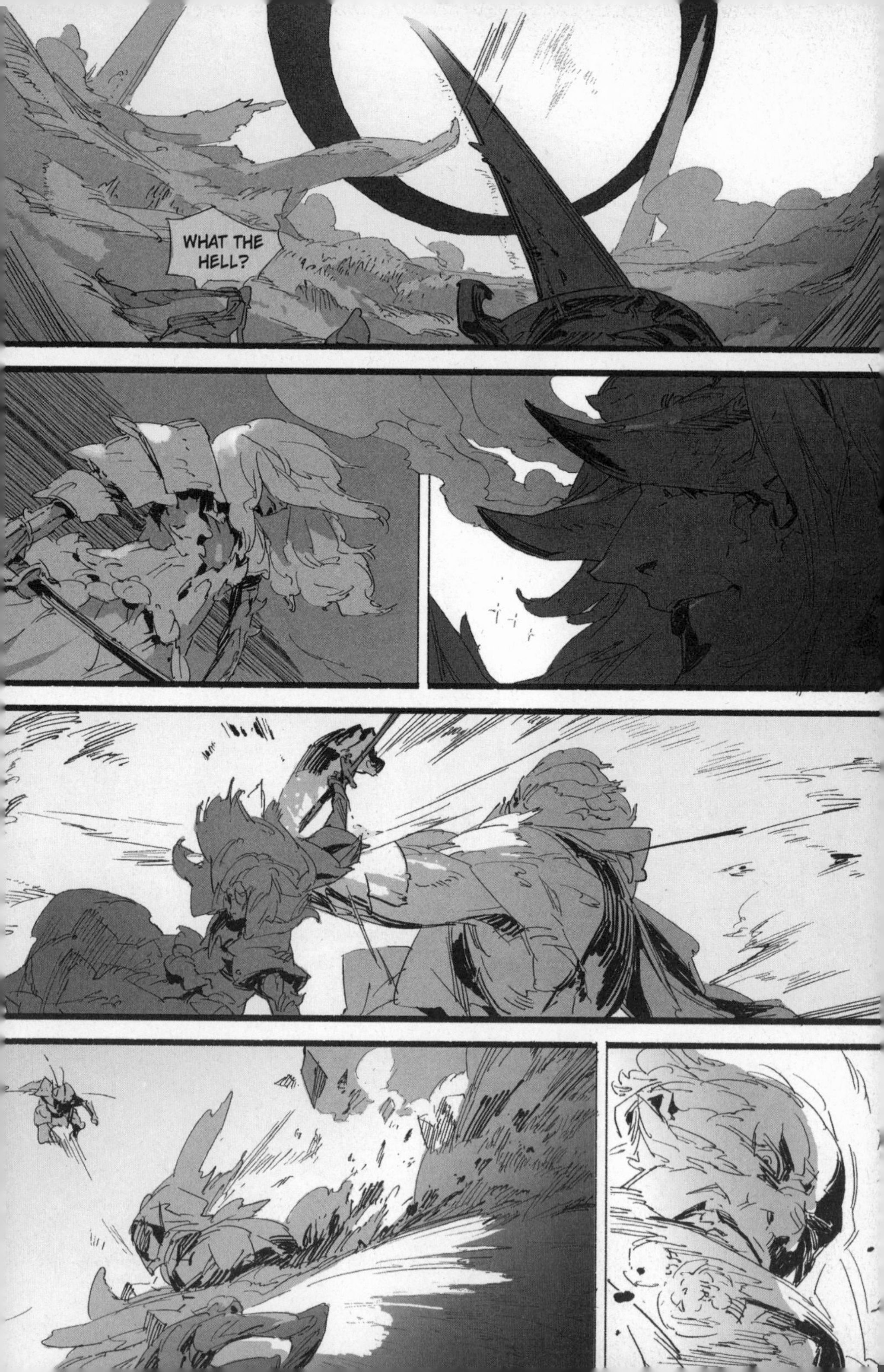
WHAT THE HELL?

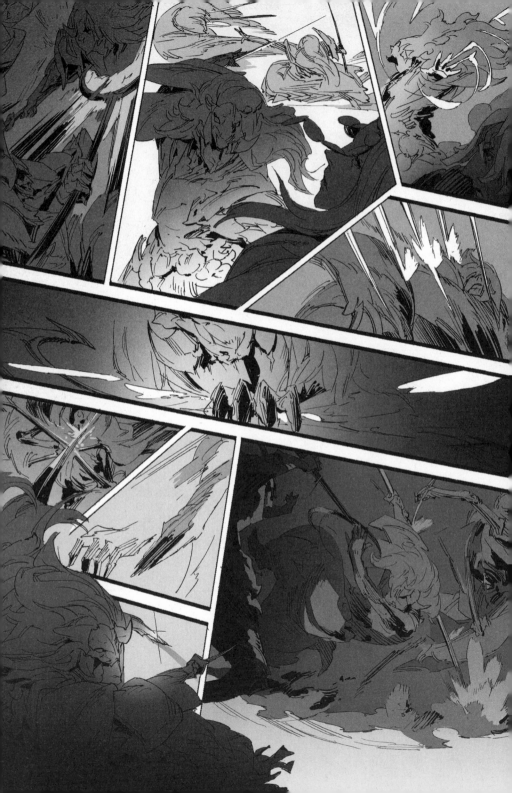

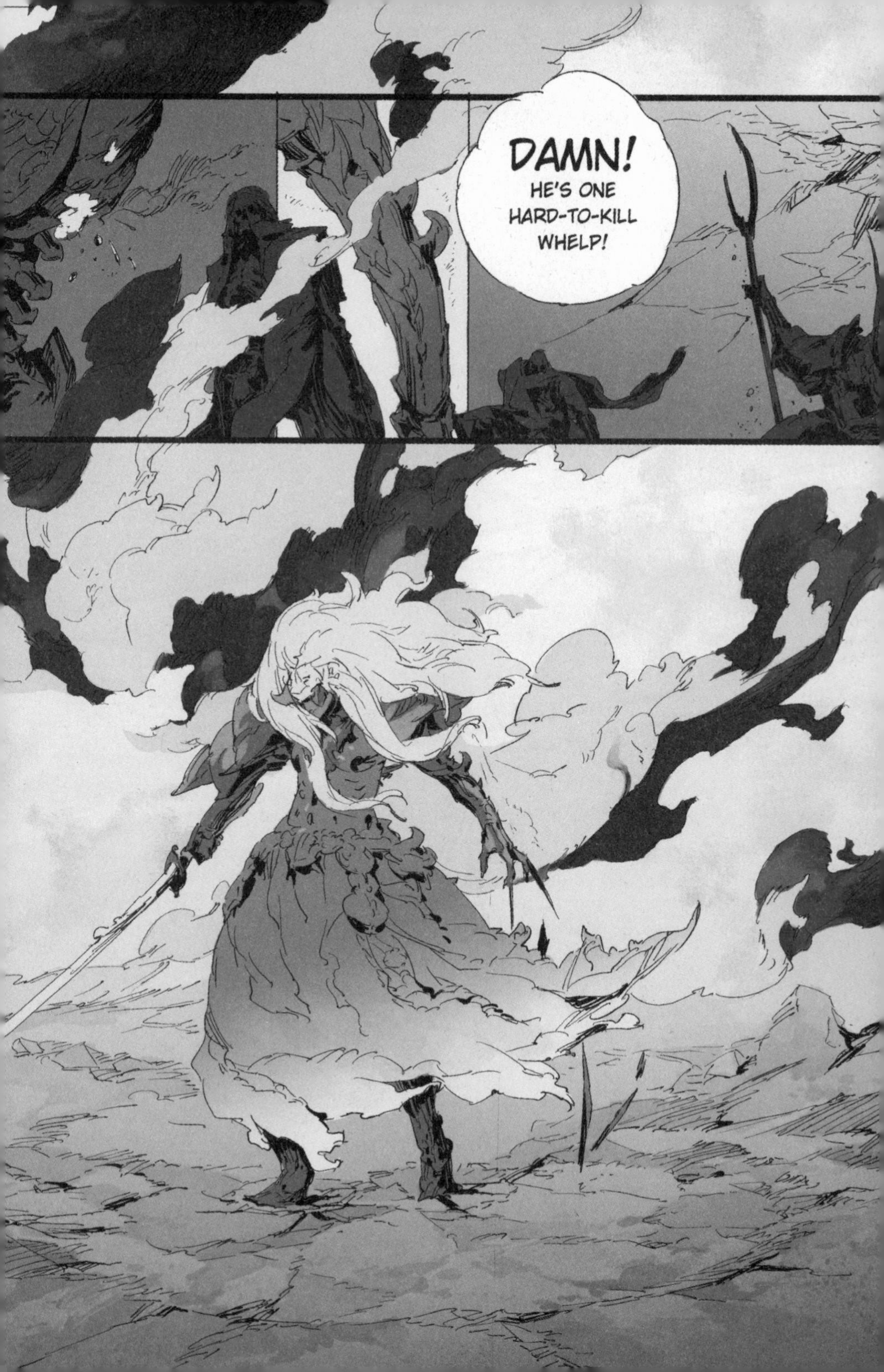
DAMN!
HE'S ONE HARD-TO-KILL WHELP!

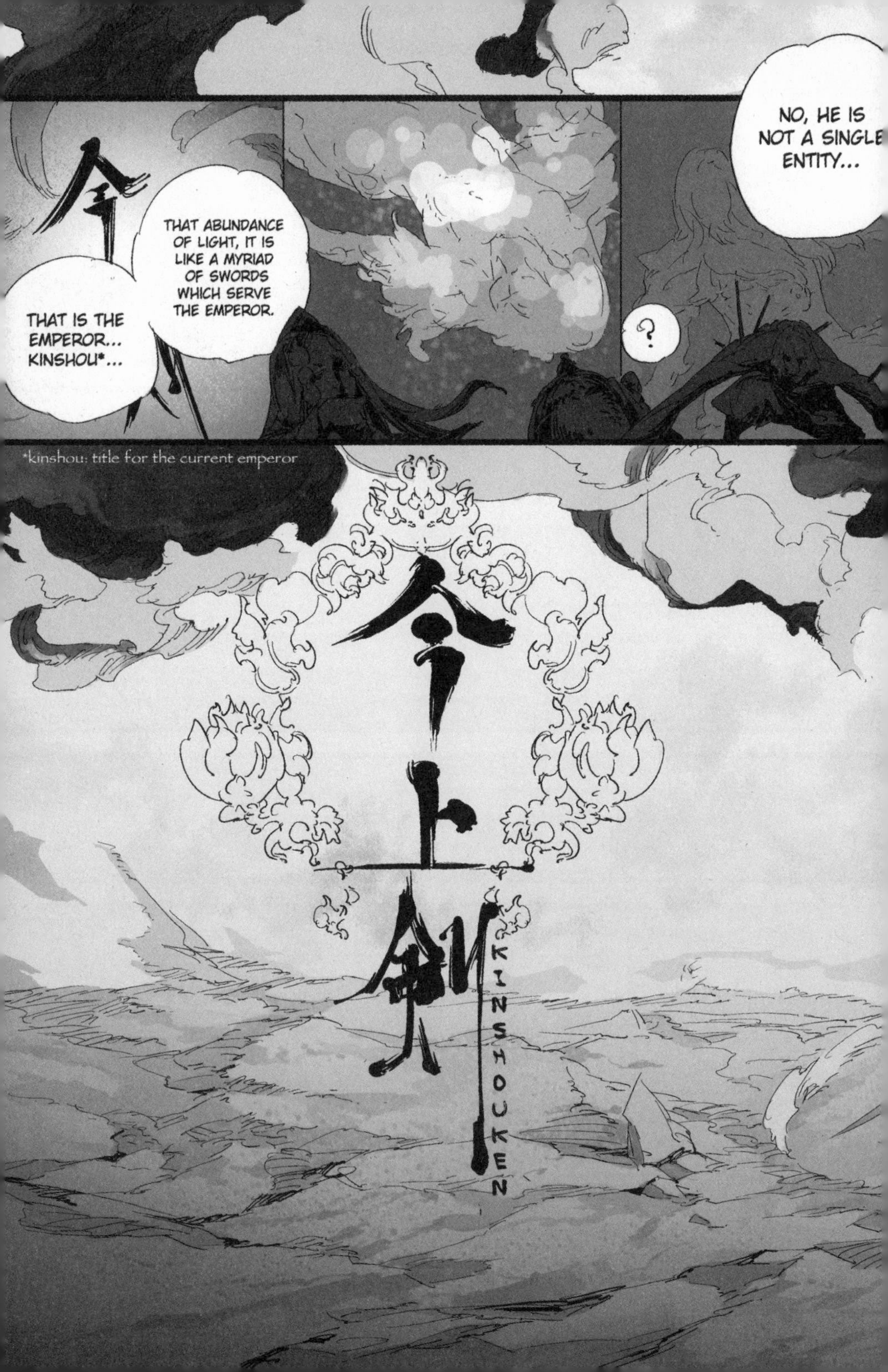
THAT IS THE EMPEROR... KINSHOU*...
THAT ABUNDANCE OF LIGHT, IT IS LIKE A MYRIAD OF SWORDS WHICH SERVE THE EMPEROR.
?
NO, HE IS NOT A SINGLE ENTITY...
今上剣
KINSHOUKEN
*kinshou: title for the current emperor

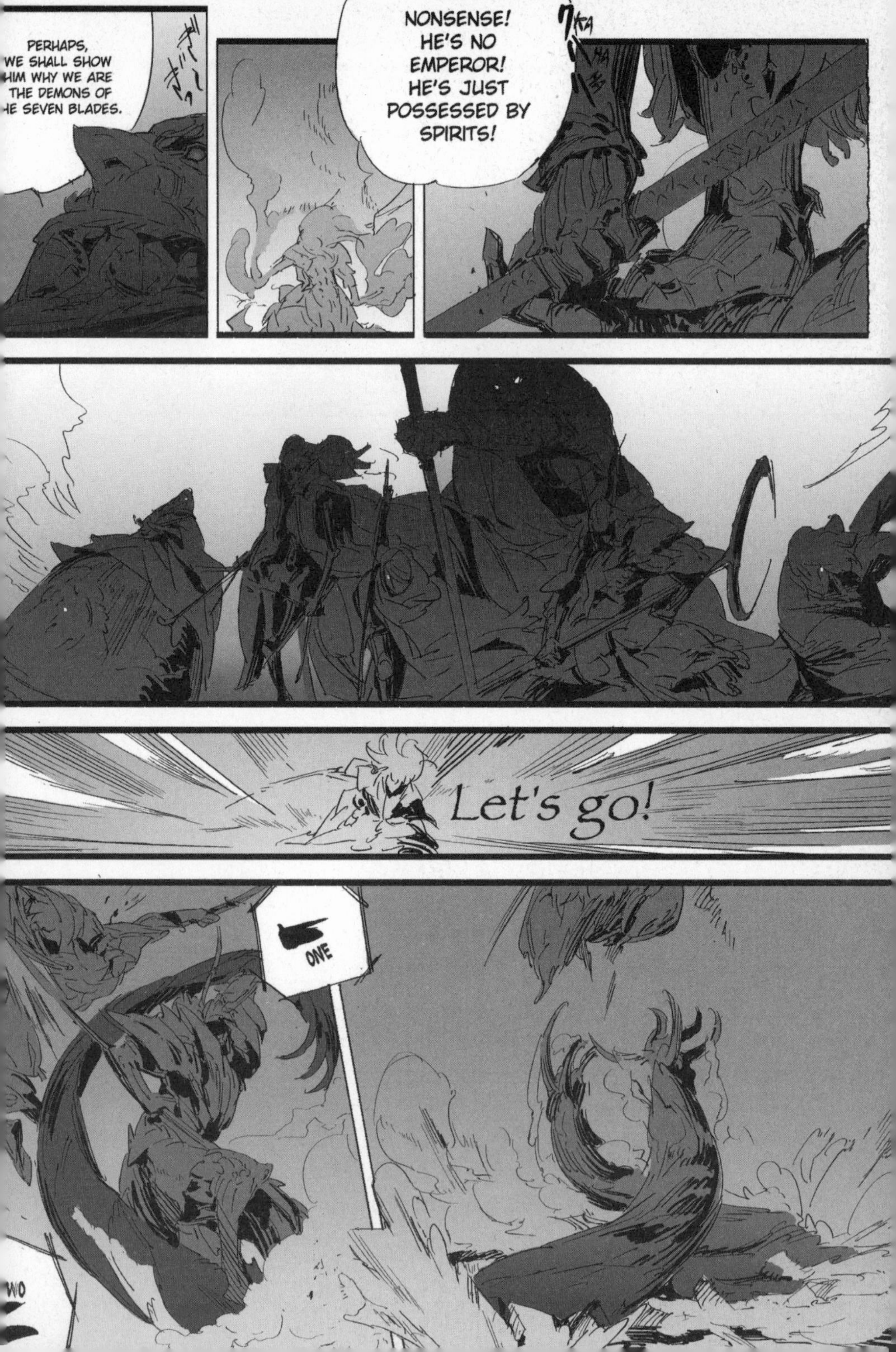
PERHAPS, WE SHALL SHOW HIM WHY WE ARE THE DEMONS OF HE SEVEN BLADES.
NONSENSE! HE'S NO EMPEROR! HE'S JUST POSSESSED BY SPIRITS!
Let's go!
ONE

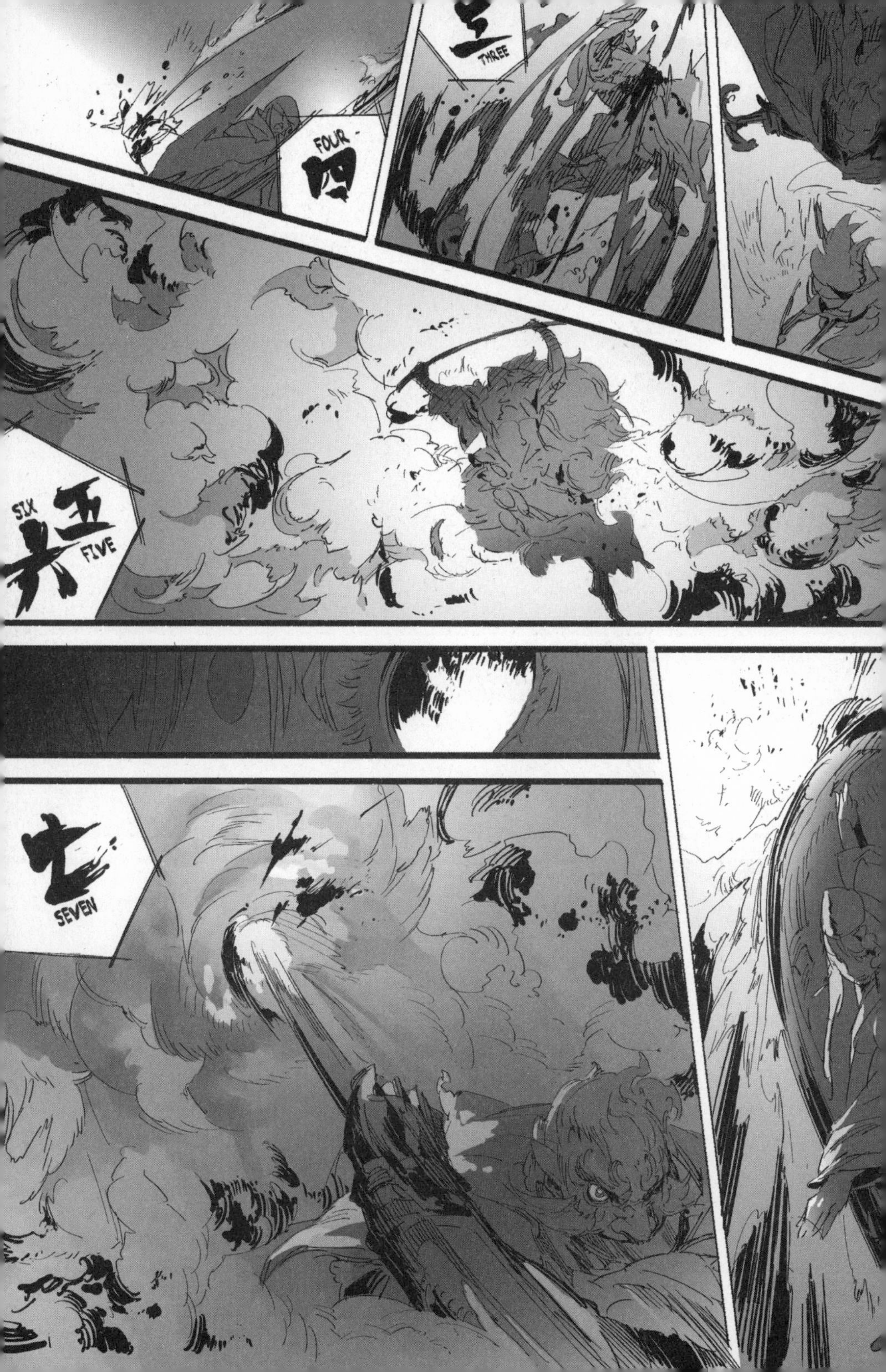

三 THREE
FOUR 四
五 FIVE
SIX 六
七 SEVEN

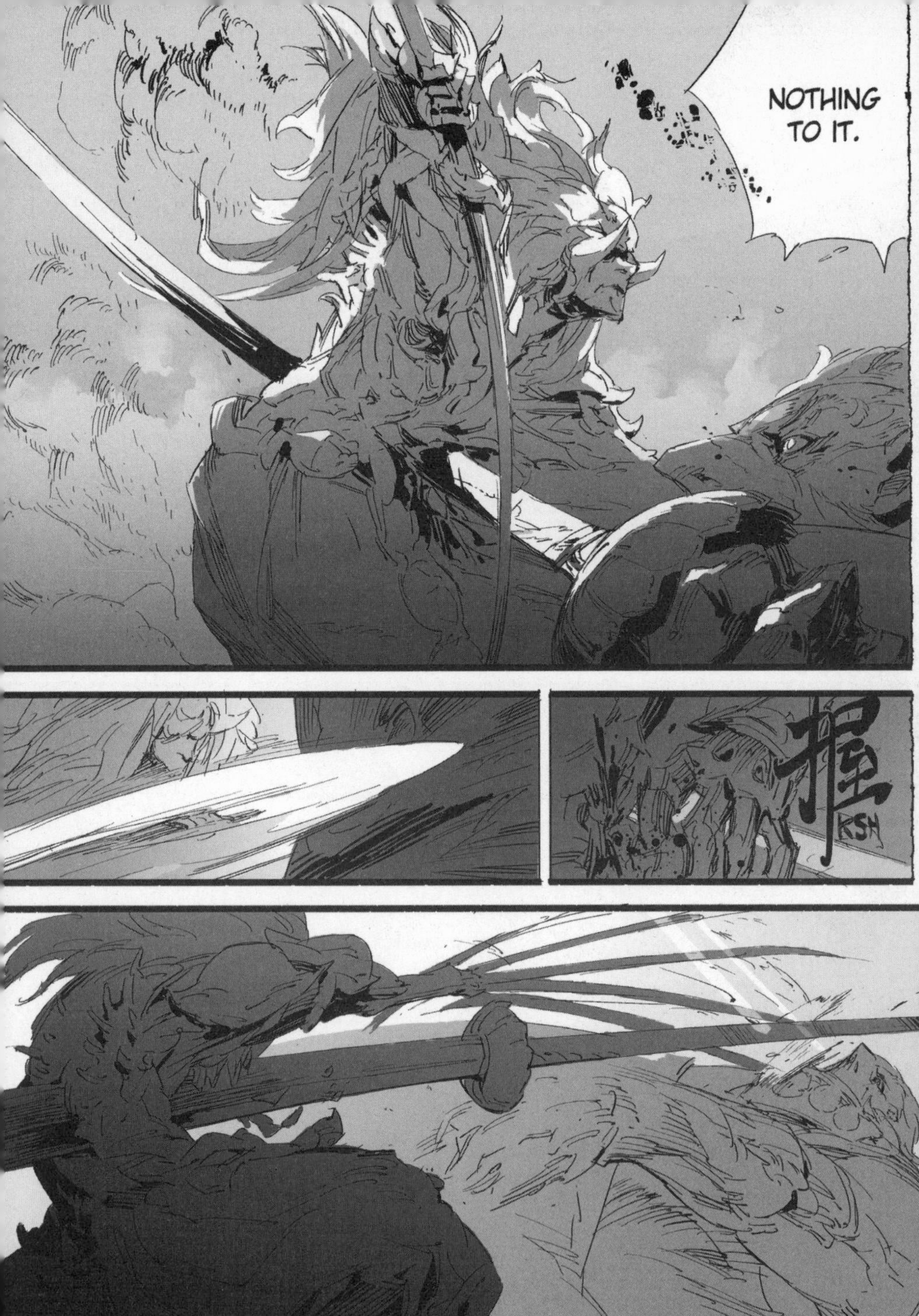
NOTHING TO IT.
握
KSH

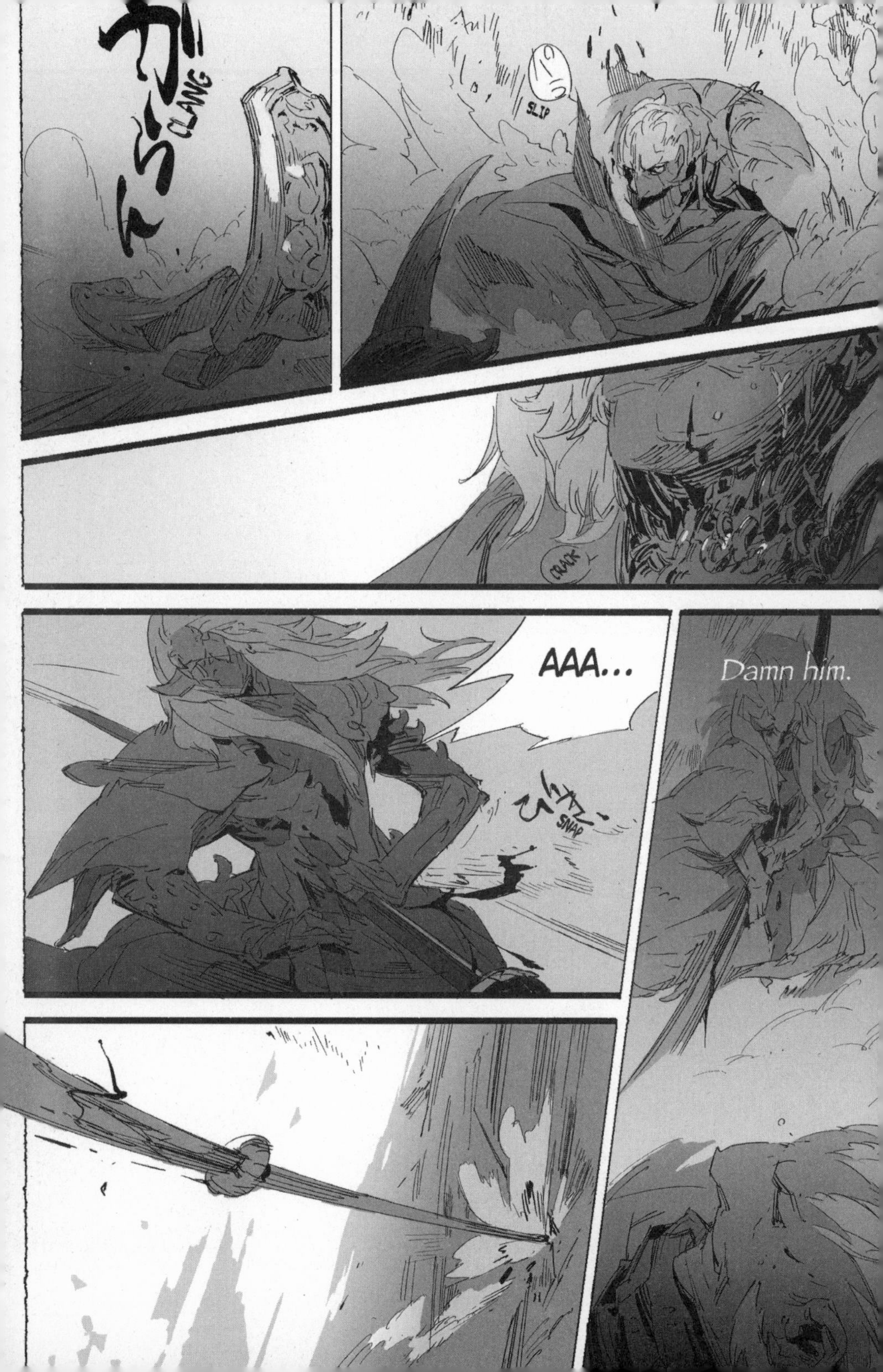

CLANG
SLIP
CRACK
AAA...
SNAP
Damn him.

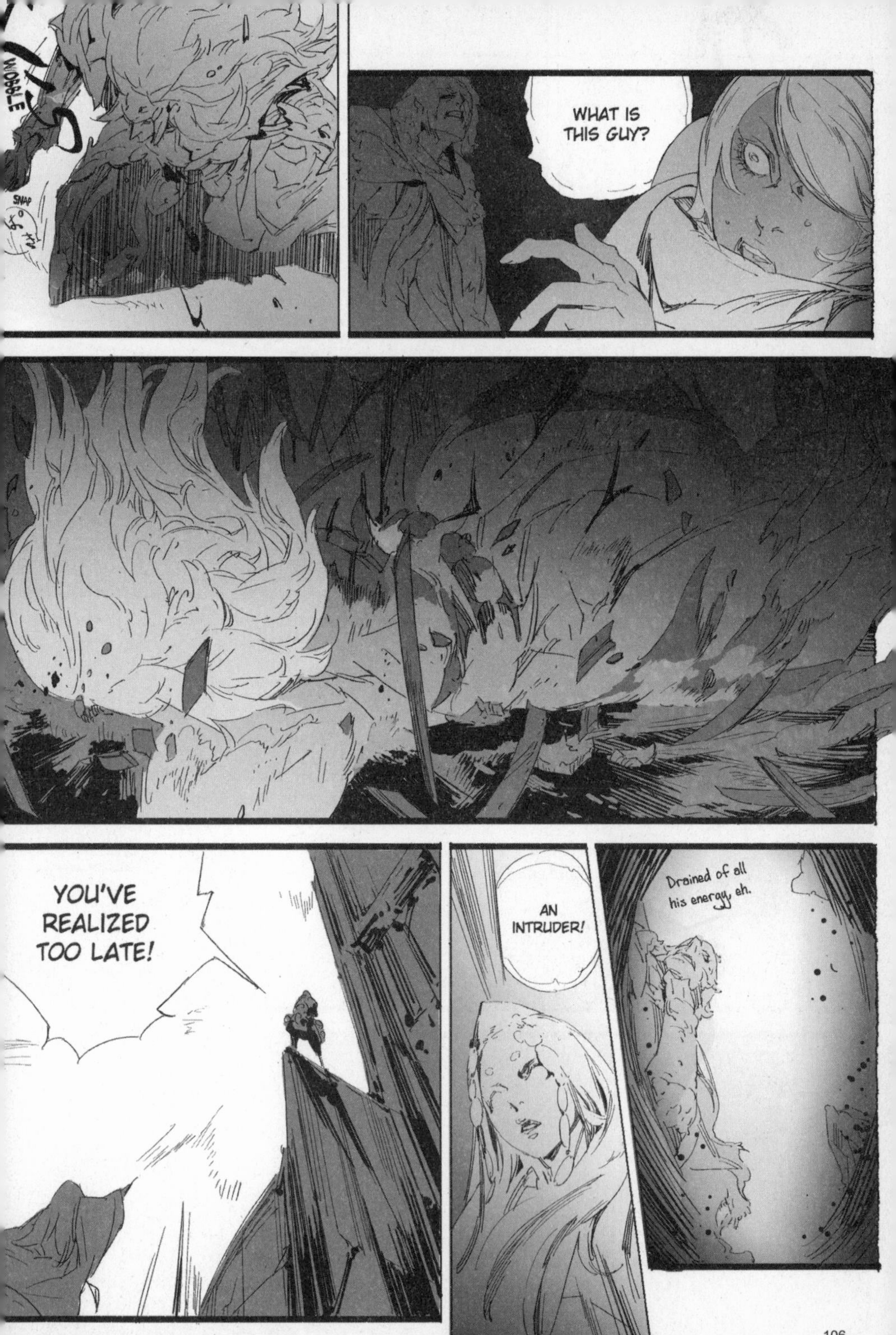
WOBBLE
SNAP
WHAT IS THIS GUY?
YOU'VE REALIZED TOO LATE!
AN INTRUDER!
Drained of all his energy, eh.

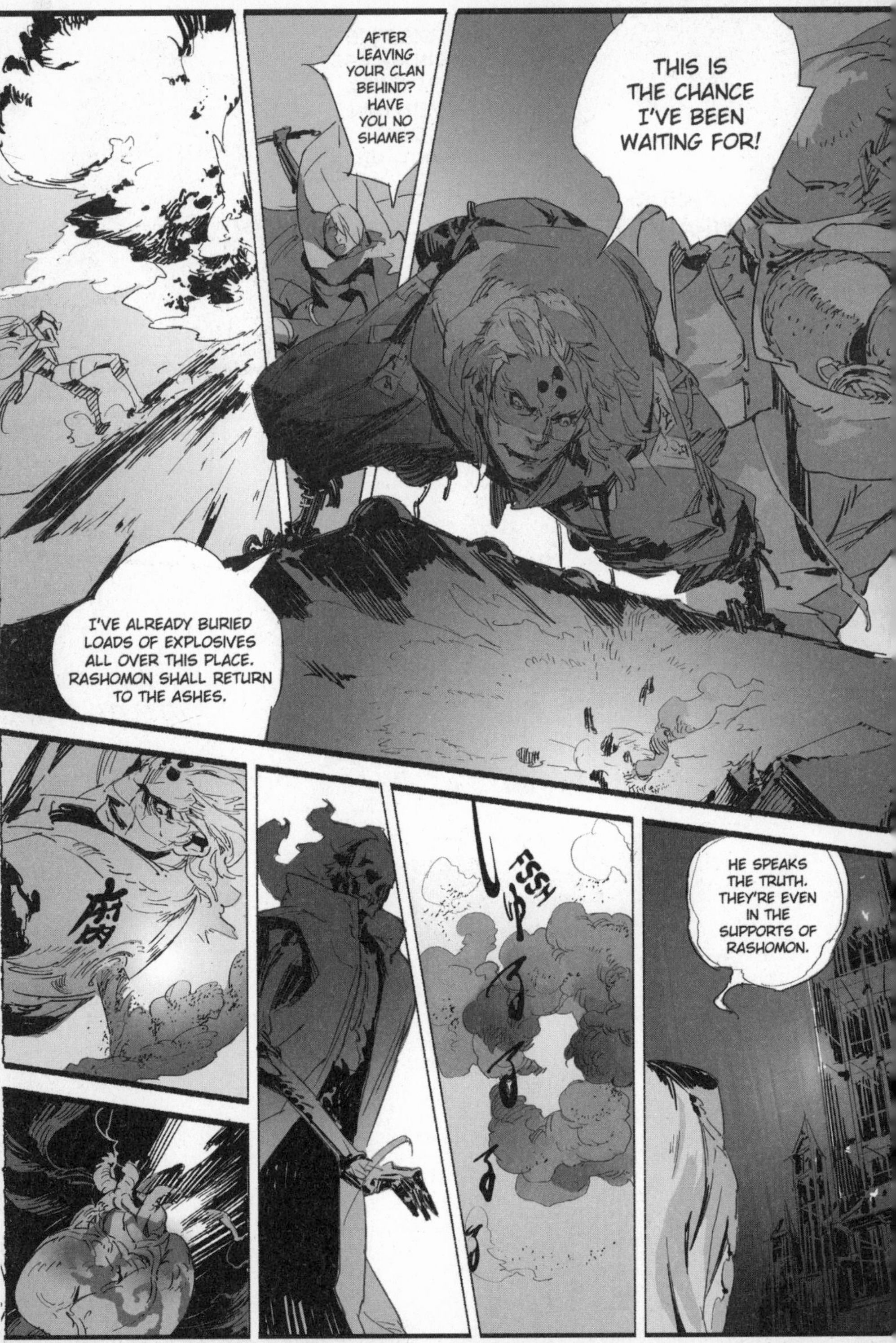
AFTER LEAVING YOUR CLAN BEHIND? HAVE YOU NO SHAME?
THIS IS THE CHANCE I'VE BEEN WAITING FOR!
I'VE ALREADY BURIED LOADS OF EXPLOSIVES ALL OVER THIS PLACE. RASHOMON SHALL RETURN TO THE ASHES.
腐
FSSH
HE SPEAKS THE TRUTH. THEY'RE EVEN IN THE SUPPORTS OF RASHOMON.

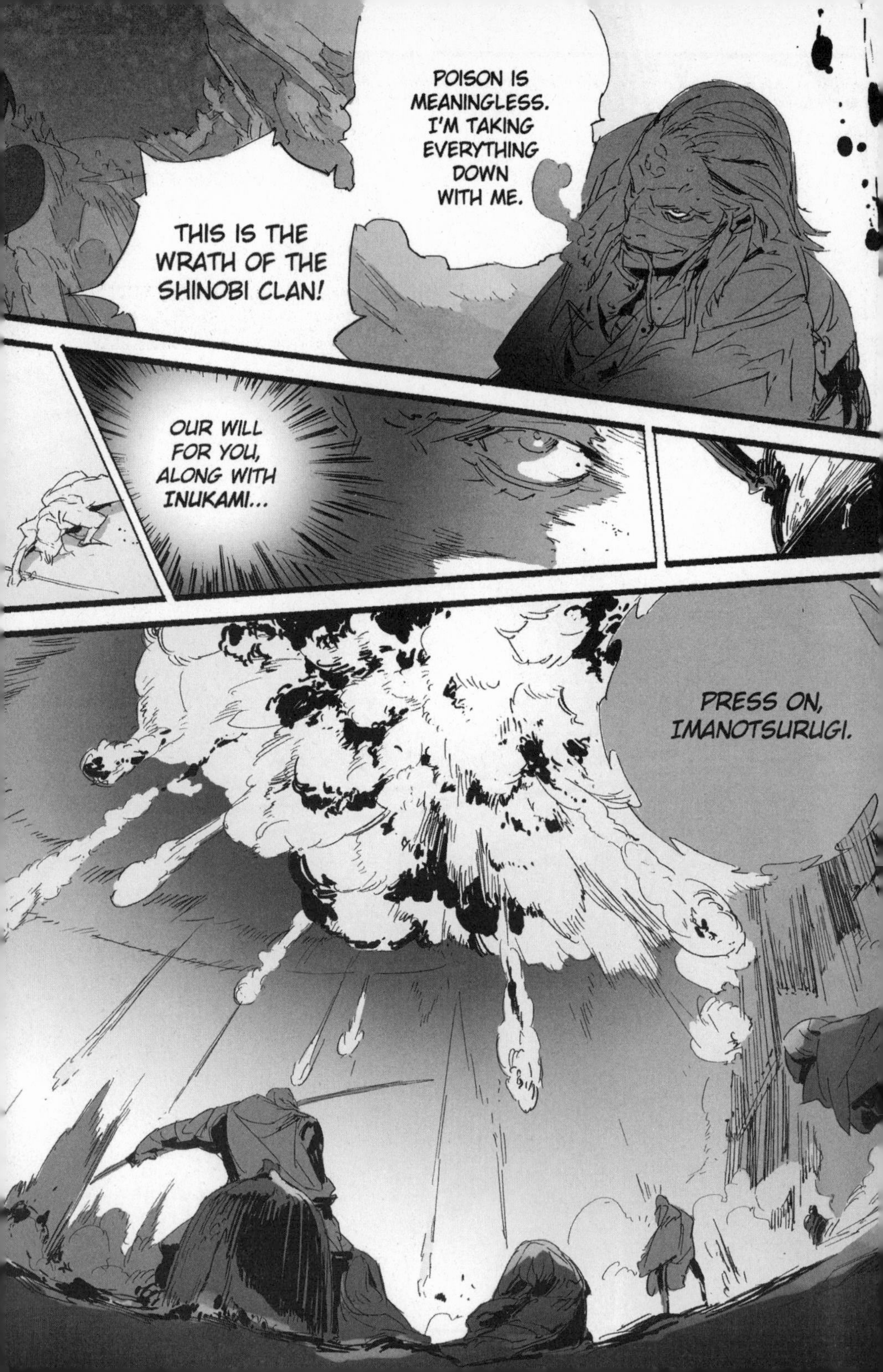
POISON IS MEANINGLESS. I'M TAKING EVERYTHING DOWN WITH ME.
THIS IS THE WRATH OF THE SHINOBI CLAN!
OUR WILL FOR YOU, ALONG WITH INUKAMI...
PRESS ON, IMANOTSURUGI.

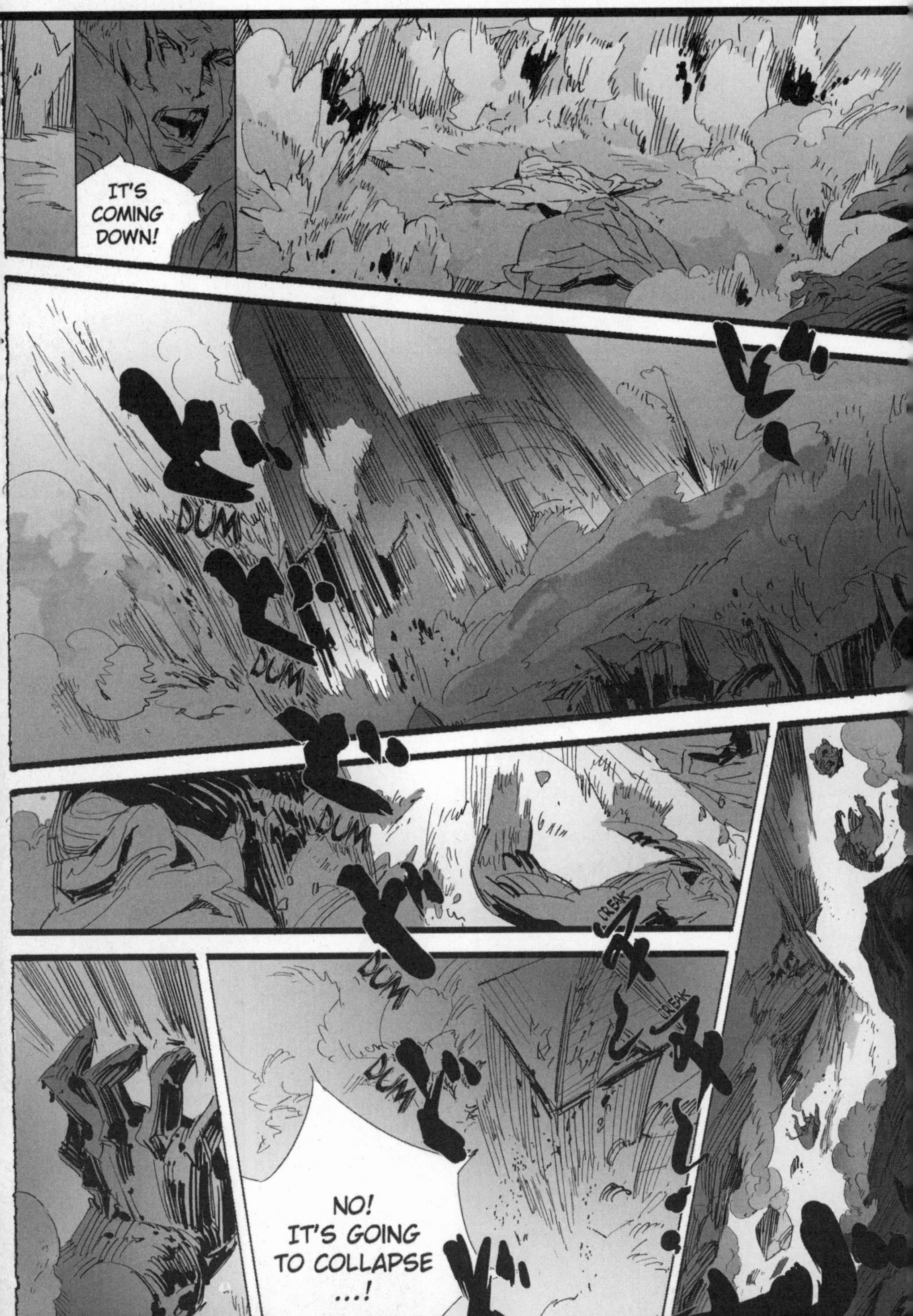
IT'S COMING DOWN!
DUM
DUM
DUM
DUM
DUM
CREAK
CREAK
NO! IT'S GOING TO COLLAPSE ...!

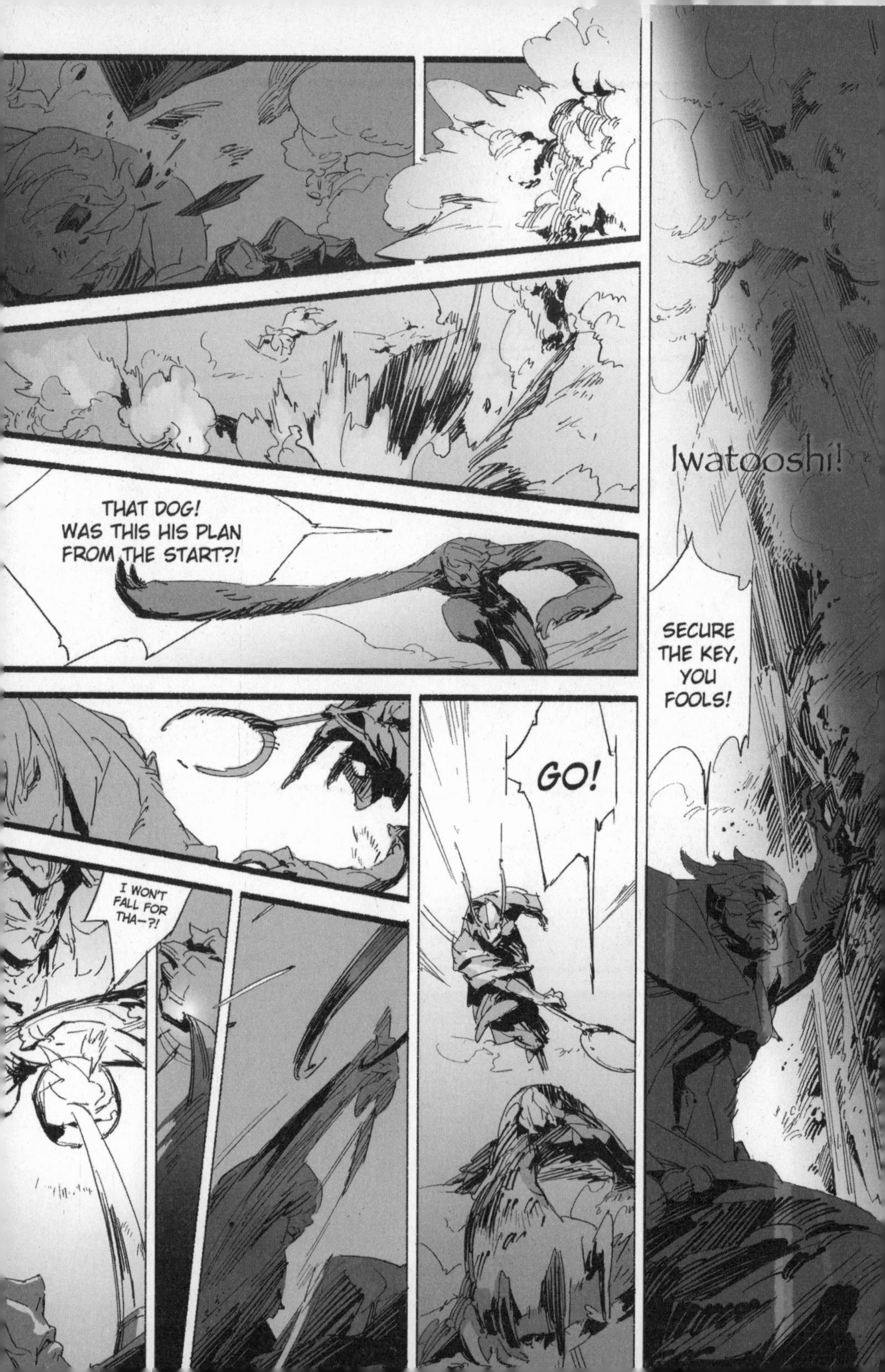
Iwatooshi!
SECURE THE KEY, YOU FOOLS!
THAT DOG! WAS THIS HIS PLAN FROM THE START?!
GO!
I WON'T FALL FOR THA--?!

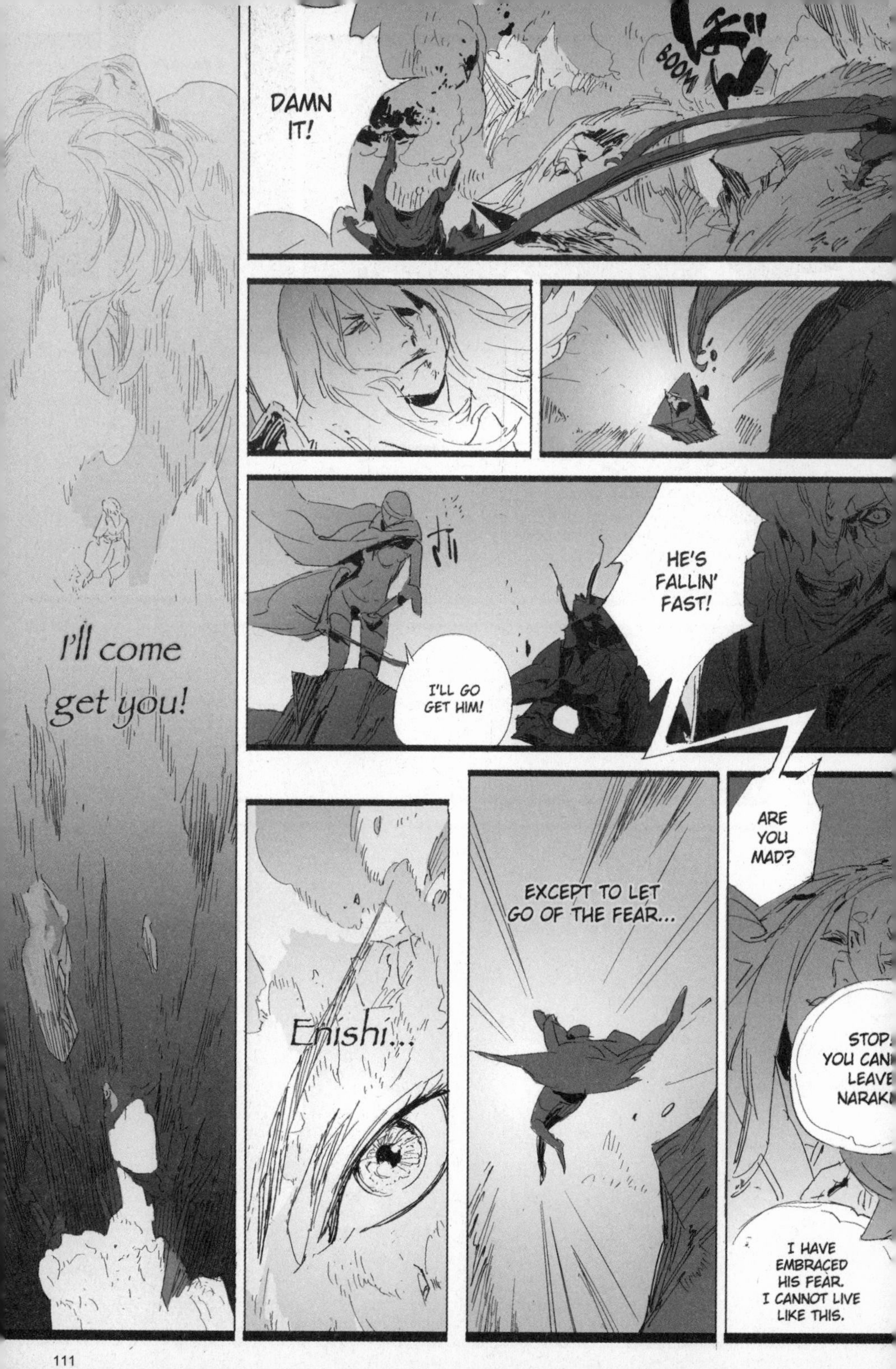
I'll come get you!
DAMN IT!
BOOM
HE'S FALLIN' FAST!
I'LL GO GET HIM!
ARE YOU MAD?
Enishi...
EXCEPT TO LET GO OF THE FEAR...
I HAVE EMBRACED HIS FEAR. I CANNOT LIVE LIKE THIS.

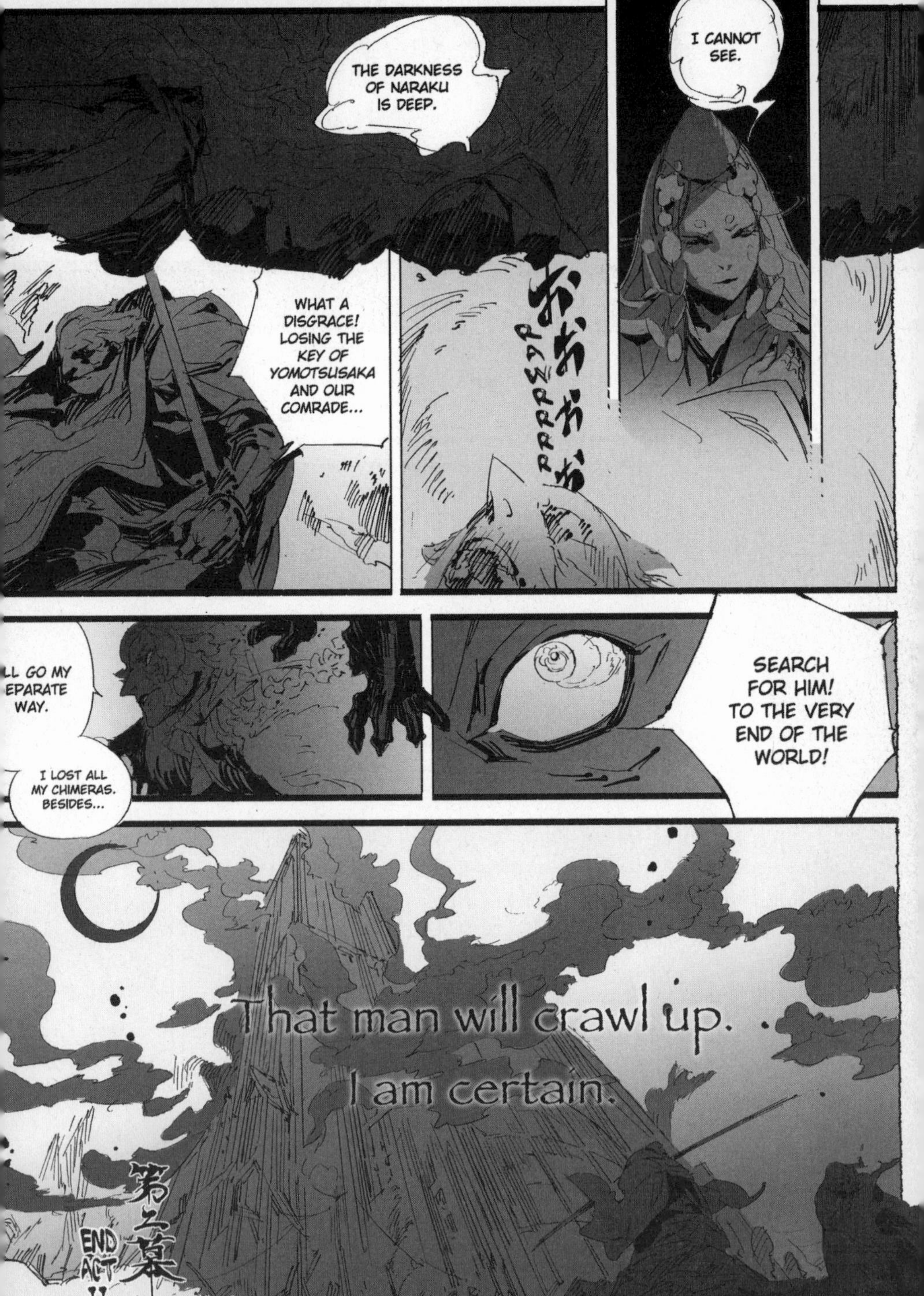
I CANNOT SEE.
THE DARKNESS OF NARAKU IS DEEP.
おおおお
RAWRRRRR
WHAT A DISGRACE! LOSING THE KEY OF YOMOTSUSAKA AND OUR COMRADE...
SEARCH FOR HIM! TO THE VERY END OF THE WORLD!
LL GO MY EPARATE WAY.
I LOST ALL MY CHIMERAS. BESIDES...
That man will crawl up.
I am certain.
第二幕 終
END ACT II

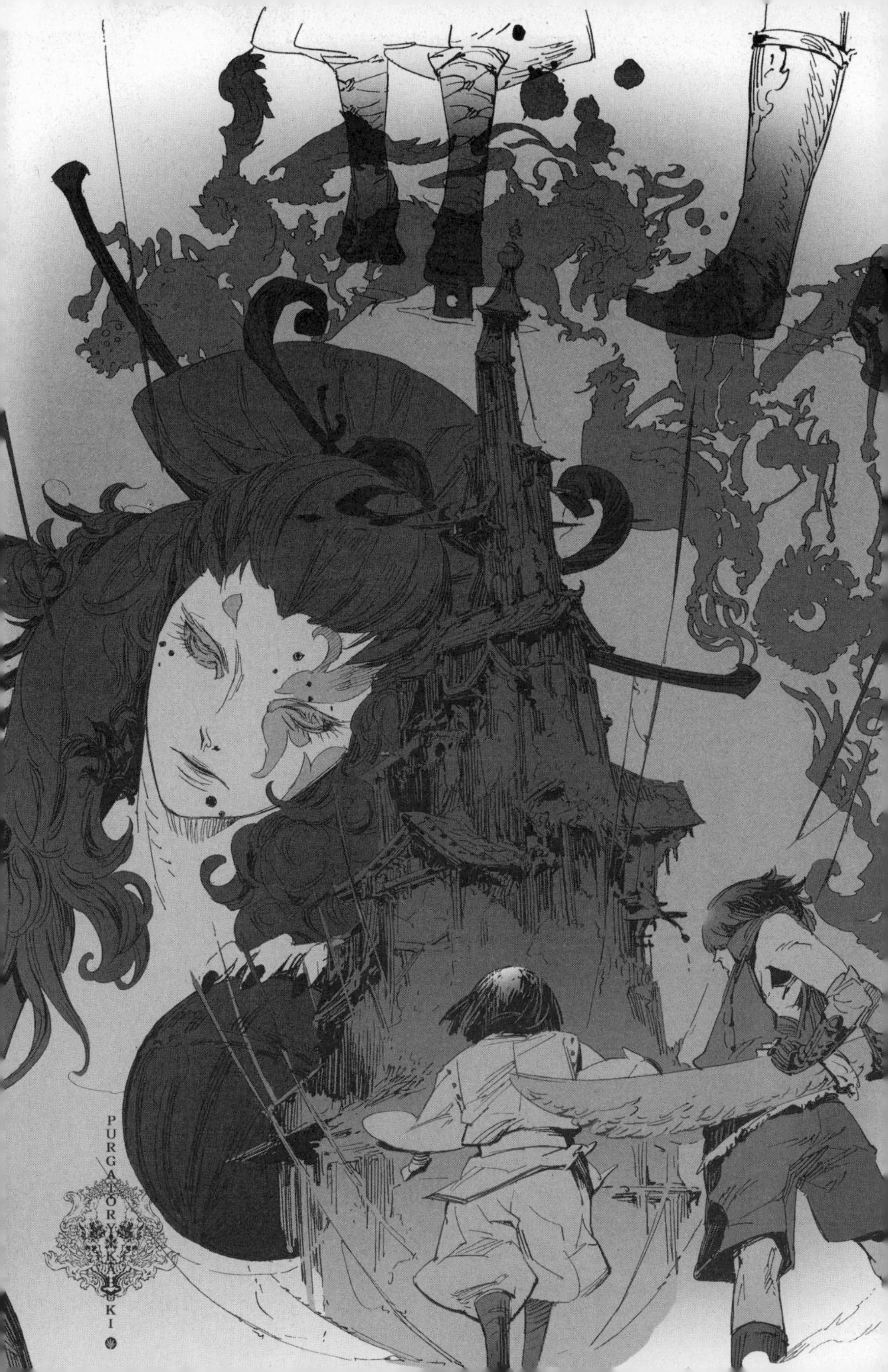
PURGATORY KABUKI

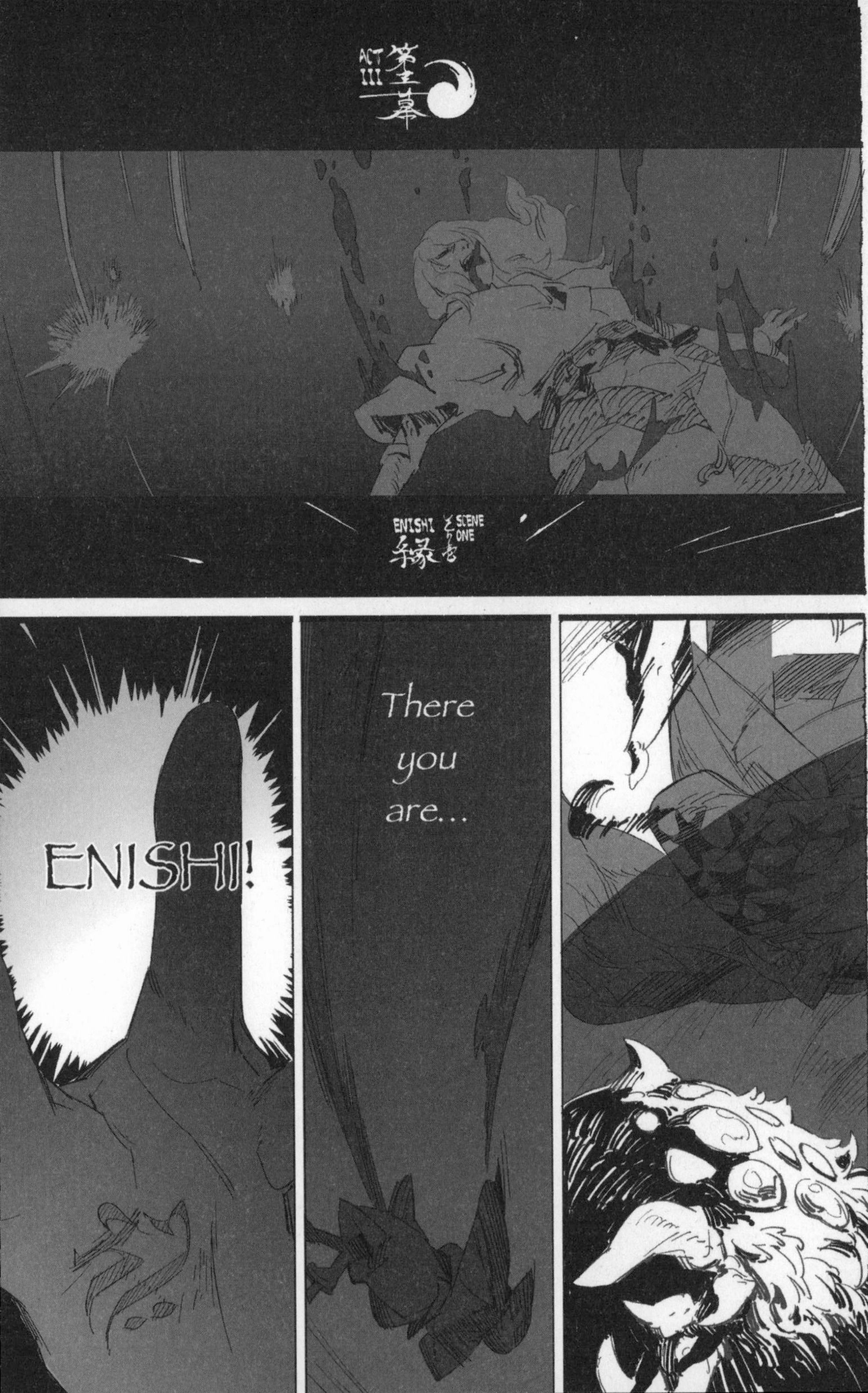
ACT III
第三幕
ENISHI SCENE ONE
縁 其の壱
ENISHI!
There you are...

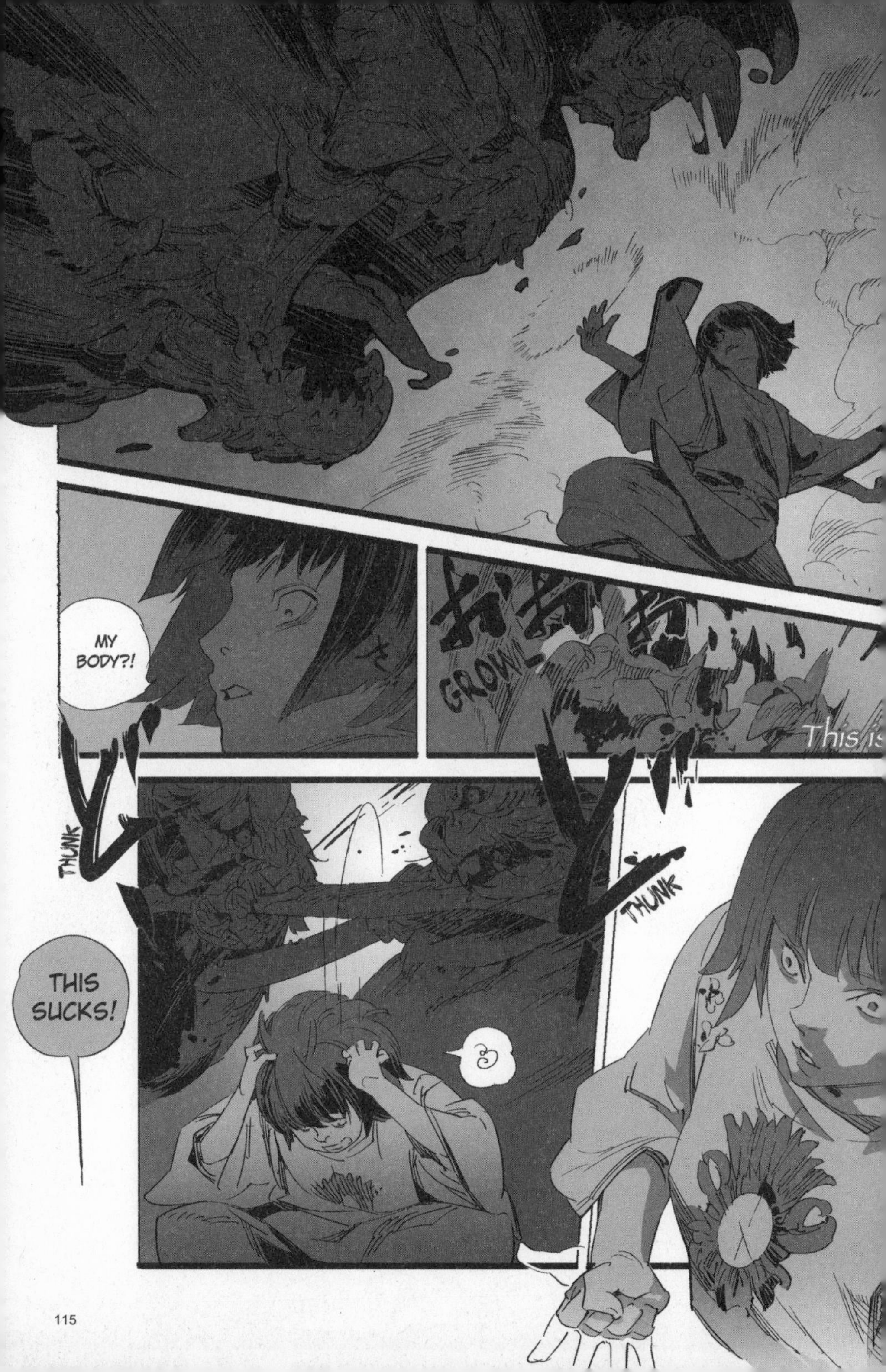
GROWL
This is
MY BODY?!
THUNK
THUNK
THIS SUCKS!

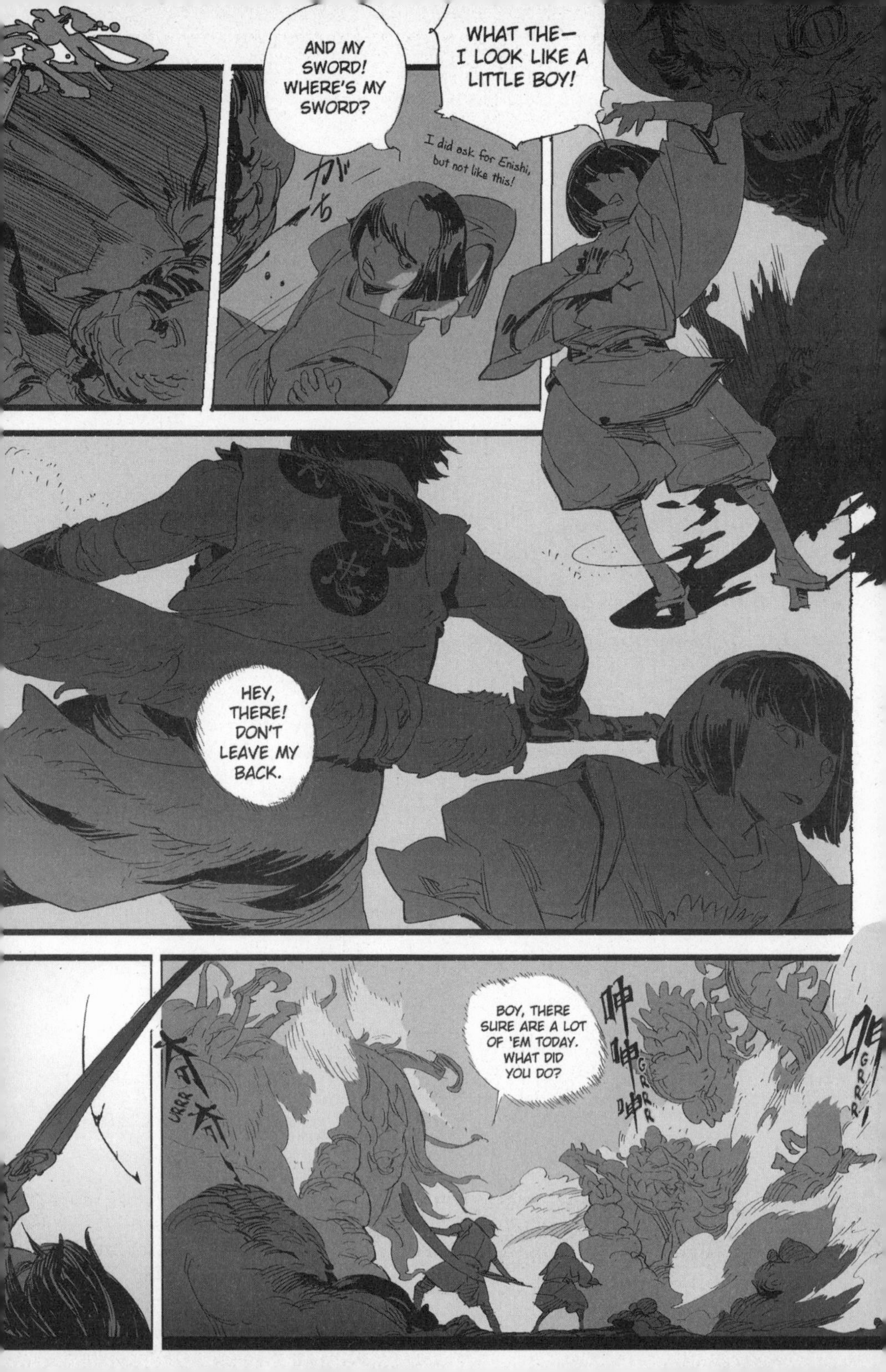
WHAT THE— I LOOK LIKE A LITTLE BOY!
AND MY SWORD! WHERE'S MY SWORD?
I did ask for Enishi, but not like this!
HEY, THERE! DON'T LEAVE MY BACK.
BOY, THERE SURE ARE A LOT OF 'EM TODAY. WHAT DID YOU DO?
GRRR
GRRR!
URRR

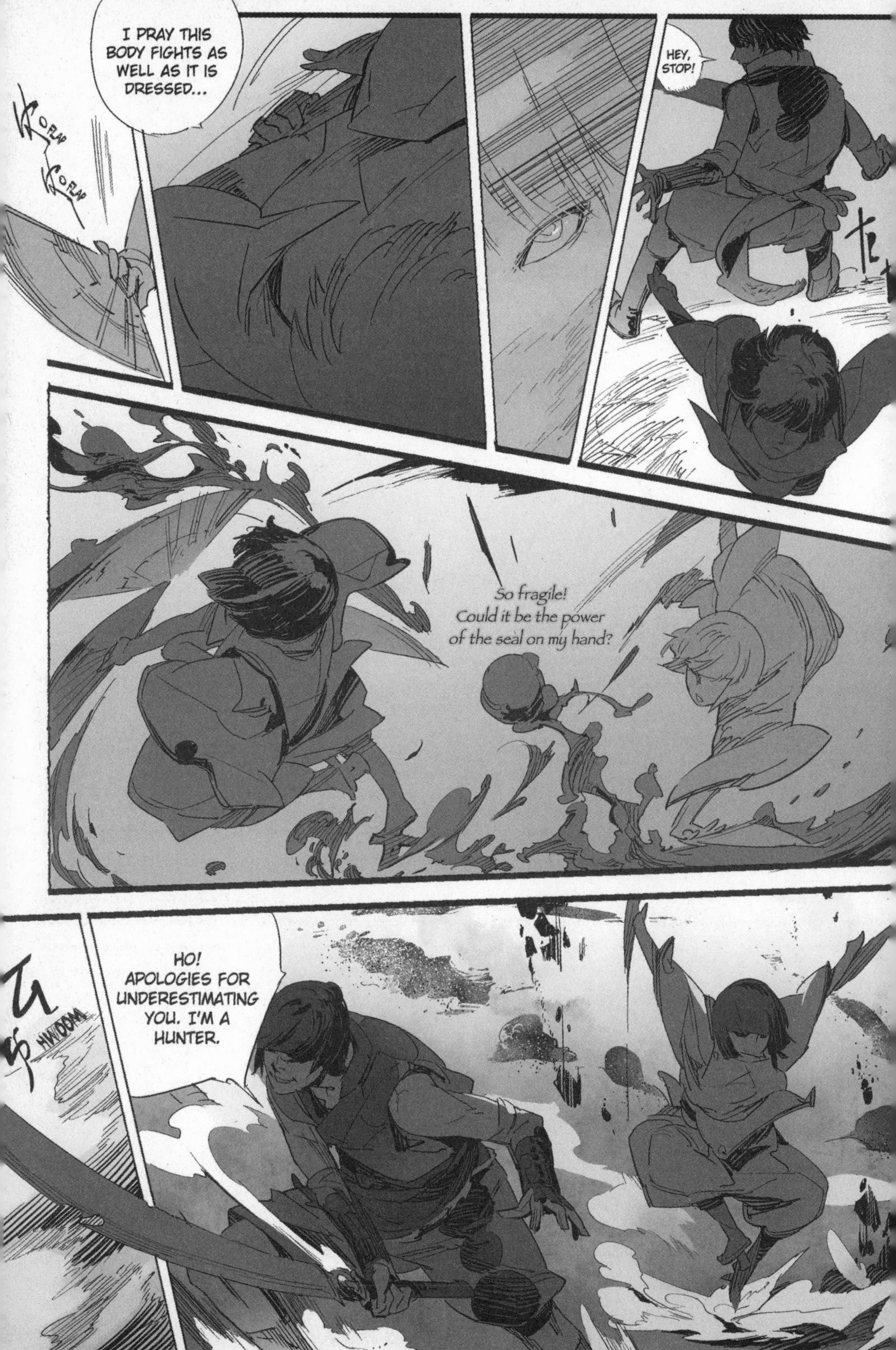
I PRAY THIS BODY FIGHTS AS WELL AS IT IS DRESSED...
FLAP
FLAP
HEY, STOP!
So fragile!
Could it be the power of the seal on my hand?
HO! APOLOGIES FOR UNDERESTIMATING YOU. I'M A HUNTER.
HWOOM

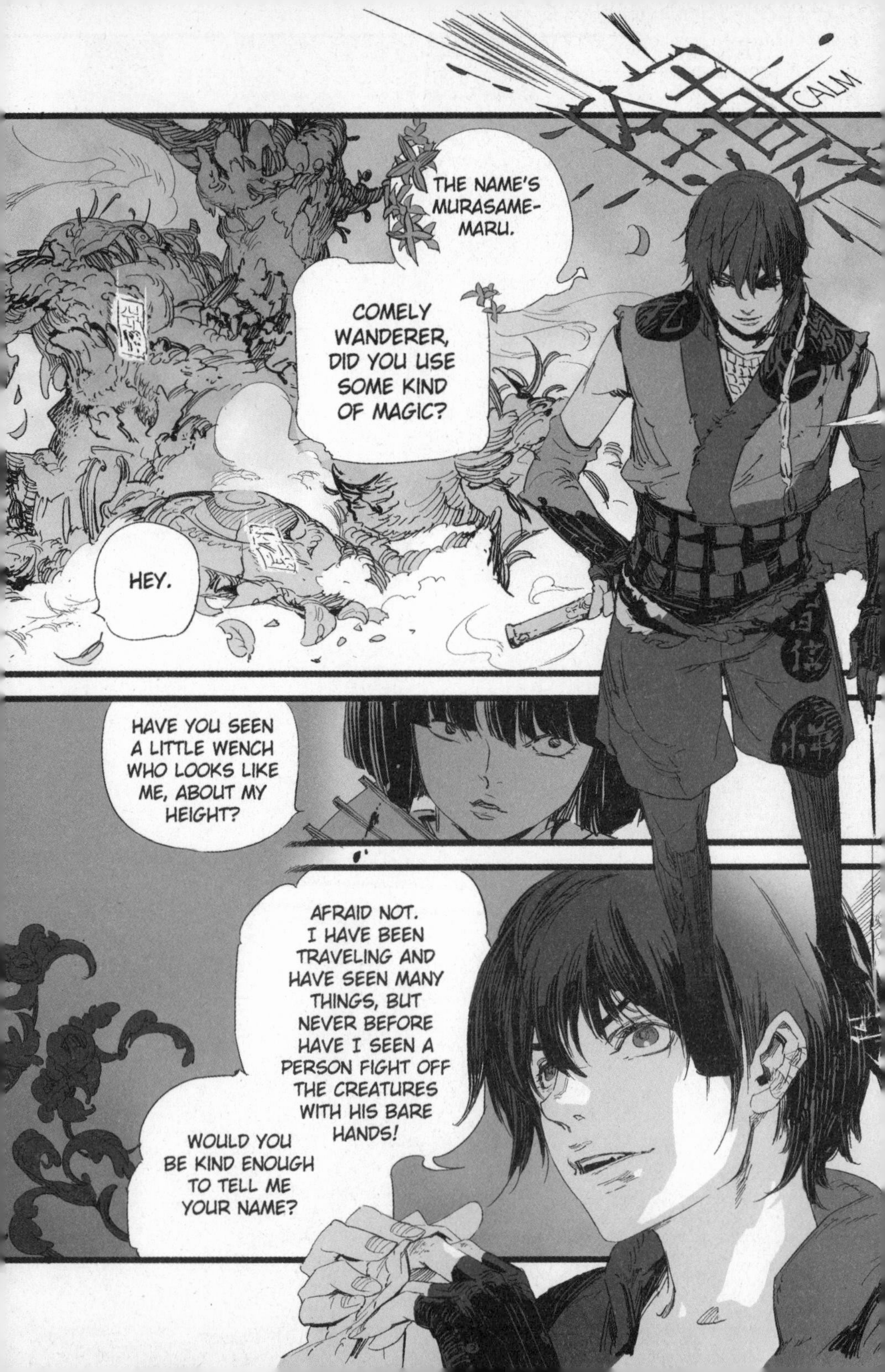
CALM
THE NAME'S MURASAME-MARU.
COMELY WANDERER, DID YOU USE SOME KIND OF MAGIC?
HEY.
HAVE YOU SEEN A LITTLE WENCH WHO LOOKS LIKE ME, ABOUT MY HEIGHT?
AFRAID NOT. I HAVE BEEN TRAVELING AND HAVE SEEN MANY THINGS, BUT NEVER BEFORE HAVE I SEEN A PERSON FIGHT OFF THE CREATURES WITH HIS BARE HANDS!
WOULD YOU BE KIND ENOUGH TO TELL ME YOUR NAME?

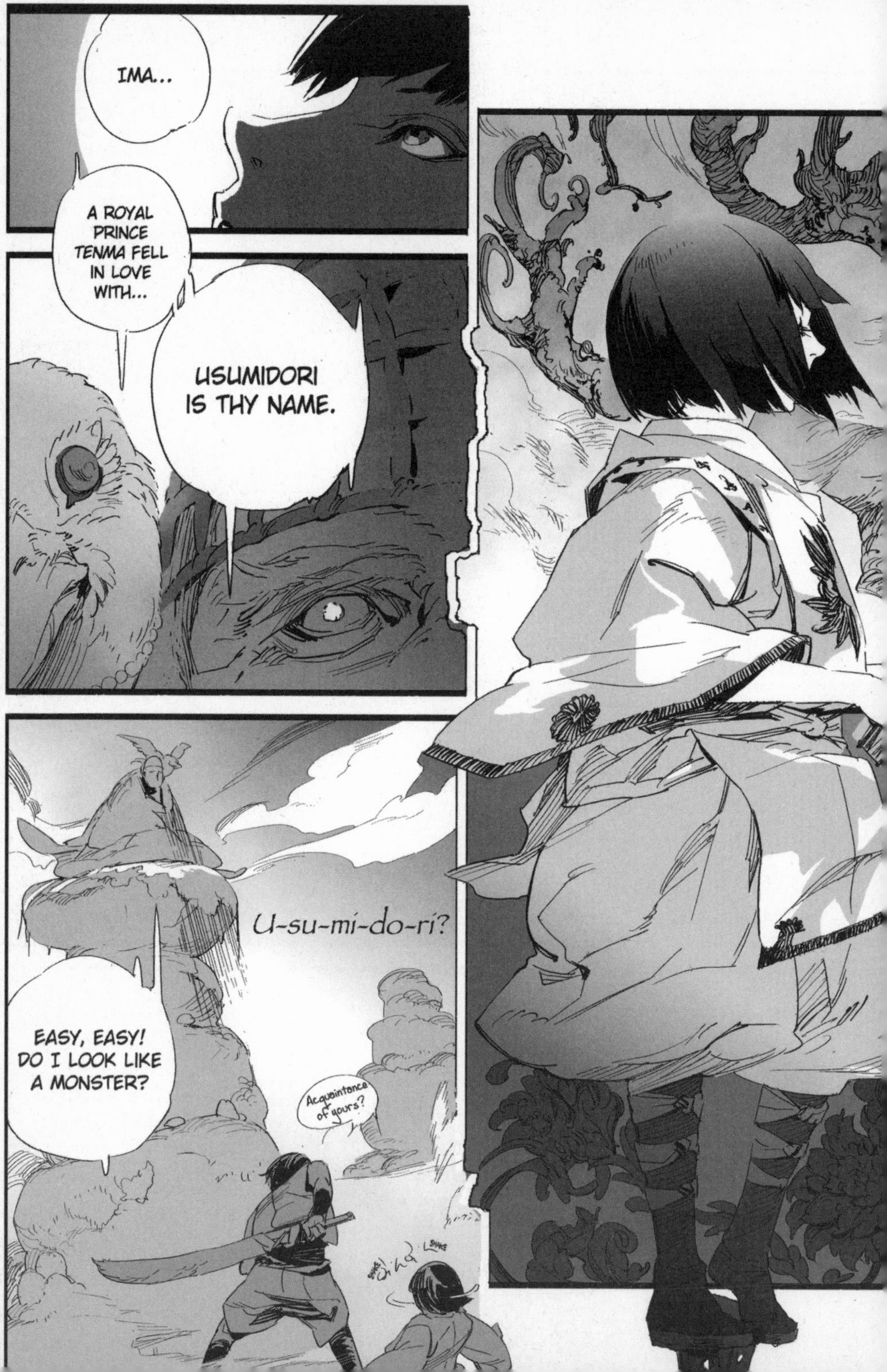
IMA...
A ROYAL PRINCE TENMA FELL IN LOVE WITH...
USUMIDORI IS THY NAME.
U-su-mi-do-ri?
EASY, EASY! DO I LOOK LIKE A MONSTER?
Acquaintance of yours?
SHAKE
SHAKE

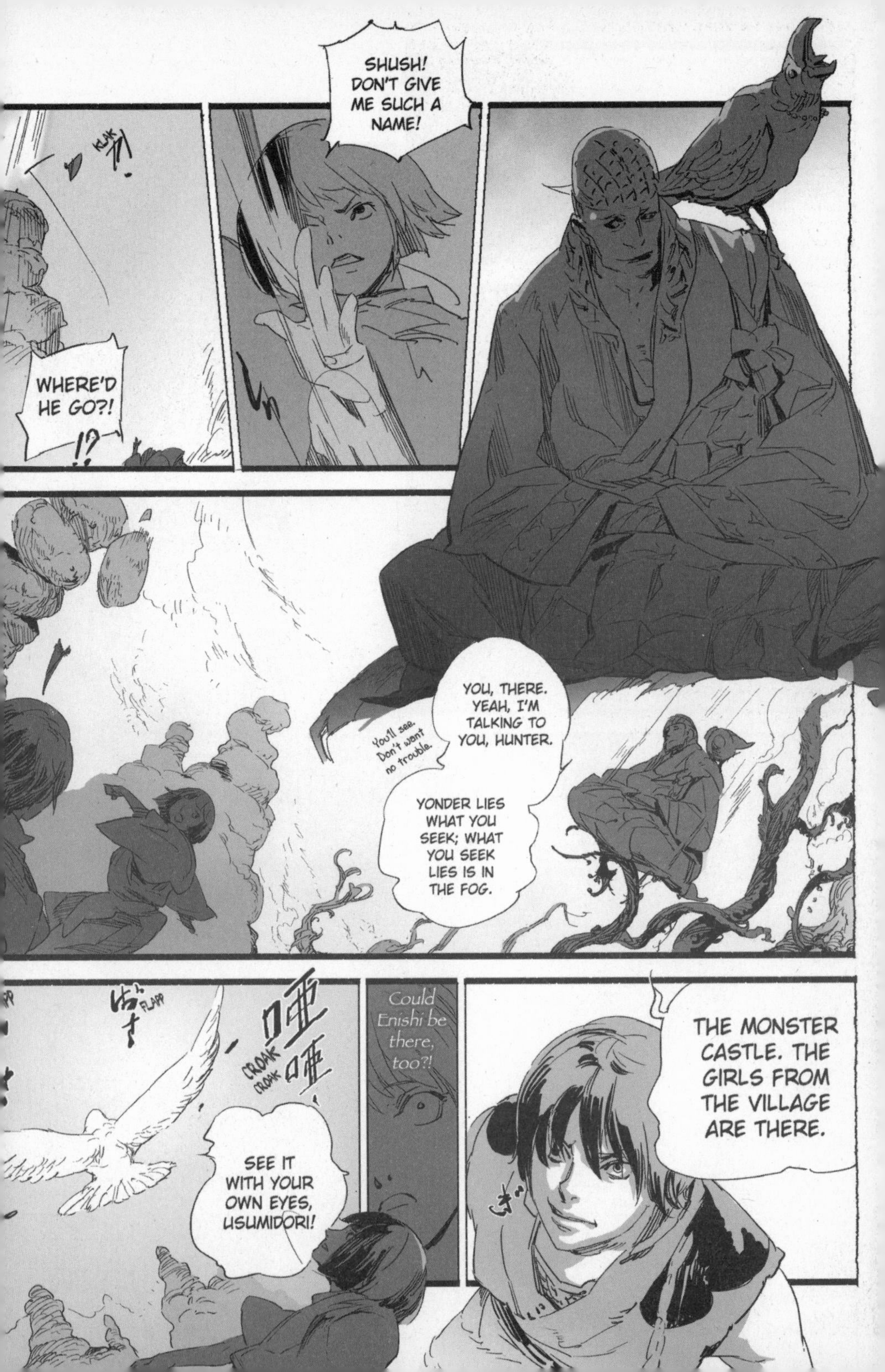
SHUSH! DON'T GIVE ME SUCH A NAME!
KLAK ?!
WHERE'D HE GO?!
!?
YOU, THERE. YEAH, I'M TALKING TO YOU, HUNTER.
You'll see. Don't want no trouble.
YONDER LIES WHAT YOU SEEK; WHAT YOU SEEK LIES IS IN THE FOG.
THE MONSTER CASTLE. THE GIRLS FROM THE VILLAGE ARE THERE.
Could Enishi be there, too?!
唖唖
CROAK CROAK
SEE IT WITH YOUR OWN EYES, USUMIDORI!
FLAPP

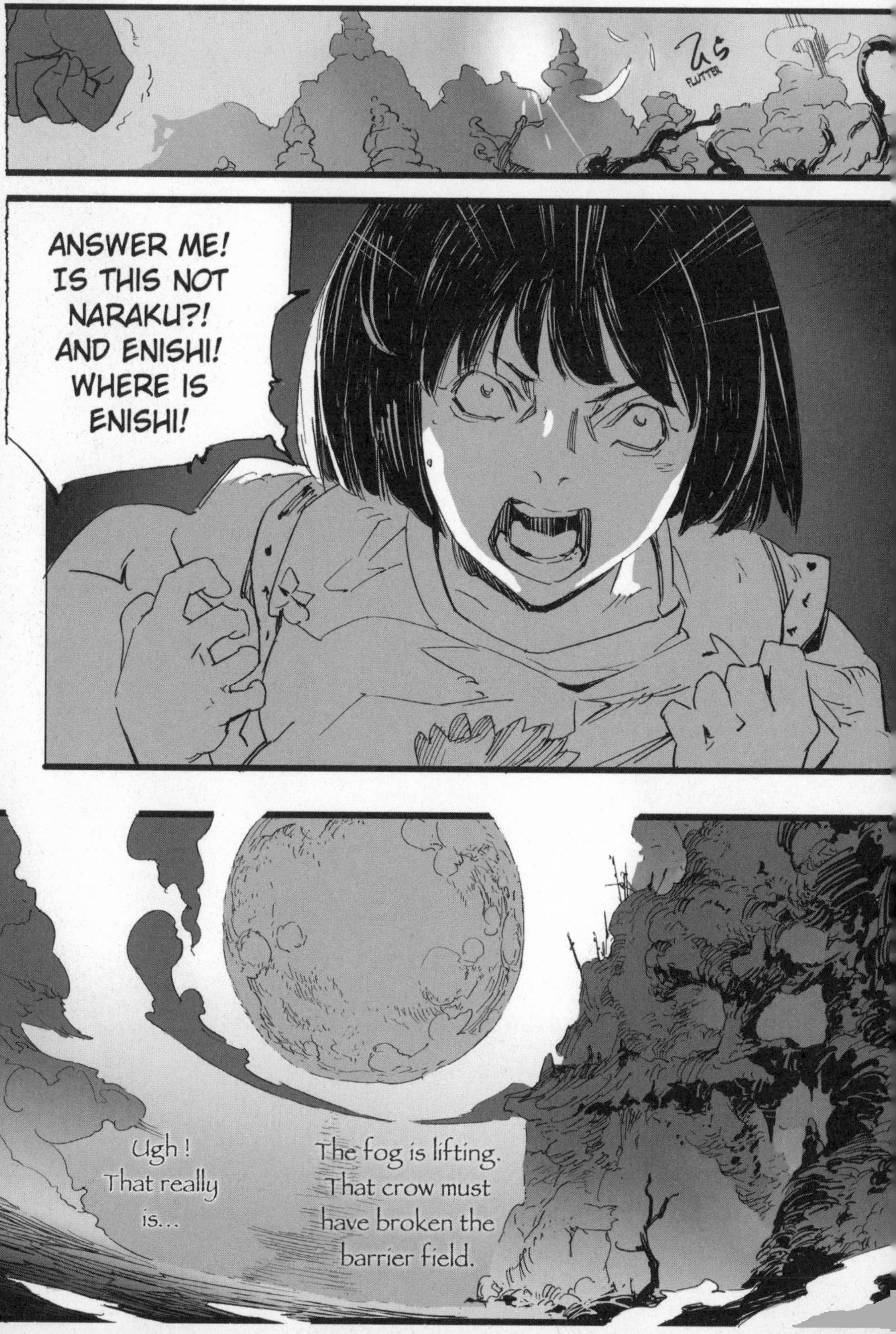
FLUTTER
ANSWER ME! IS THIS NOT NARAKU?! AND ENISHI! WHERE IS ENISHI!
The fog is lifting. That crow must have broken the barrier field.
Ugh! That really is...

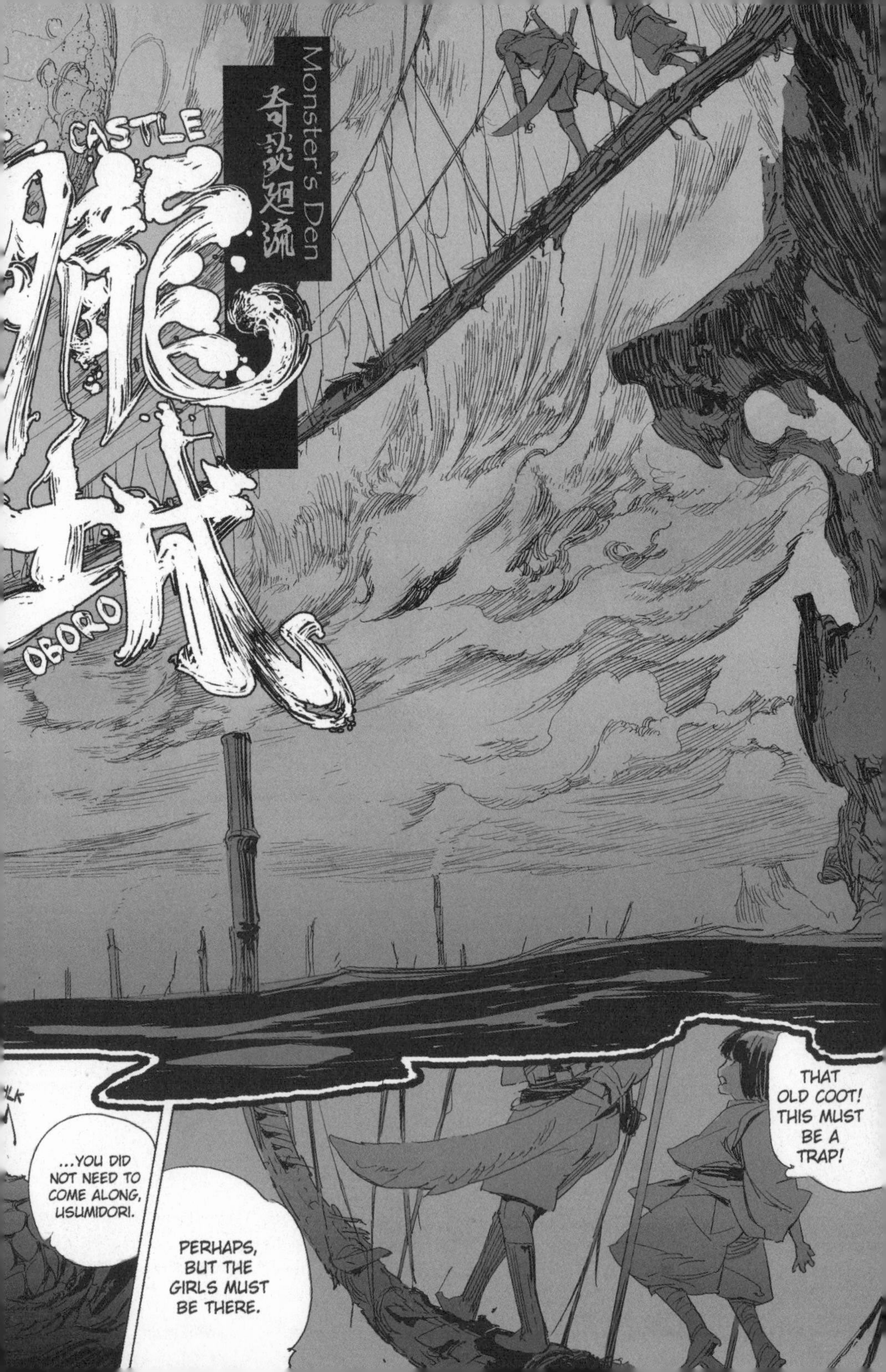
CASTLE
OBORO
Monster's Den
奇談廻流
THAT OLD COOT! THIS MUST BE A TRAP!
...YOU DID NOT NEED TO COME ALONG, USUMIDORI.
PERHAPS, BUT THE GIRLS MUST BE THERE.

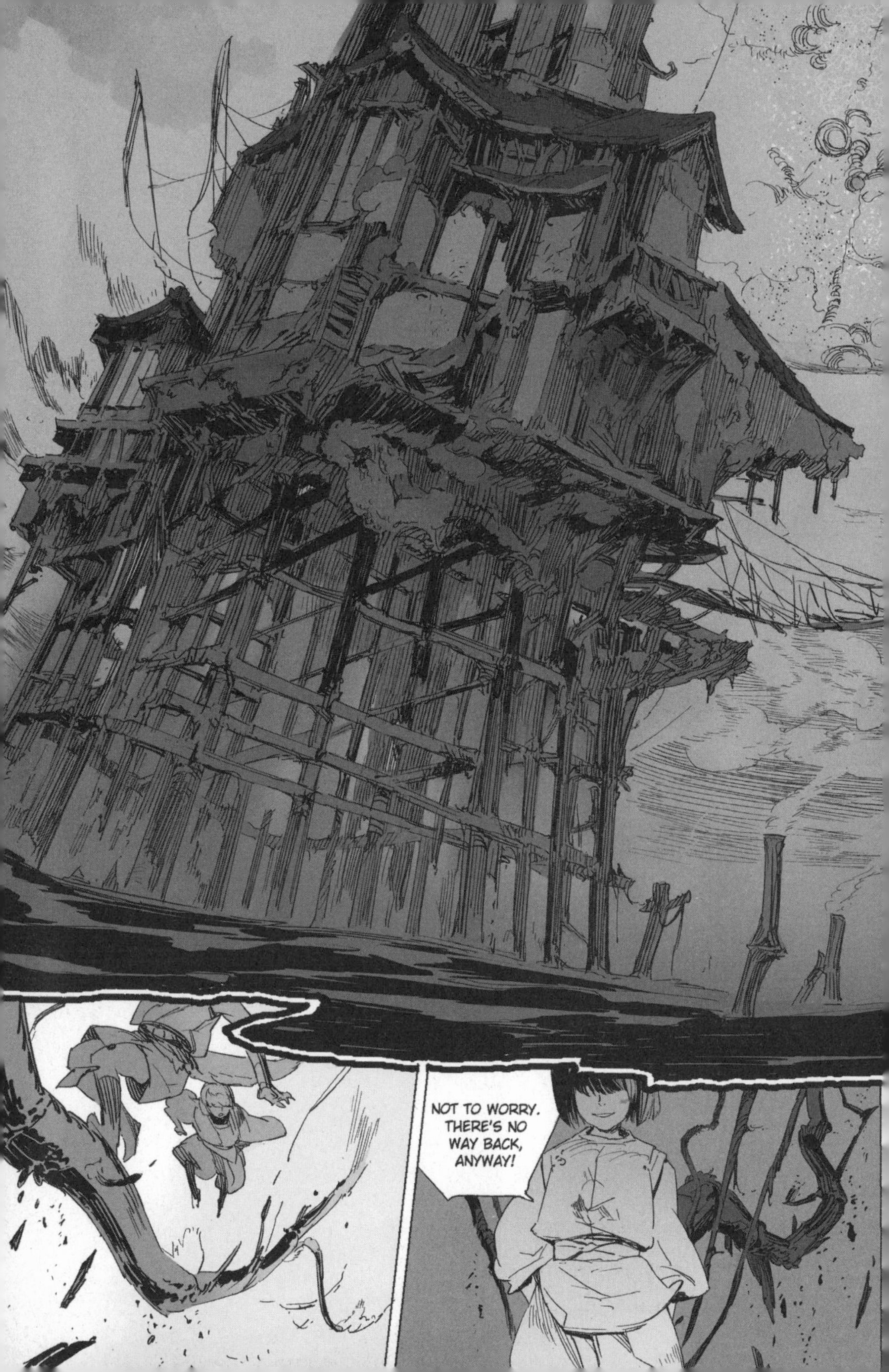
NOT TO WORRY. THERE'S NO WAY BACK, ANYWAY!

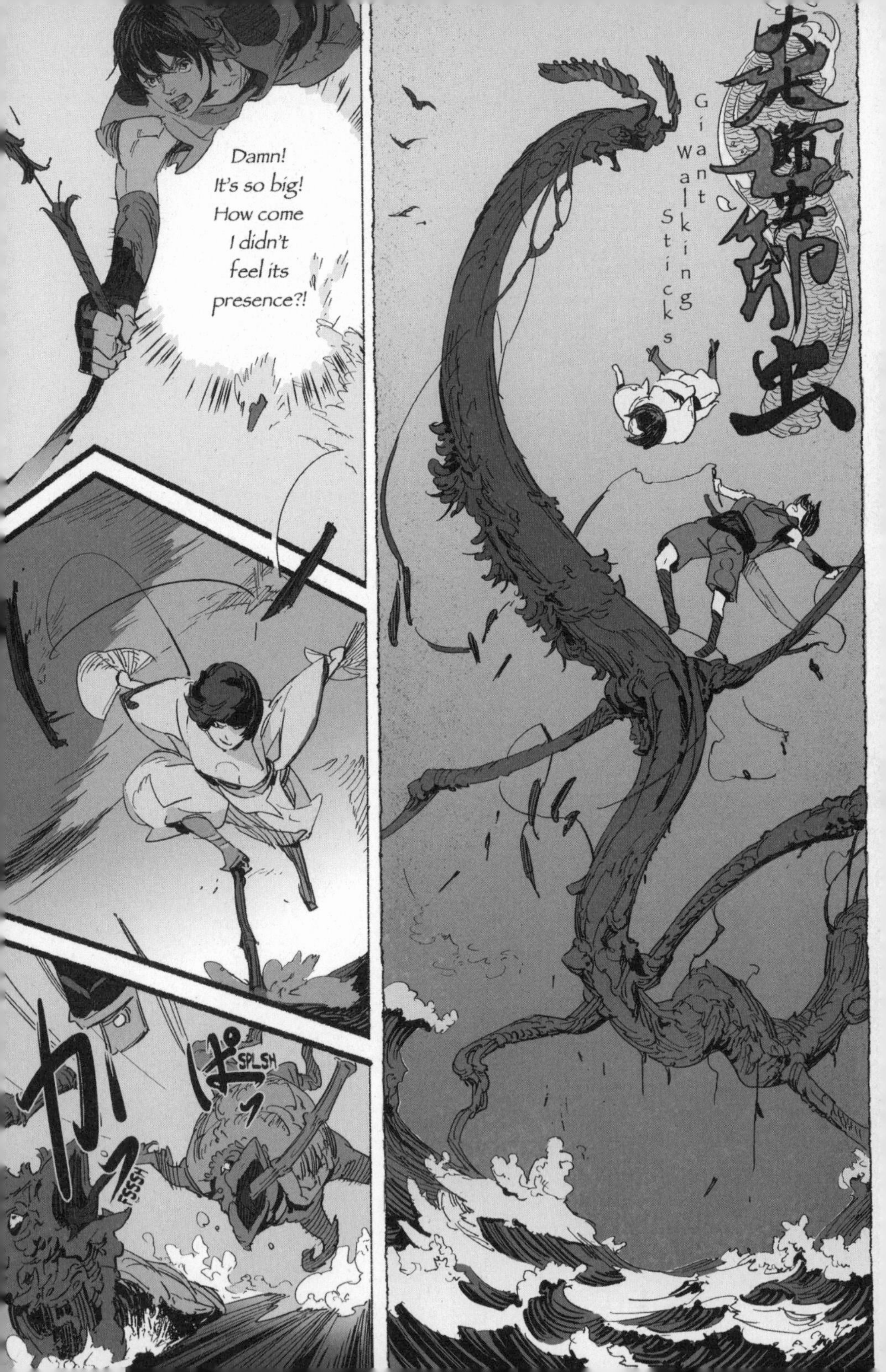
大節虫
Giant Walking Sticks
Damn! It's so big! How come I didn't feel its presence?!
ぱっ
SPLSH
かっ
FSSSH

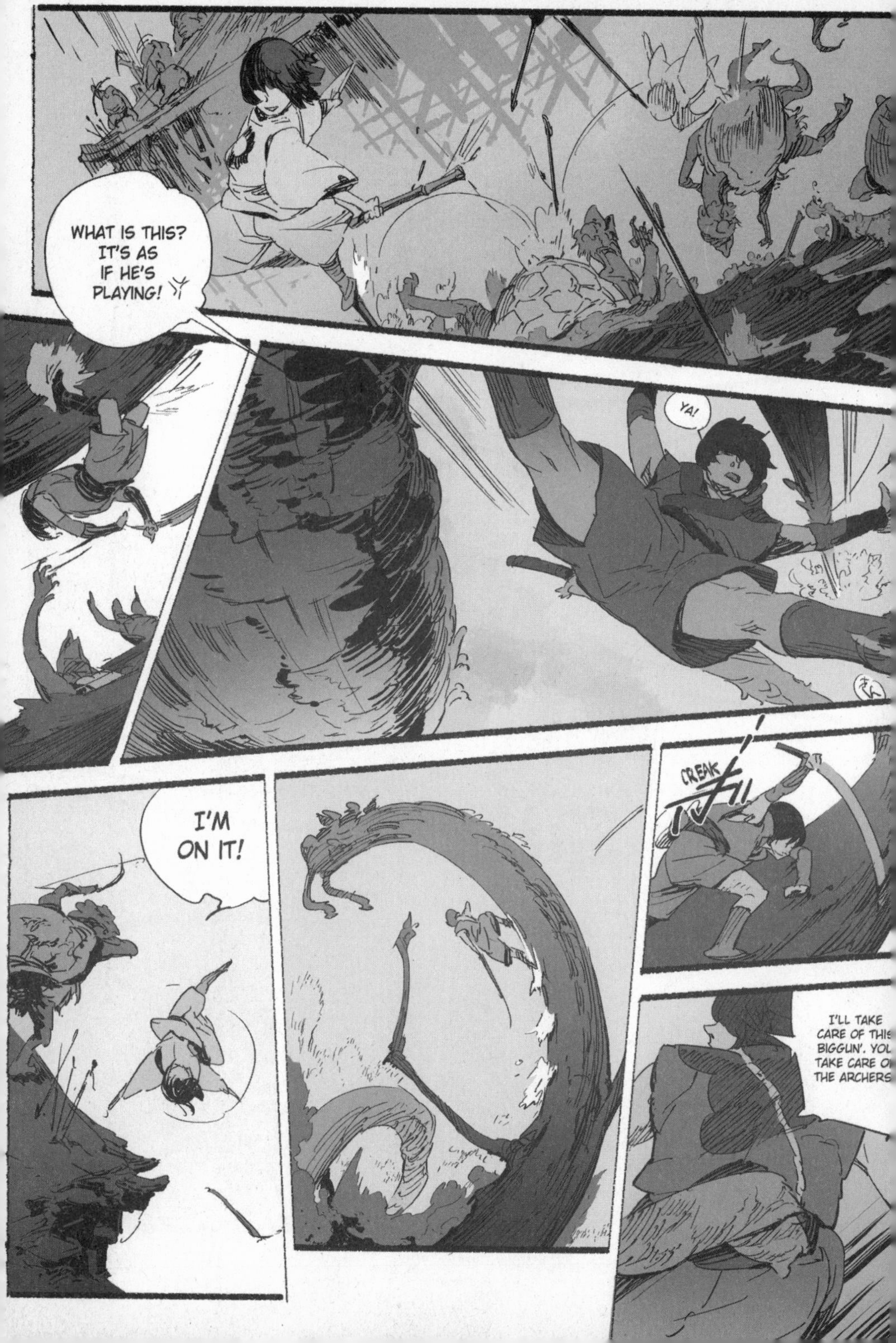
WHAT IS THIS? IT'S AS IF HE'S PLAYING!
YA!
I'M ON IT!
CREAK
I'LL TAKE CARE OF THIS BIGGUN'. YOU TAKE CARE OF THE ARCHERS

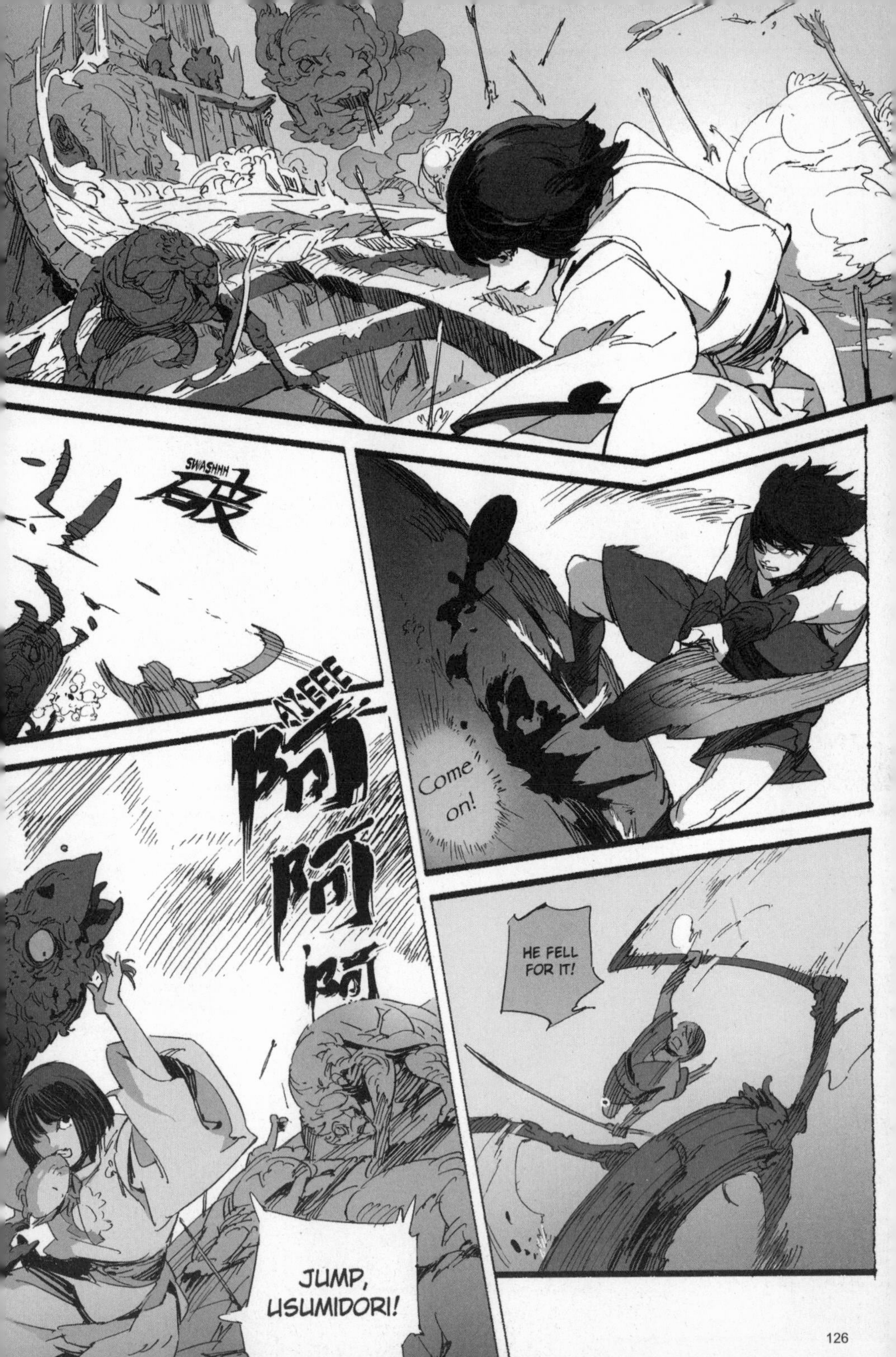
SWASHHH
破
Come on!
AIEEE
阿阿阿
HE FELL FOR IT!
JUMP, USUMIDORI!

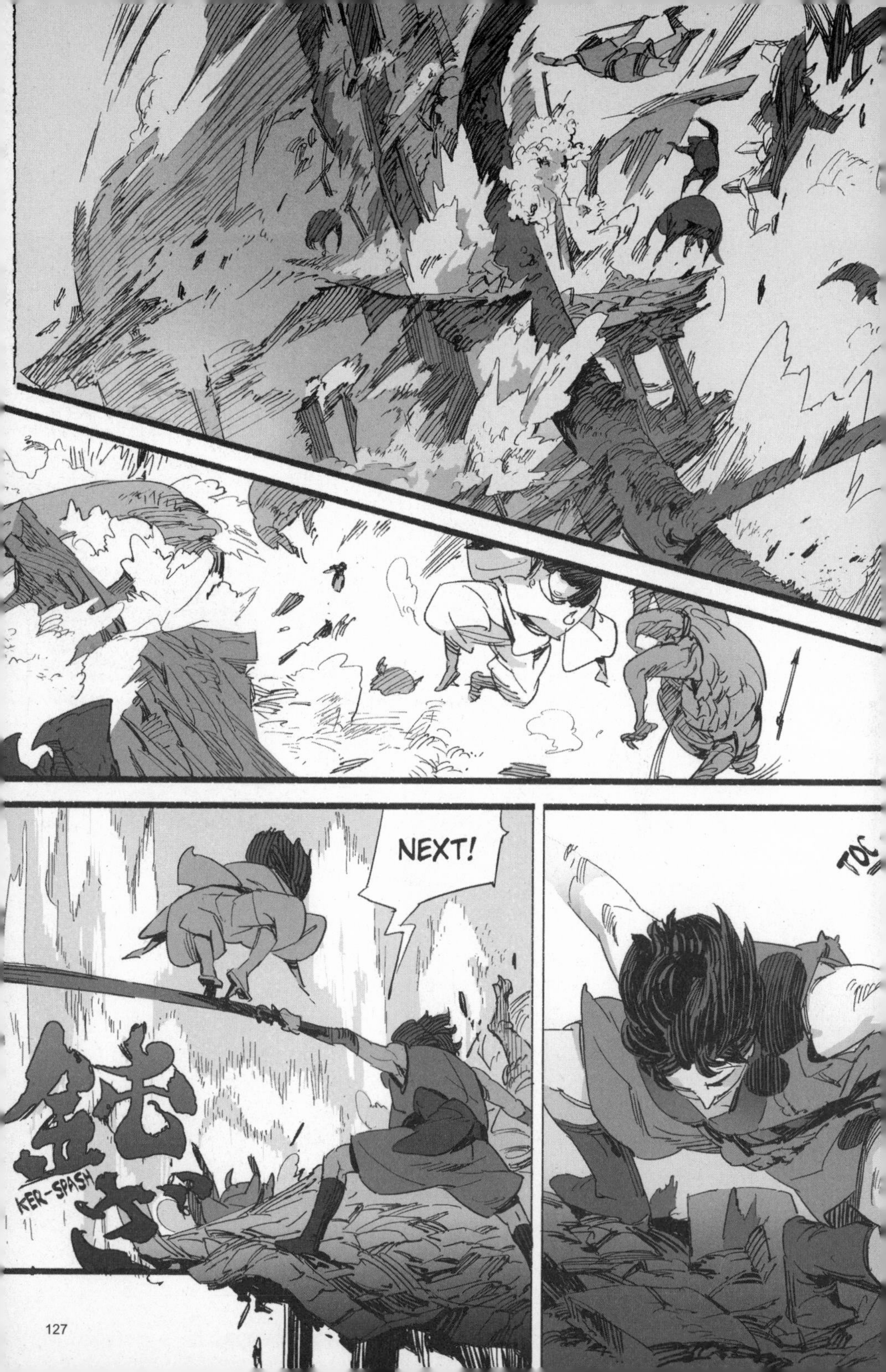
NEXT!
KER-SPASH
TOC

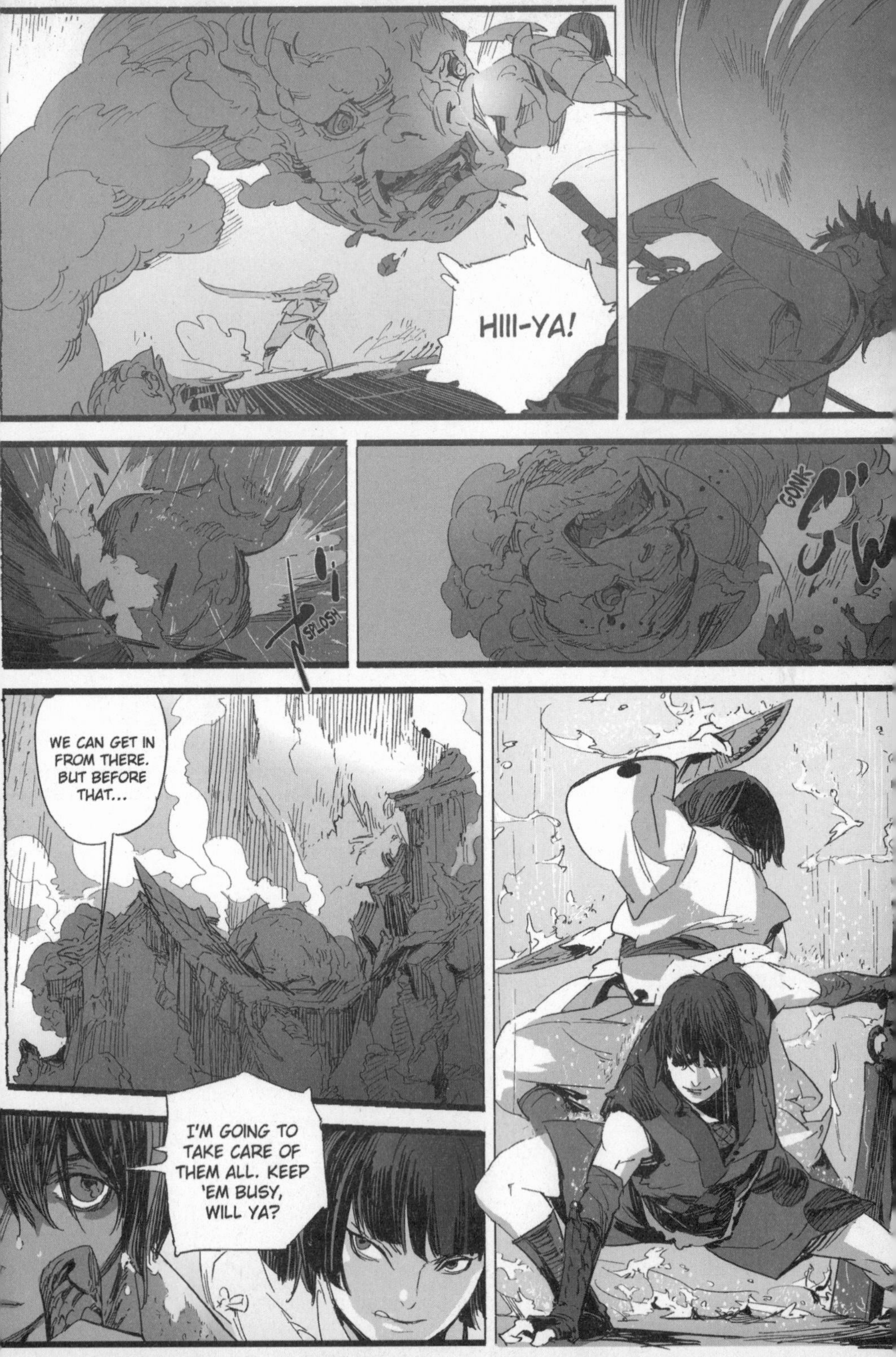
HIII-YA!
SPLOSH
GONK
WE CAN GET IN FROM THERE. BUT BEFORE THAT...
I'M GOING TO TAKE CARE OF THEM ALL. KEEP 'EM BUSY, WILL YA?

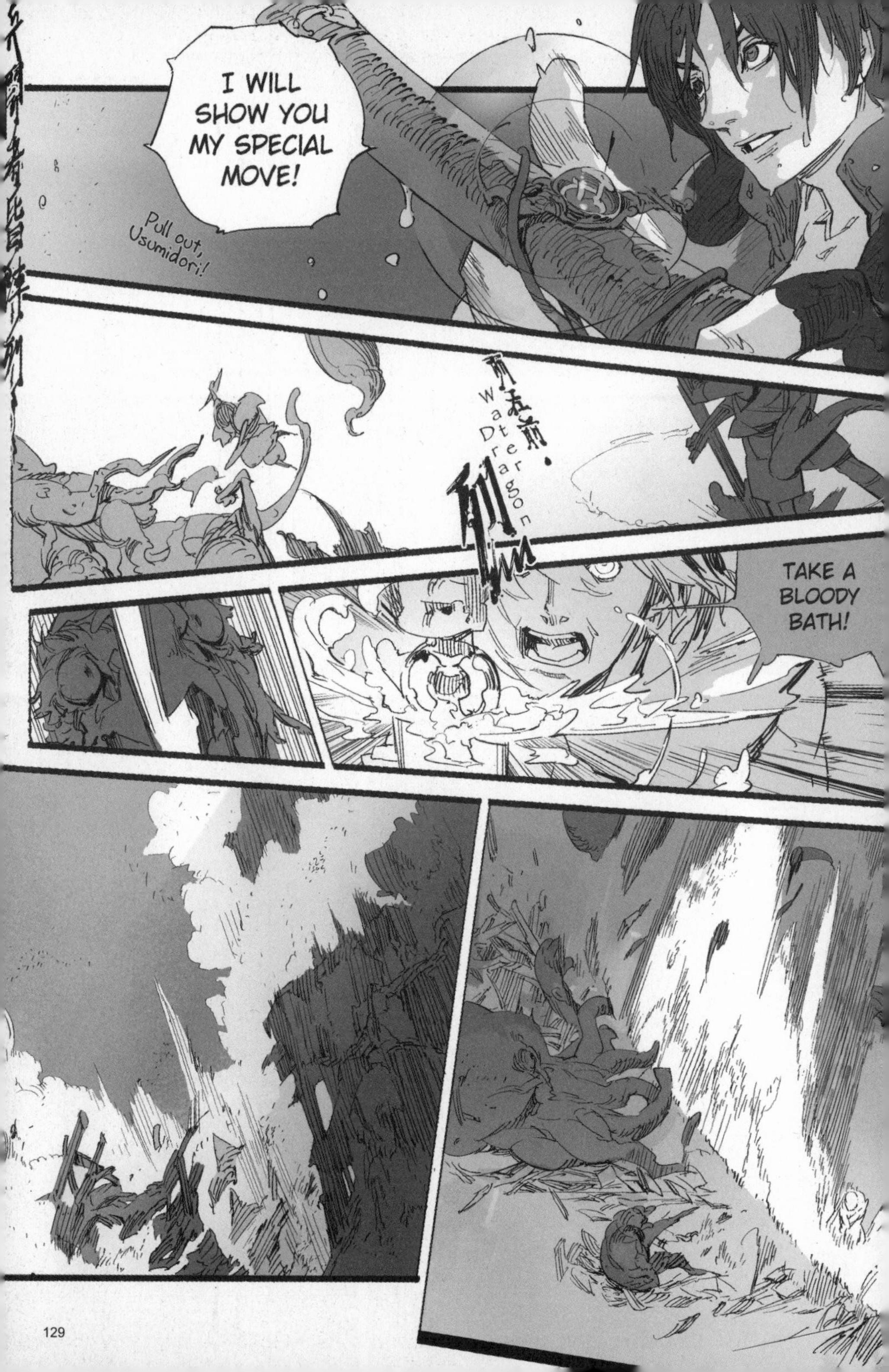
I WILL SHOW YOU MY SPECIAL MOVE!
Pull out, Usumidori!
Water Dragon
TAKE A BLOODY BATH!

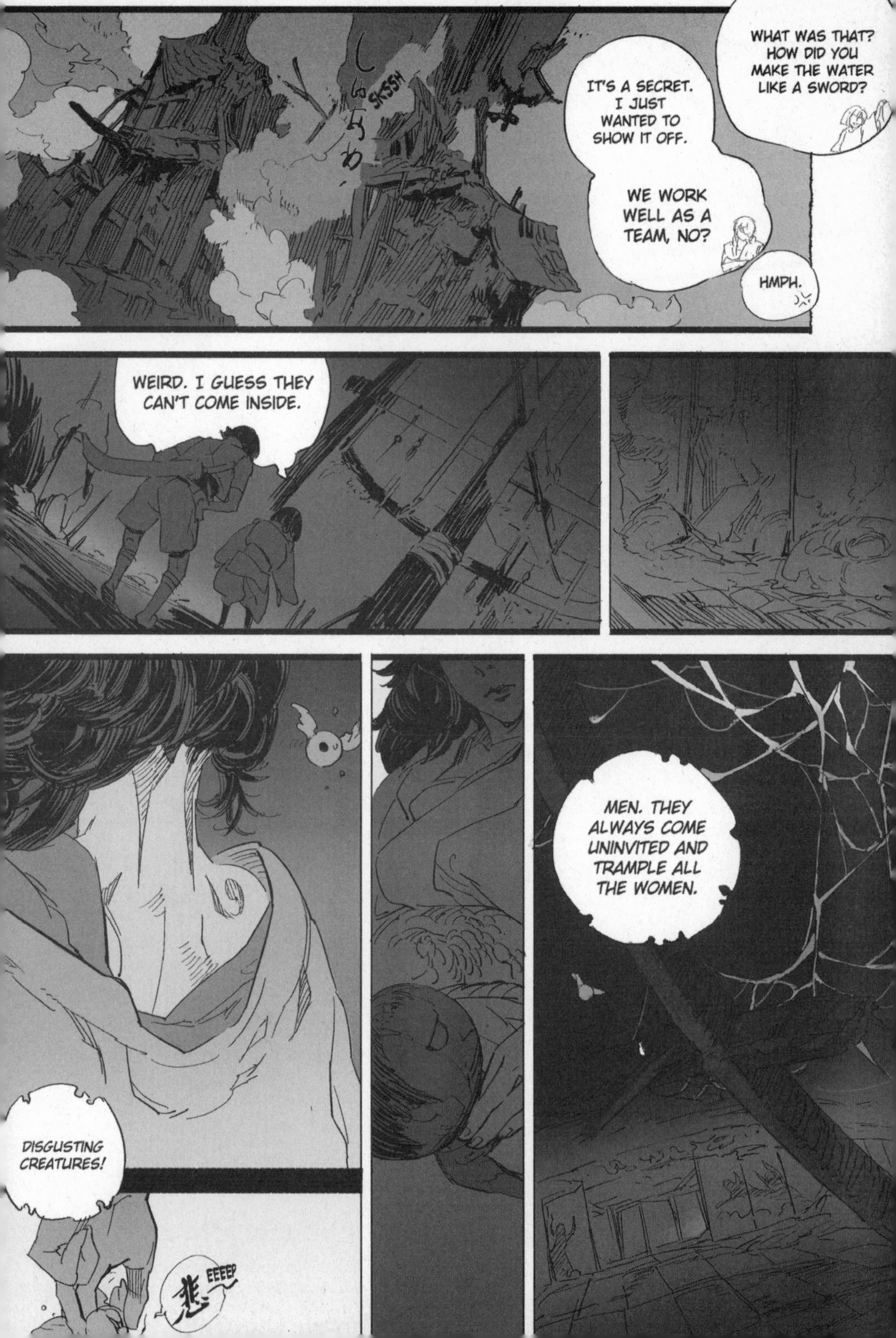
SKSSH
WHAT WAS THAT? HOW DID YOU MAKE THE WATER LIKE A SWORD?
IT'S A SECRET. I JUST WANTED TO SHOW IT OFF.
WE WORK WELL AS A TEAM, NO?
HMPH.
WEIRD. I GUESS THEY CAN'T COME INSIDE.
MEN. THEY ALWAYS COME UNINVITED AND TRAMPLE ALL THE WOMEN.
DISGUSTING CREATURES!
EEEEP

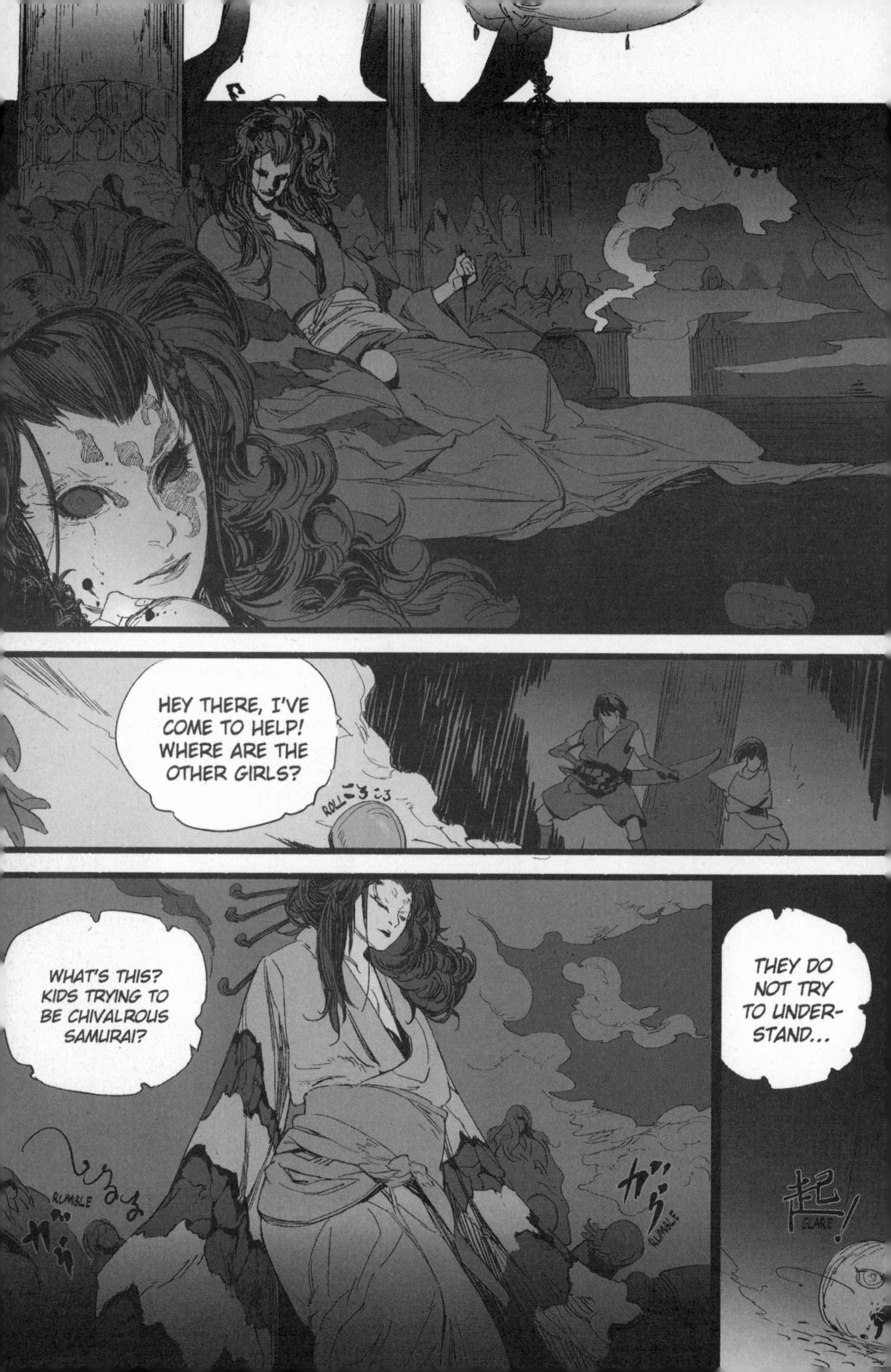
HEY THERE, I'VE COME TO HELP! WHERE ARE THE OTHER GIRLS?
ROLL ころころ
WHAT'S THIS? KIDS TRYING TO BE CHIVALROUS SAMURAI?
RUMBLE
RUMBLE
THEY DO NOT TRY TO UNDER-STAND...
起
GLARE!

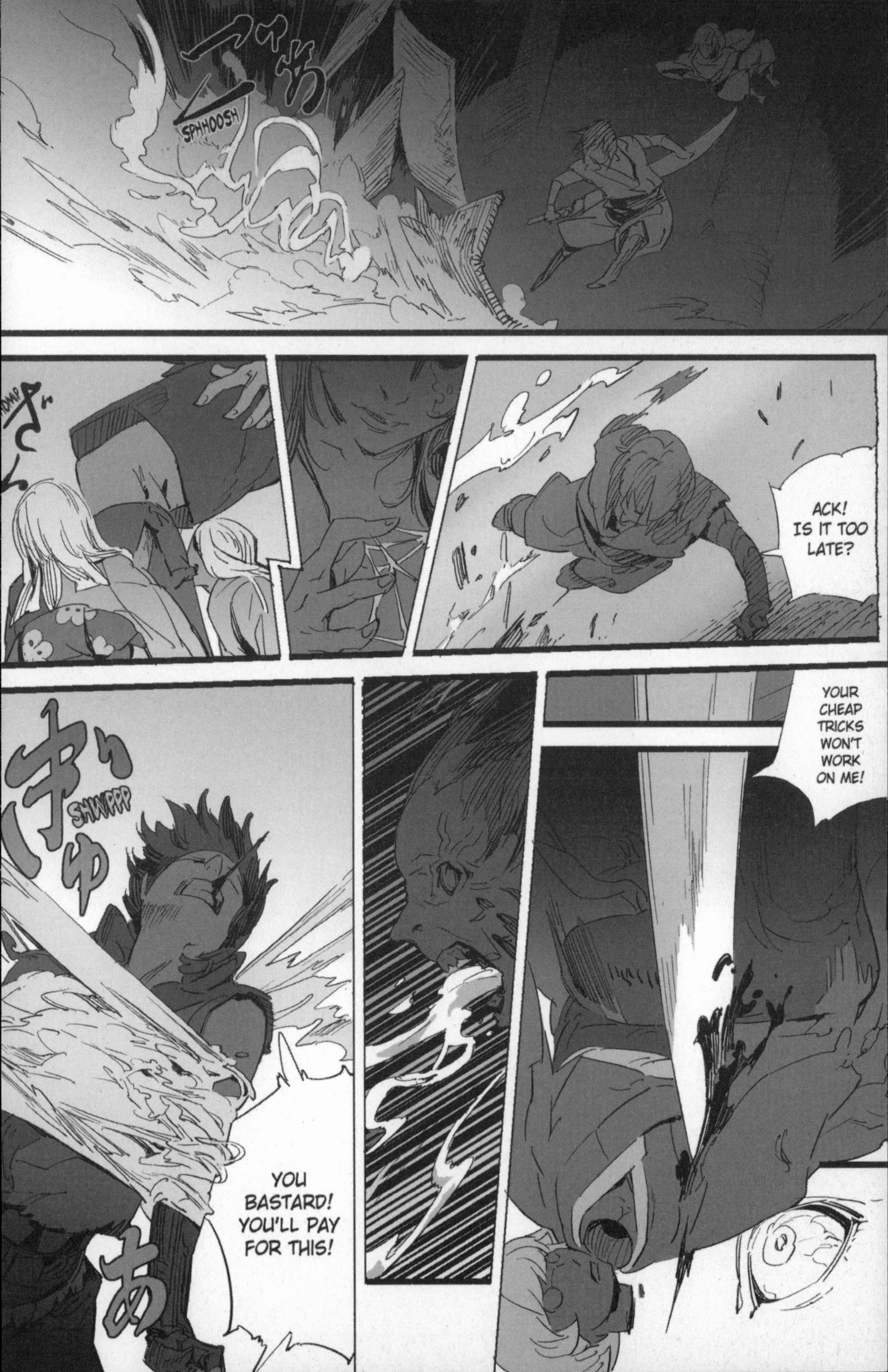
SPHOOSH
ACK! IS IT TOO LATE?
YOUR CHEAP TRICKS WON'T WORK ON ME!
SHWPPP
YOU BASTARD! YOU'LL PAY FOR THIS!

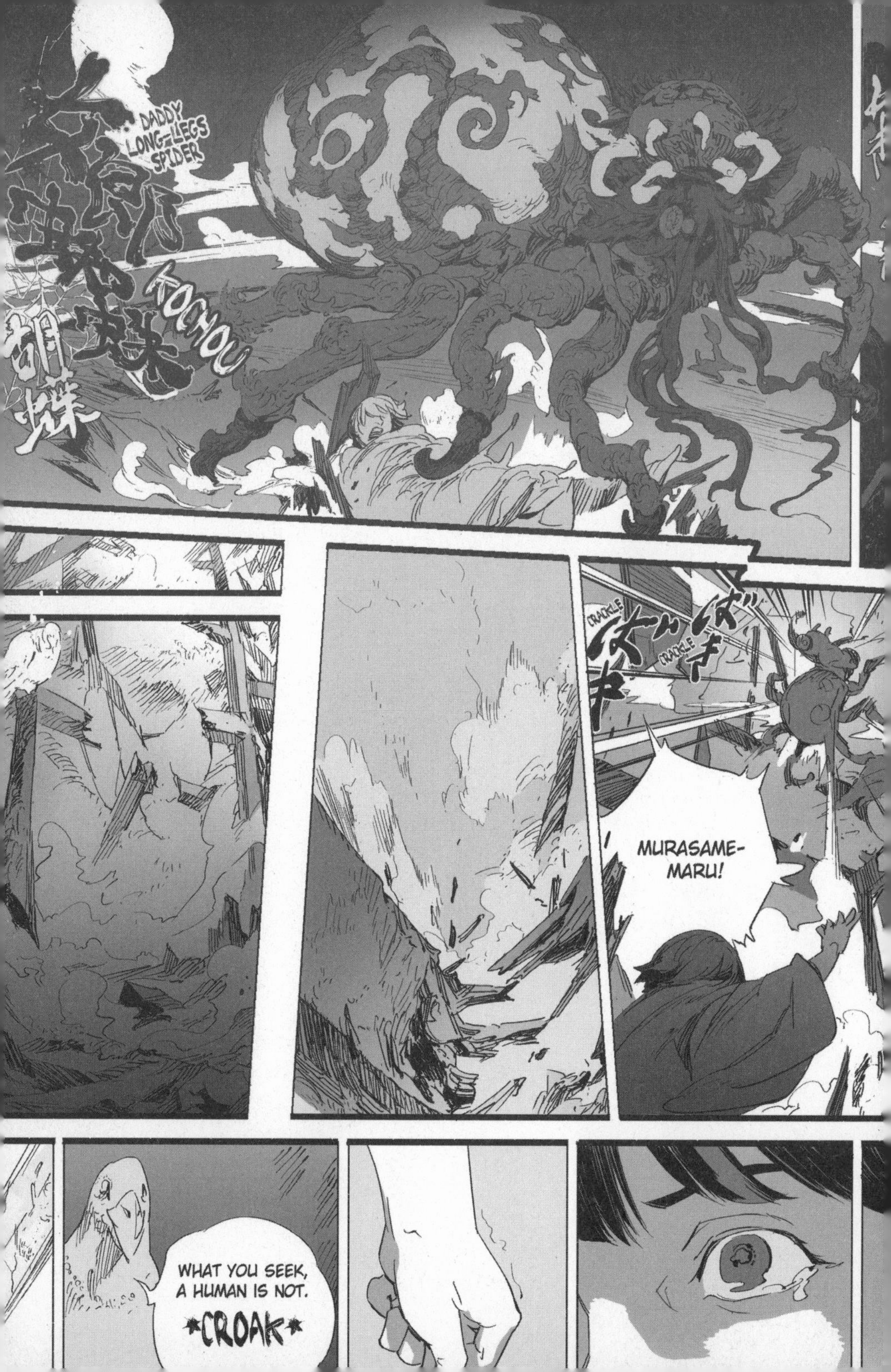
DADDY LONG-LEGS SPIDER
KOCHOU
CRACKLE
CRACKLE
MURASAME-MARU!
WHAT YOU SEEK, A HUMAN IS NOT.
CROAK

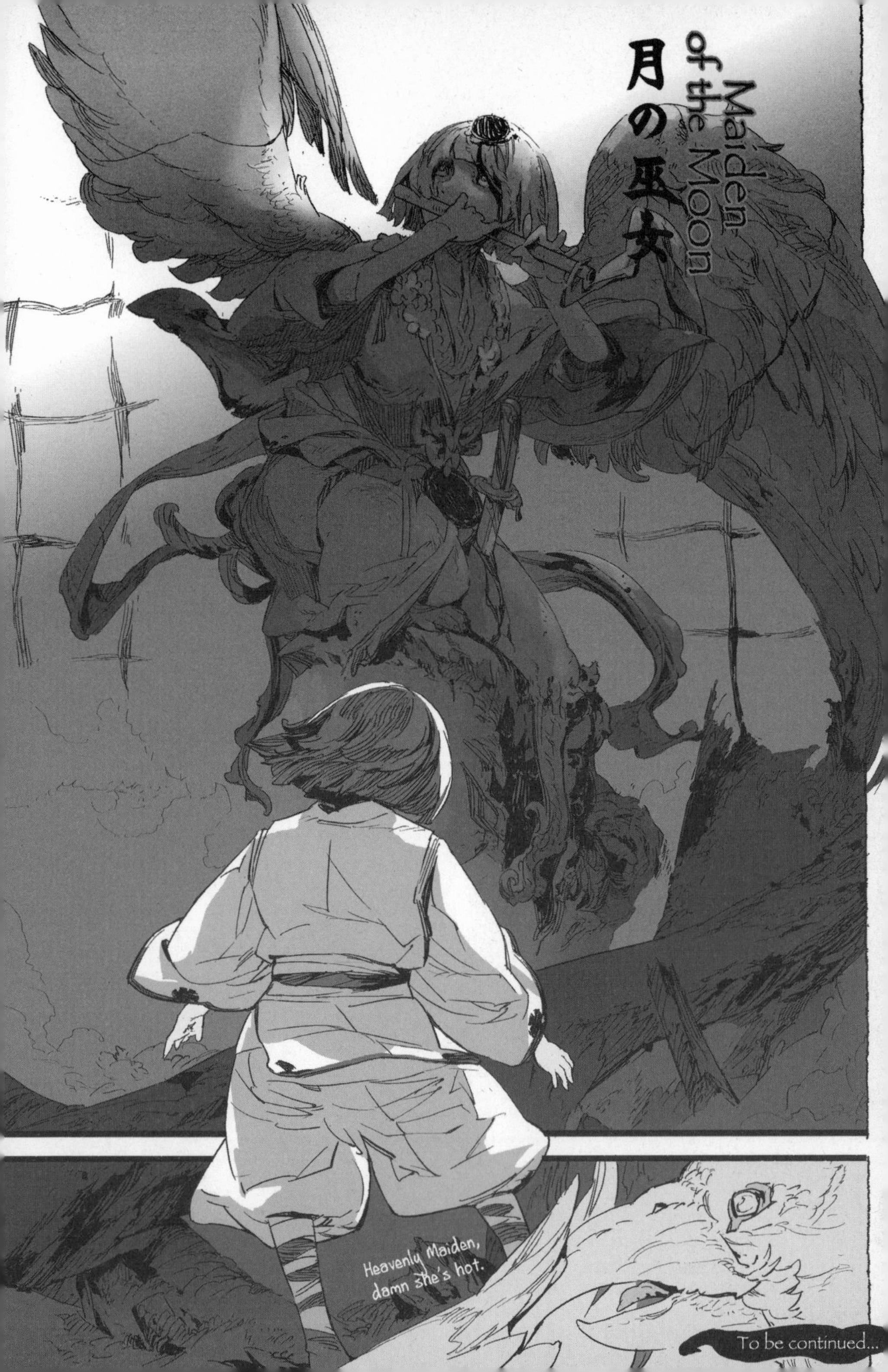
月の巫女
Maiden of the Moon
Heavenly Maiden, damn she's hot.
To be continued...

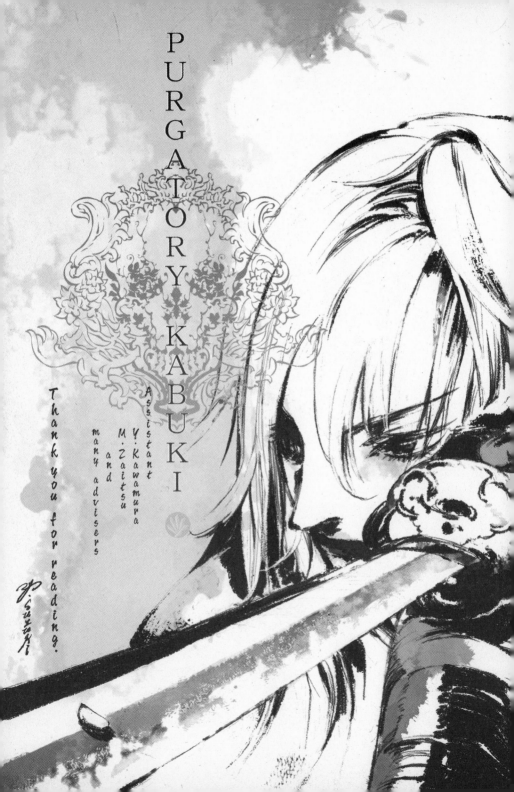

PURGATORY KABUKI

Assistant

Y. Kawamura
M. Zaitsu

and

many advisers

Thank you for reading.

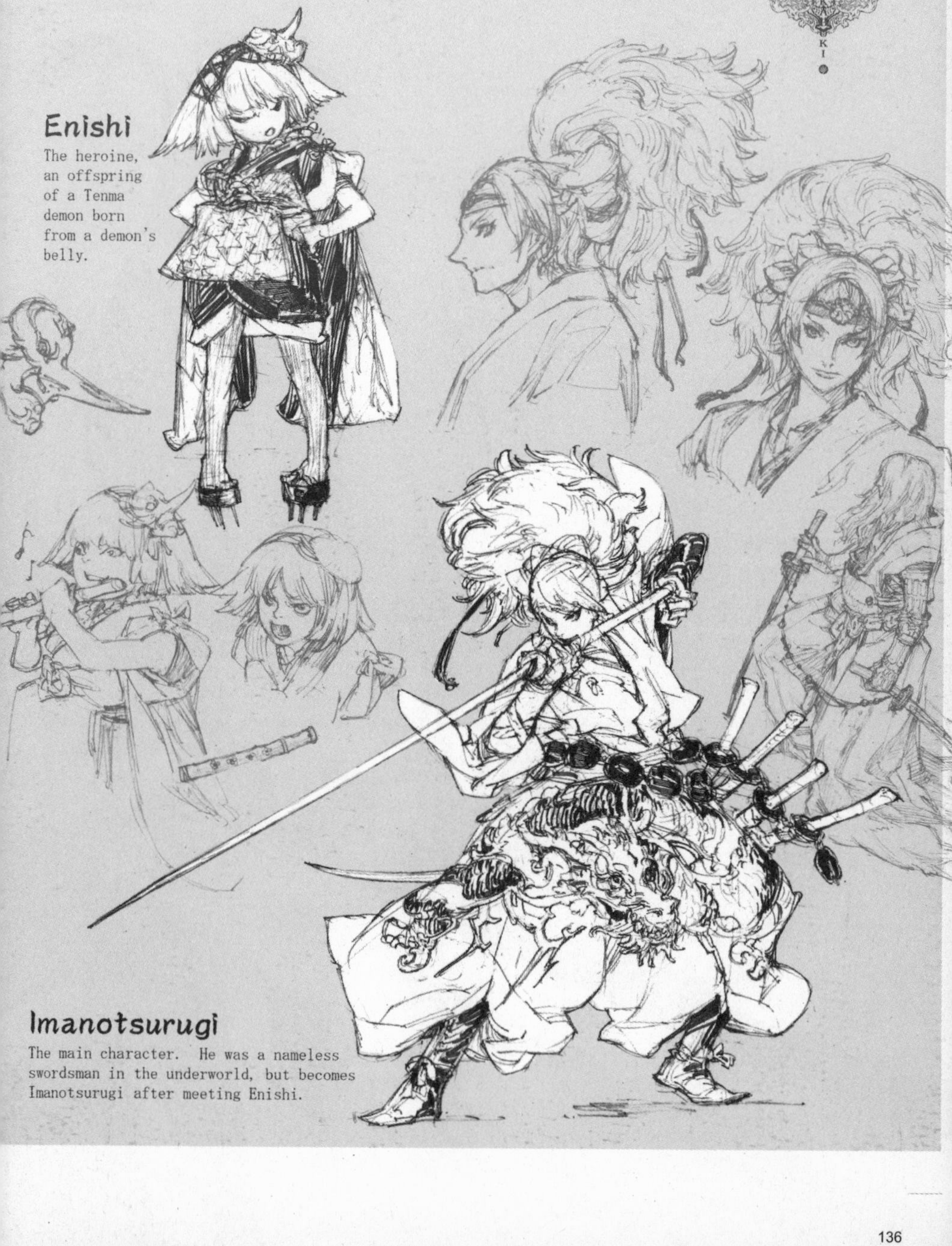

Enishi

The heroine, an offspring of a Tenma demon born from a demon's belly.

Imanotsurugi

The main character. He was a nameless swordsman in the underworld, but becomes Imanotsurugi after meeting Enishi.

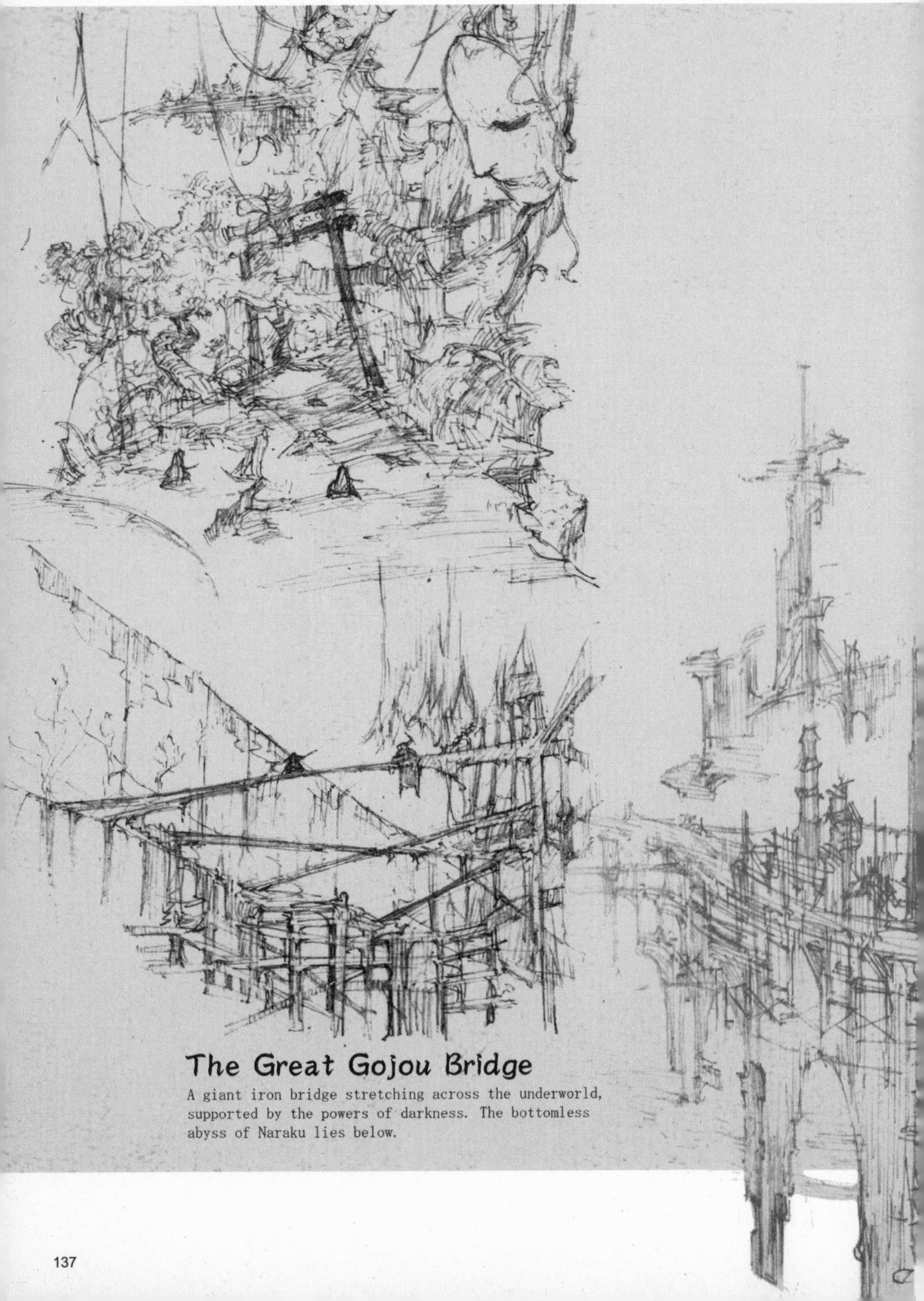

The Great Gojou Bridge

A giant iron bridge stretching across the underworld, supported by the powers of darkness. The bottomless abyss of Naraku lies below.

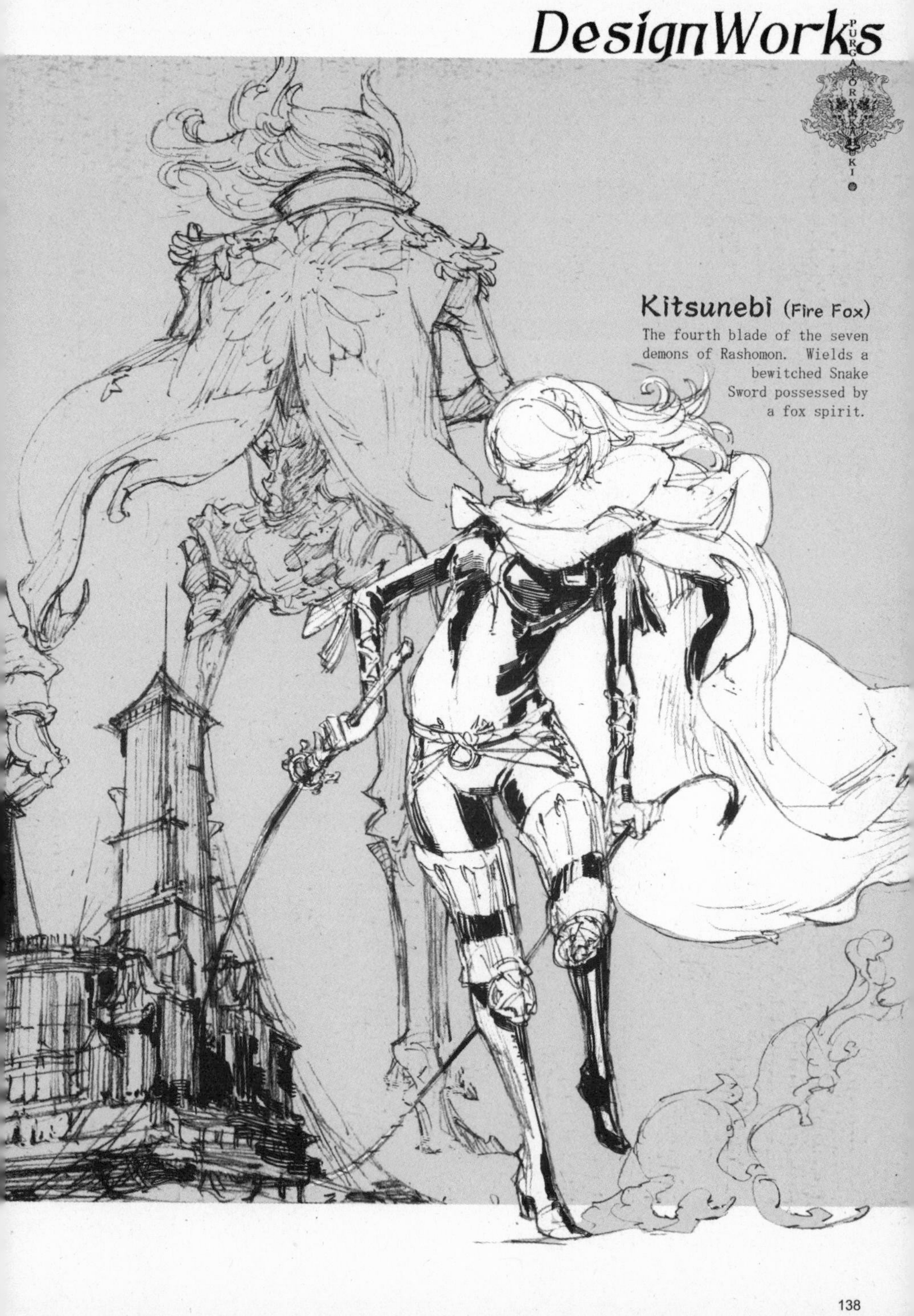

Kitsunebi (Fire Fox)

The fourth blade of the seven demons of Rashomon. Wields a bewitched Snake Sword possessed by a fox spirit.

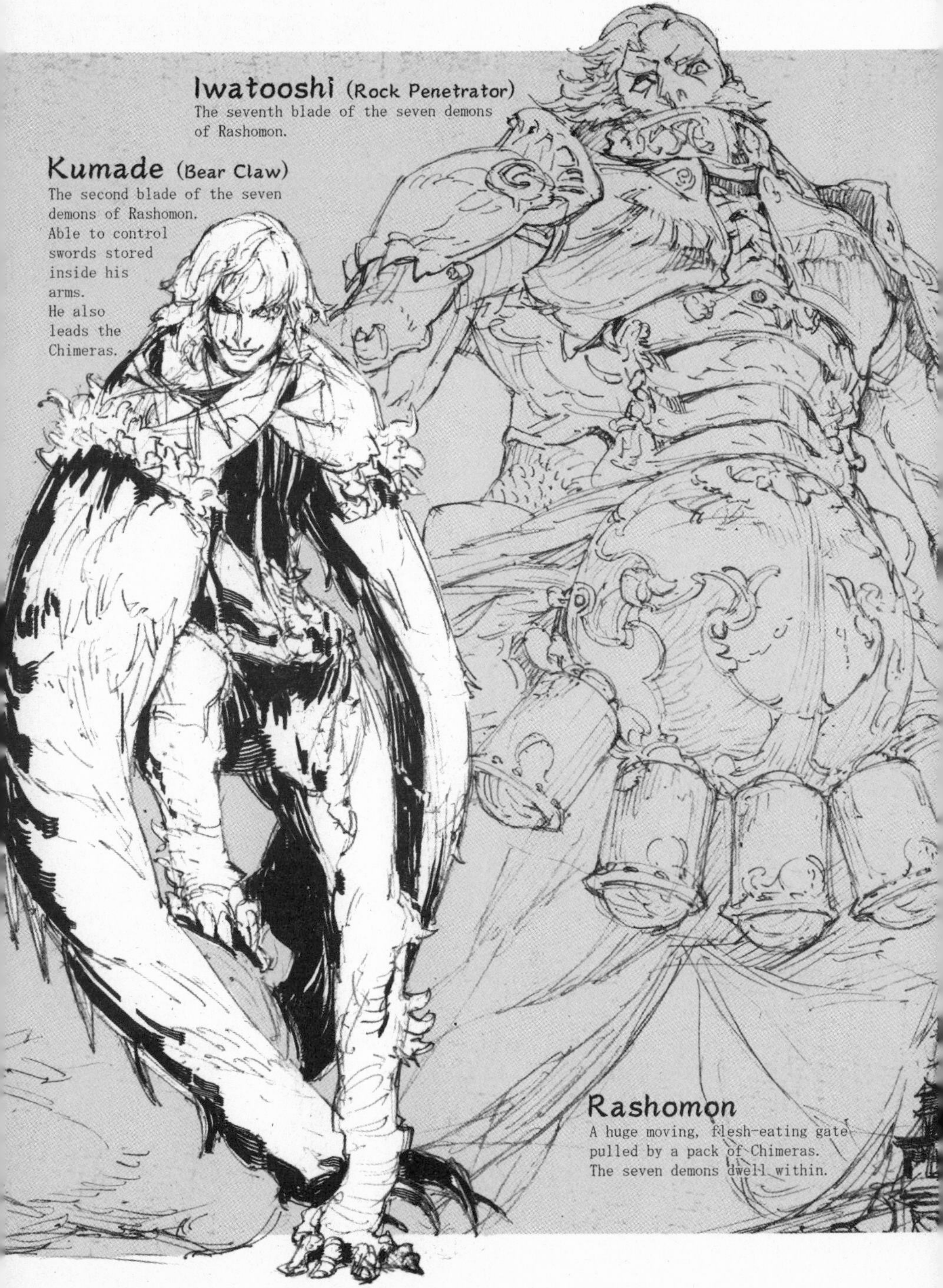

Iwatooshi (Rock Penetrator)

The seventh blade of the seven demons of Rashomon.

Kumade (Bear Claw)

The second blade of the seven demons of Rashomon.
Able to control swords stored inside his arms.
He also leads the Chimeras.

Rashomon

A huge moving, flesh-eating gate pulled by a pack of Chimeras.
The seven demons dwell within.

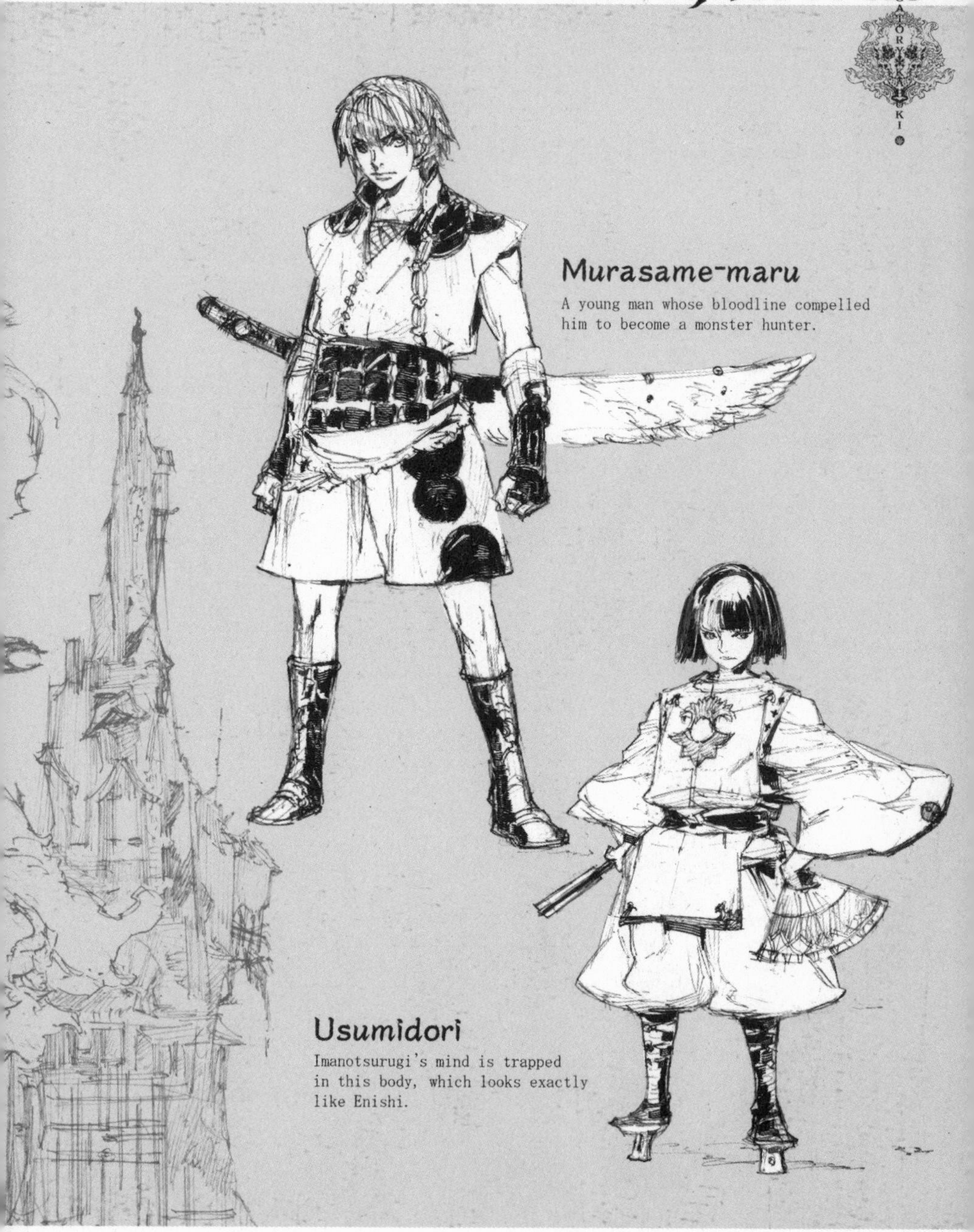

Murasame-maru

A young man whose bloodline compelled him to become a monster hunter.

Usumidori

Imanotsurugi's mind is trapped in this body, which looks exactly like Enishi.

ただ生ける刃の如く、力果てた男の懐を狙うもの妖鋼。妖鋼との争いの中、男は自身の剣への執着を知る。妖鋼を追って現れた言葉無しの鬼、鬼童丸と男は対峙する。捨て身の技をも使い辛くも鬼童丸を斬り倒す。つかの間、鬼の腹より奇しき子が現れた。それは男の剣をはるかに凌ぐ天魔の子。倒れ伏した男に語りかける天魔の子「ここは無縁地獄の橋の上果てなく殺しあうが必然～ただしかし千の刀手にするの者ならば無縁なろうと斬りはらし天への道も開けよう」天魔の子は自分を天に送ることを条件に裂けた男のの体を縫い接化する。天魔の子は蛾。男の誓いの名は今剣。

女を追う忍の一団。しかし女の正体は妖艶な闘士だった、瞬く間に形勢は逆転…。集めた刀を使い鍛錬中であった今剣のもとへ一人逃げ落ちた忍がまい込む。人を喰う門、羅生門の話を語る忍。無念を嘆く忍を今剣は嫌う、しかし忍の宝刀、犬神に興味を抱き羅生門へと向う。羅生門鬼を称す異様な闘士達は命がけの小競り合いを繰り返していた。羅生門へと乗り込んだ今剣はその生き物が如くうごめく建物に飲み込まれるすでのところ忍の宝刀、犬神を見つけ辛くも脱出する。そこで待ち受けていたのは羅生門の七鬼の一人、狐火だった。

今剣と狐火の対決。狐火の蛇剣に翻弄されながらも辛うじて立ち回る今剣。一方、鵺の大群を相手にする鵺の前に新たな刺客、熊手。戦いの中で今剣は犬神の扱いに慣れていく。しかし付利を隠せない状態に鵺と今剣は互いの位置を入れ替え攻勢へとに転じる。得体の知れぬ相手に苛立ち暴走する狐火。今剣に鵺を壊滅され深手も負う熊手。業を煮やし岩融が加勢に。鵺は串刺しに。そして奈落へと転落する。駆けよる今剣、だが前に立ちはだかる岩融。

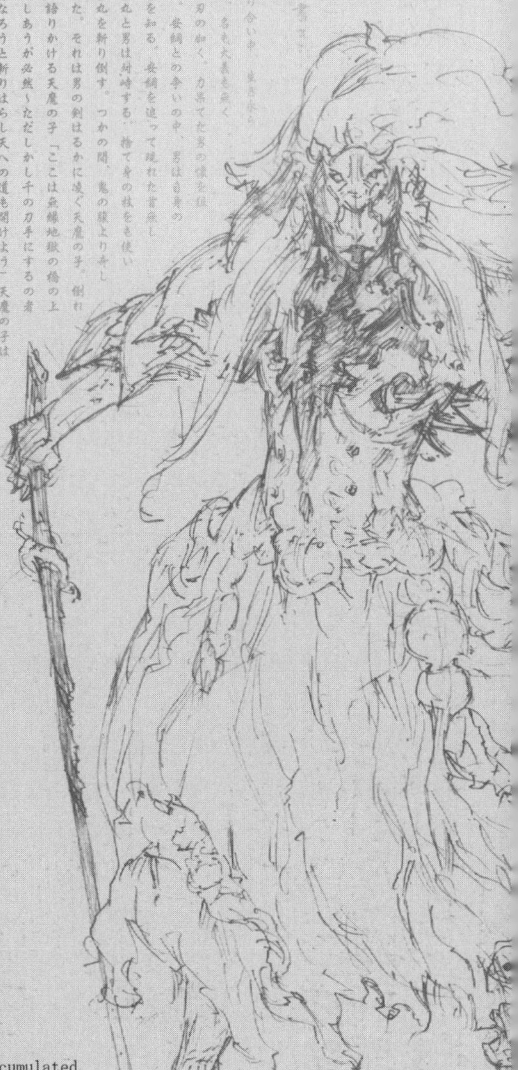

Kinshouno-tsurugi

The transformation of Imanotsurugi.

The collective body of all the swords he has accumulated.

The Legend
The story takes place on a giant bridge named Gojou Bridge,
reaching across from one end of the Underworld to the other.
A great warrior monk named Benkei had posted himself at Gojou
Bridge, dueling every passing swordsman and eventually collect-
ing 999 swords. On his 1000th duel, however, he was defeated by
Minamoto no Yoshitune, who wielded the sword Imanotsurugi.

The Location
Yomi, or the underworld, has a few different masks.
The Chinese believed there was a world of the dead below
the earth and called it Yomi. Literally written "yellow spring," the
color yellow symbolizes earth in the Wu Xing, or Five Elements
and reminded them of the world that was underneath theirs.

The Demons
Oni-The Guardians of the Gate
In Purgatory Kabuki, oni take on completely different shapes
and forms than the classic Japanese monster with bovine horns,
fangs, claws, complete with tiger-skin loincloth.
Each one possesses special powers. They communicate with
each other telepathically. They serve under no deity, unlike the
oni in Buddhism, where they serve under Enma Daio-O, judge
of the dead, and torture the sinners in purgatory. They are the
ronin of oni, the drifters in purgatory who have united for one
mysterious cause.

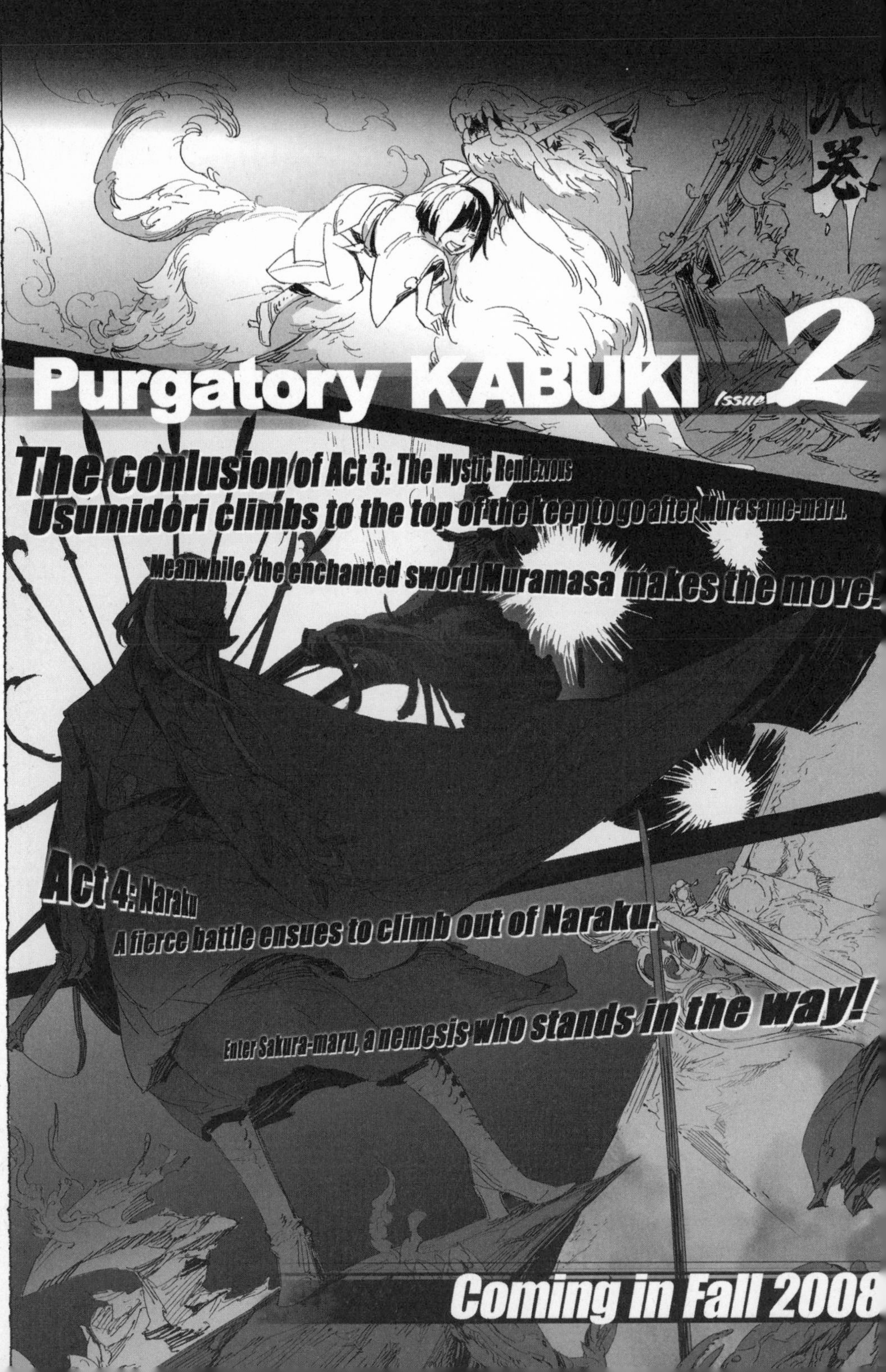

Purgatory KABUKI Issue 2
The conlusion of Act 3: The Mystic Rendezvous
Usumidori climbs to the top of the keep to go after Murasame-maru.
Meanwhile, the enchanted sword Muramasa makes the move!
Act 4: Naraku
A fierce battle ensues to climb out of Naraku.
Enter Sakura-maru, a nemesis who stands in the way!
Coming in Fall 2008

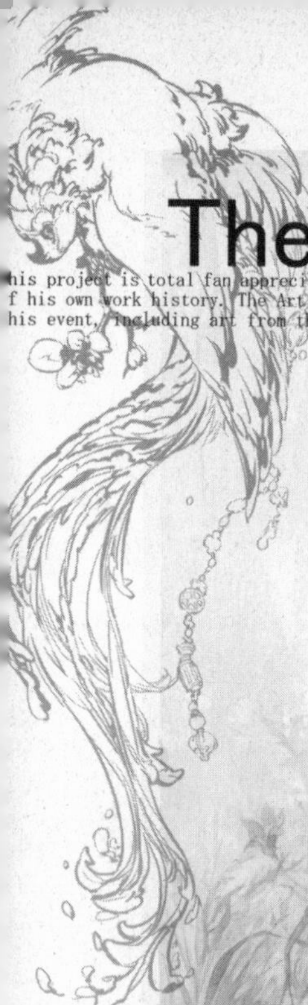

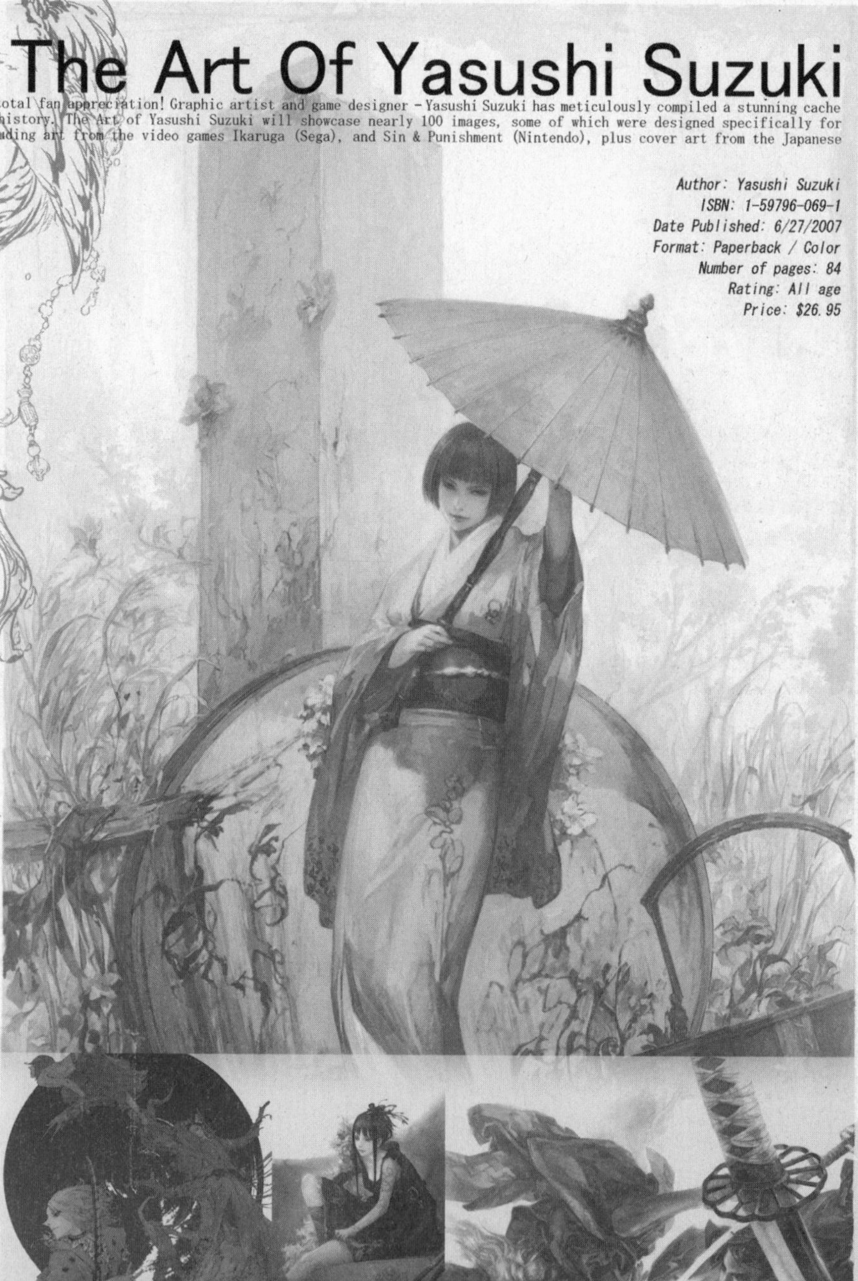

The Art Of Yasushi Suzuki

his project is total fan appreciation! Graphic artist and game designer - Yasushi Suzuki has meticulously compiled a stunning cache f his own work history. The Art of Yasushi Suzuki will showcase nearly 100 images, some of which were designed specifically for his event, including art from the video games Ikaruga (Sega), and Sin & Punishment (Nintendo), plus cover art from the Japanese

Author: Yasushi Suzuki
ISBN: 1-59796-069-1
Date Published: 6/27/2007
Format: Paperback / Color
Number of pages: 84
Rating: All age
Price: $26.95

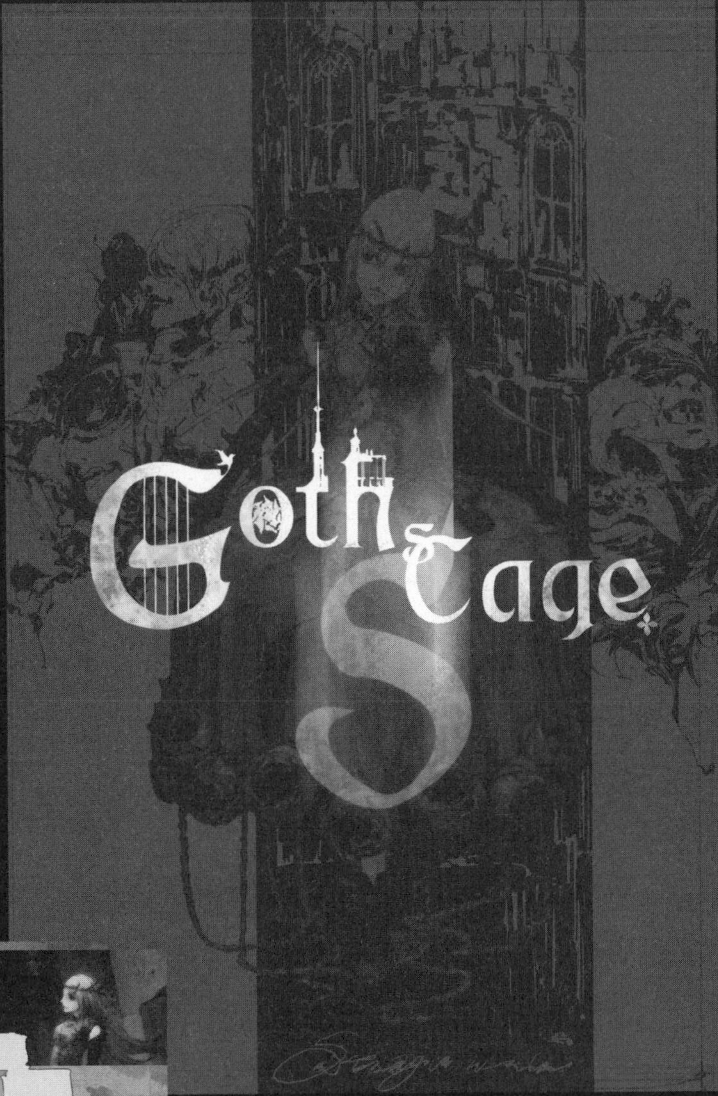
Goth Stage

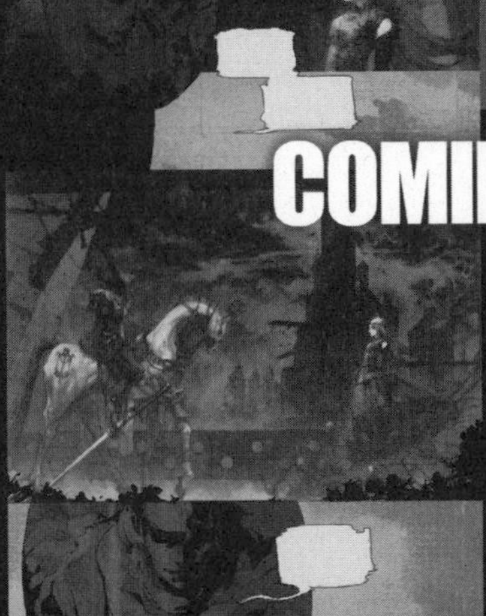

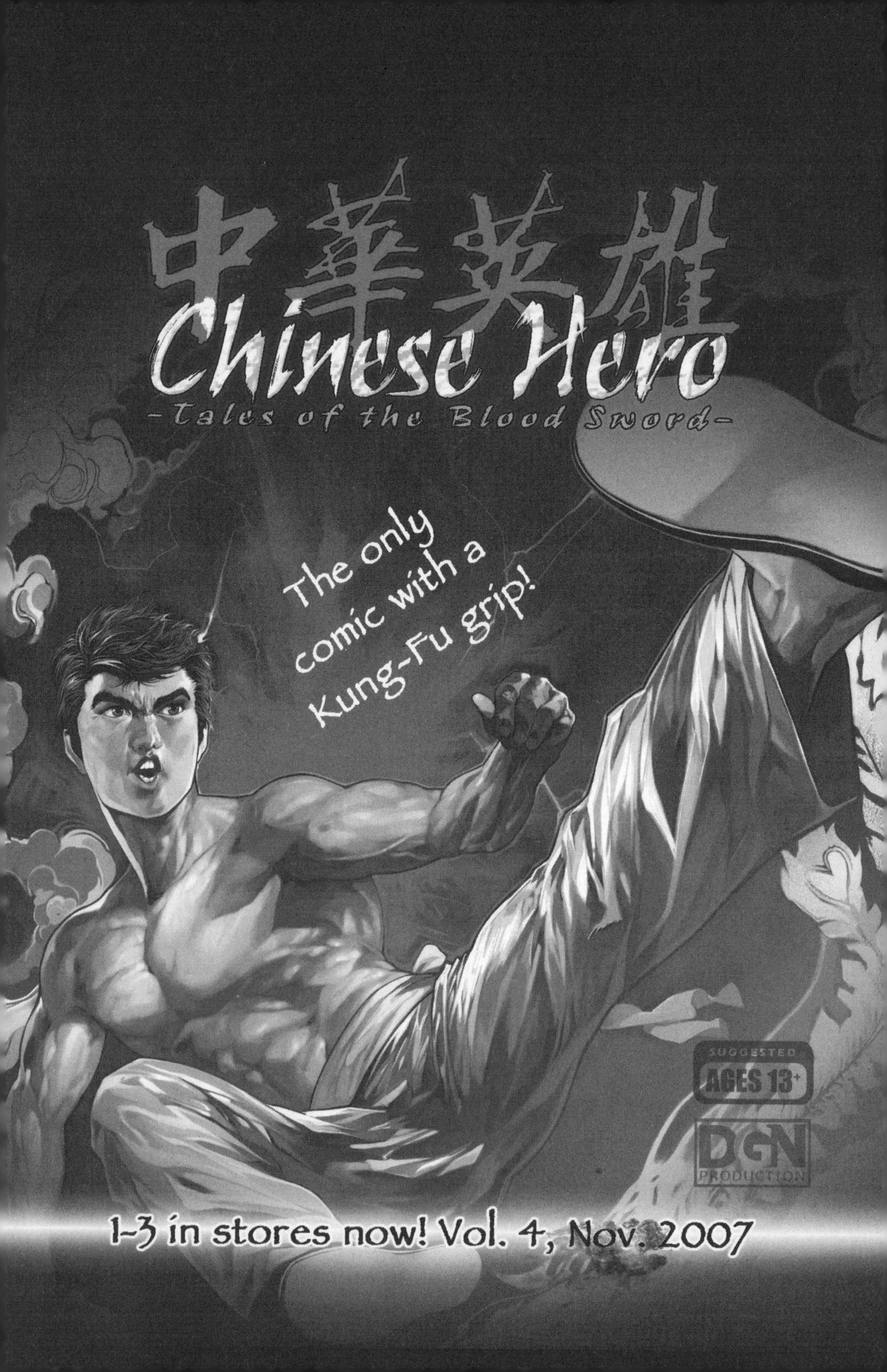
中華英雄
Chinese Hero
-Tales of the Blood Sword-
The only comic with a Kung-Fu grip!
SUGGESTED AGES 13+
DGN PRODUCTION
1-3 in stores now! Vol. 4, Nov. 2007

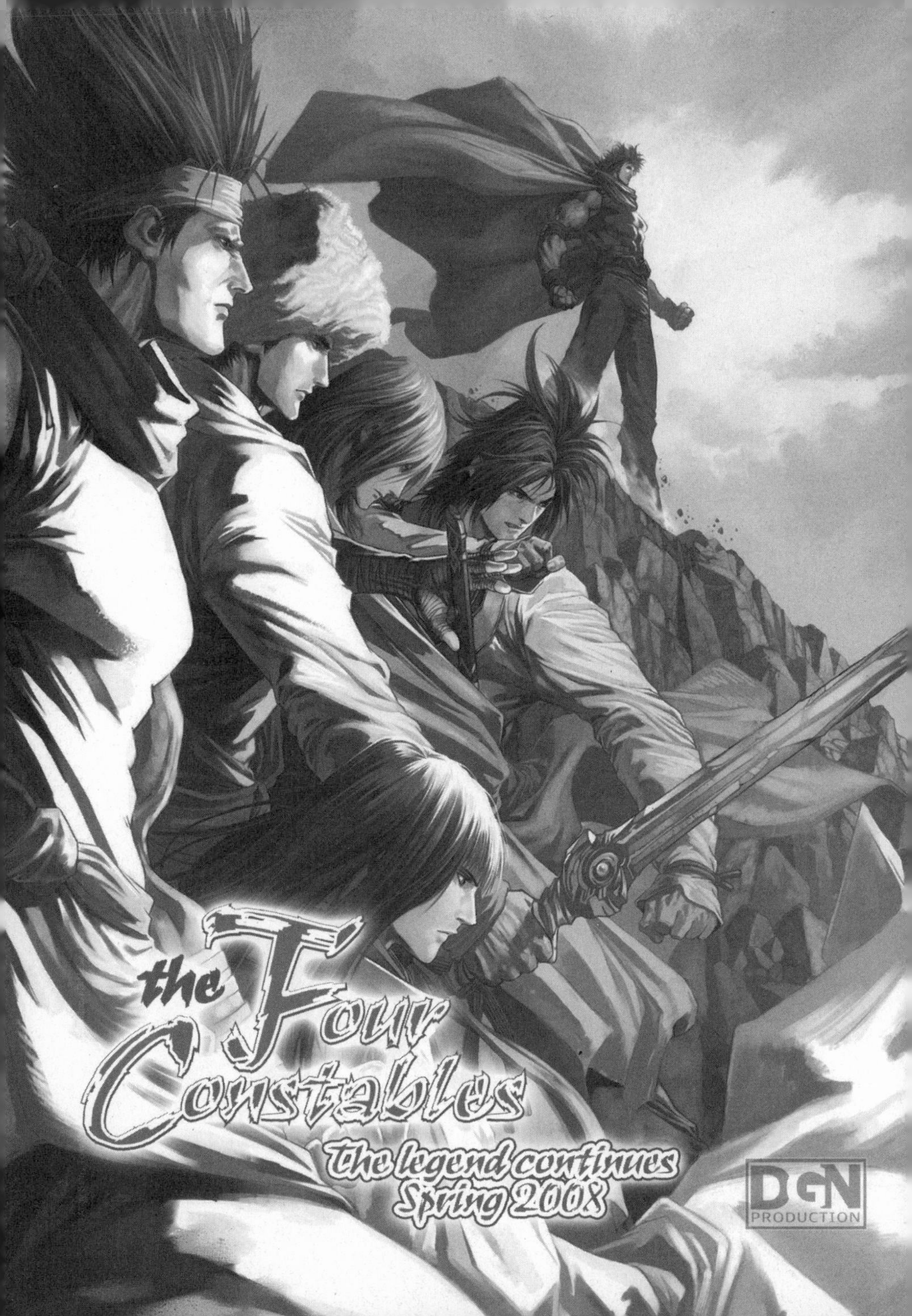

the Four Constables
The legend continues
Spring 2008
DGN PRODUCTION

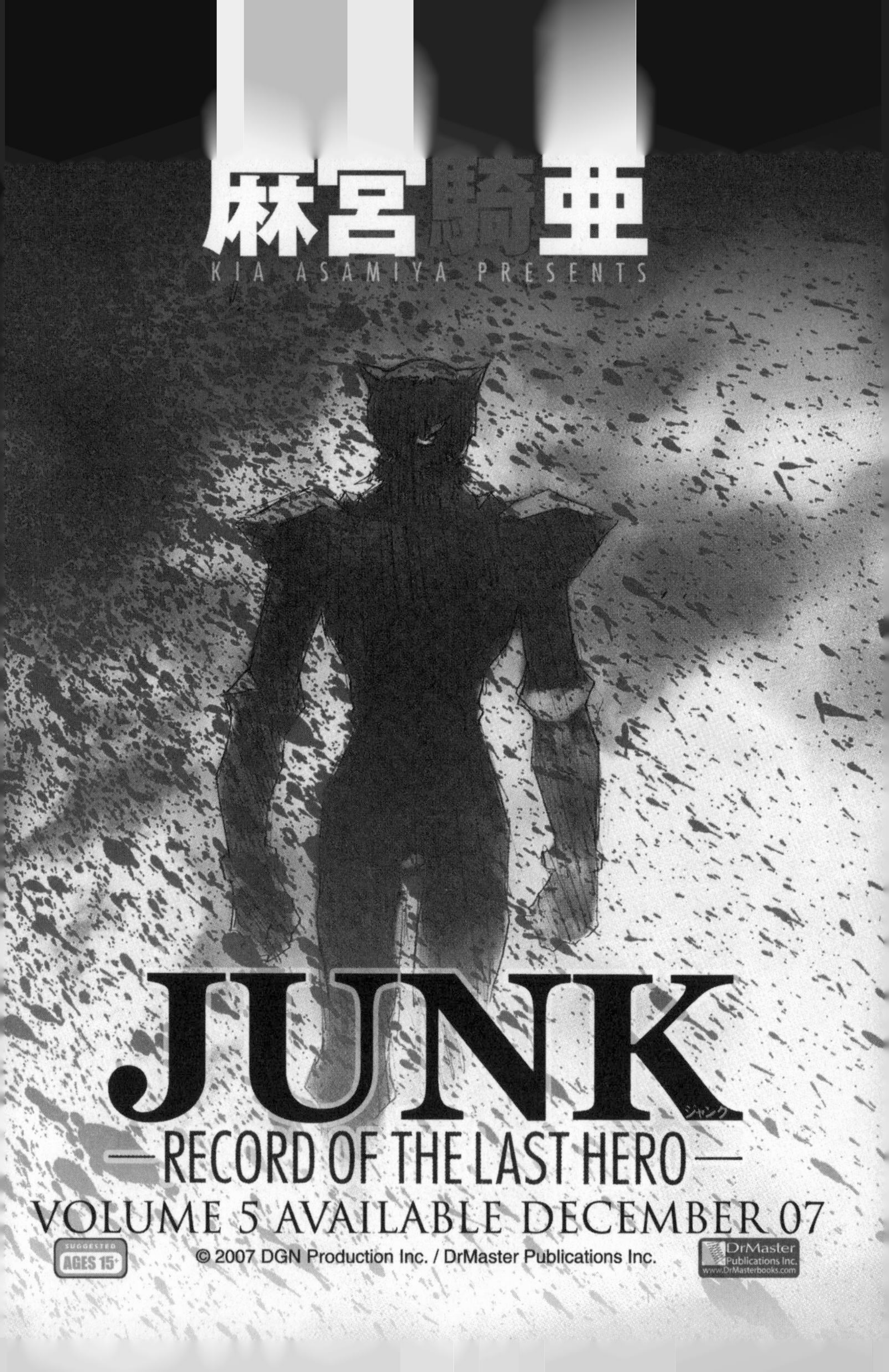
麻宮騎亜
KIA ASAMIYA PRESENTS
JUNK
ジャンク
—RECORD OF THE LAST HERO—
VOLUME 5 AVAILABLE DECEMBER 07
SUGGESTED AGES 15+
© 2007 DGN Production Inc. / DrMaster Publications Inc.
DrMaster Publications Inc.
www.DrMasterbooks.com

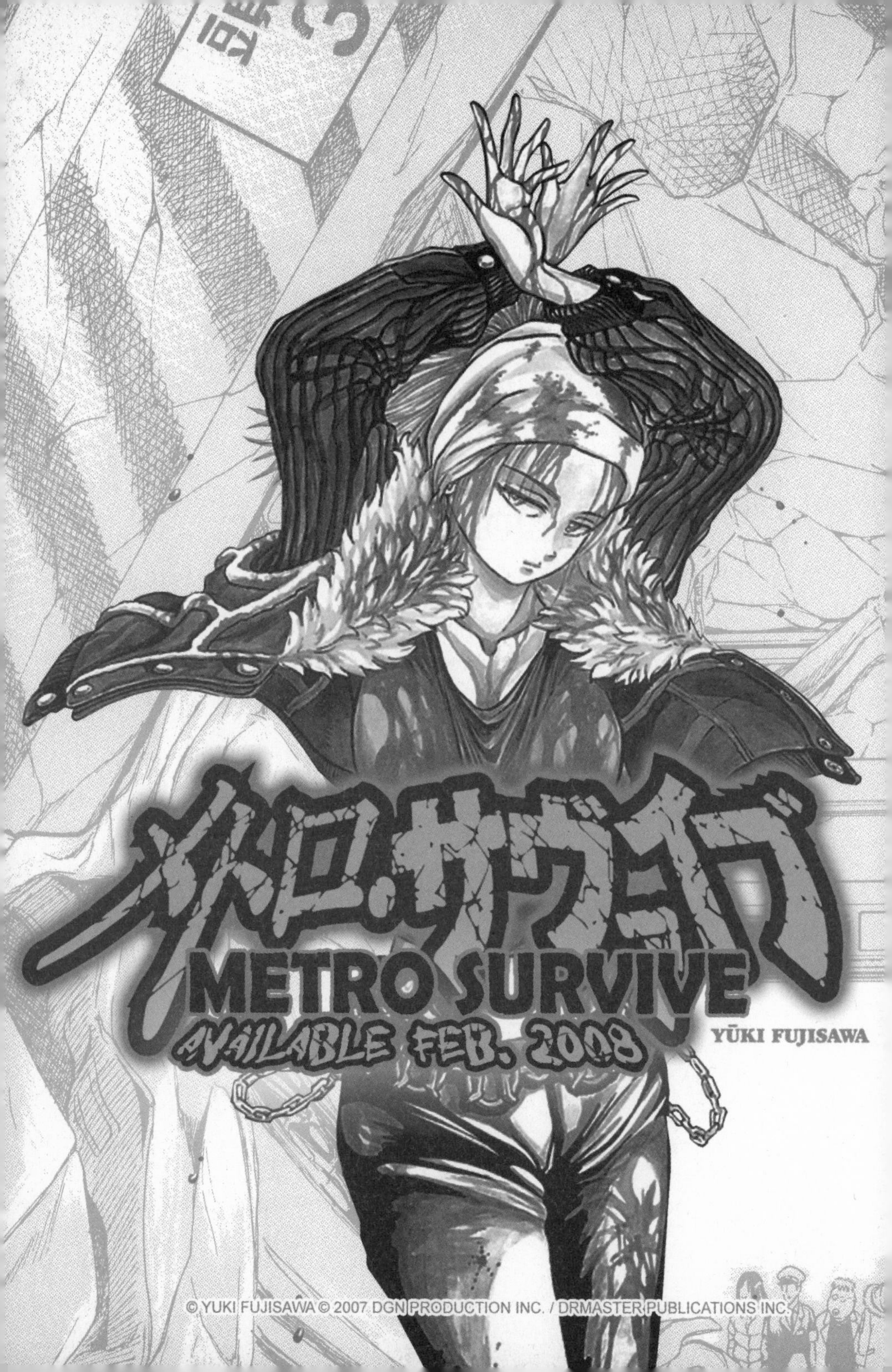
METRO SURVIVE
AVAILABLE FEB. 2008
YŪKI FUJISAWA
© YUKI FUJISAWA © 2007 DGN PRODUCTION INC. / DRMASTER PUBLICATIONS INC.

Wait, Don't Forget!

This book was printed in the original/Asian format. Please read panels from right to left.

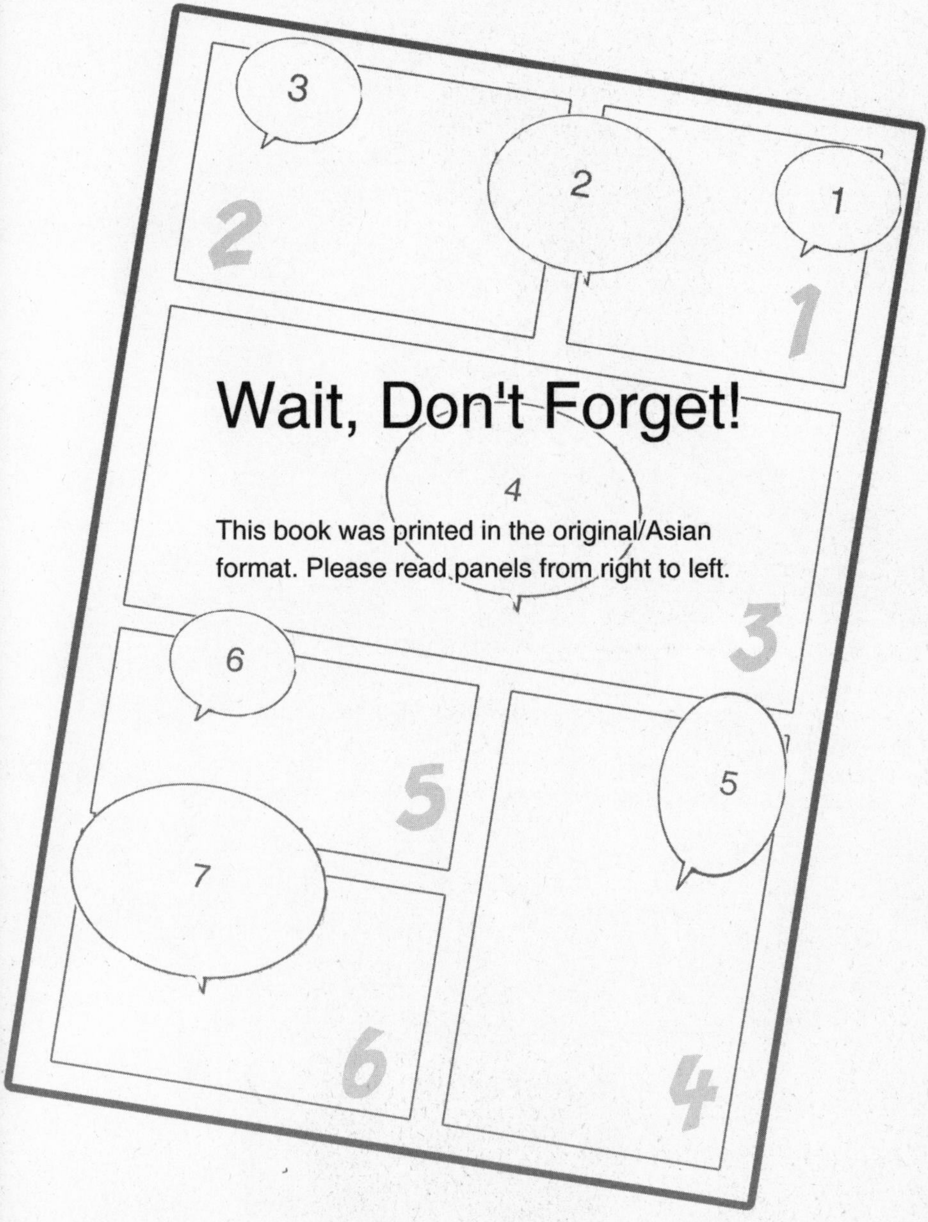

1
2
3
4
5
6
7
1
2
3
4
5
6